WESTERN MONTANA

A Portrait of The Land and Its People

NUMBER FIVE

BY JOHN A. ALWIN
Associate Professor of Geography
Department of Earth Sciences
Montana State University

Published By

MONTANA MAGAZINE, INC.

Helena, Montana 59604

Rick Graetz, Publisher
Mark Thompson, Publications Director
Carolyn Cunningham, Editor

This series intends to fill the need for in-depth information about Montana subjects. The geographic concept explores the historical color, the huge landscape and the resilient people of a single Montana subject or area. Design by Len Visual Design, Helena, Montana. All camera prep work and layout production completed in Helena, Montana. Typesetting by Thurber Printing, Helena, Montana. Color Lithography — Dai Nippon, San Francisco. Printed in Japan.

PREFACE

There is a little bit of geographer in each of us. We are fascinated with places. We wonder what makes them different from other places and how they came to be the way they are. We are curious about the relationship between the environment and people and how they have used and sometimes abused that natural landscape.

Eastern Montana, number two in this series, focuses on the often misunderstood great plains of Montana. *Western Montana*, a companion volume, examines the other Montana, the mountainous western third. It is a region of the most complimentary superlative filled with colorful history, spectacular scenery, pristine wilderness, abundant wildlife, environmental controversy and fiercely loyal citizenry. In the minds of its residents and many of its more than a million visitors each year, it is a place without equal.

Dedication

This book is dedicated to my parents. To my father for instilling a curiosity about almost everything, which I later found fit well under the heading of geography, and to my mother for the example of the rewards of pursuing a university education.

Montana Magazine, Inc., Publisher
Box 5630, Helena, MT 59604
ISBN 0-938314-07-6

A

C

D

E

CONTENTS

WESTERN MONTANA

A PORTRAIT OF THE LAND AND ITS PEOPLE

Photo Credits — Page 2: (A) Jerome Rock Lakes, Spanish Peaks Wilderness—Pat O'Hara; (B) Haying crew, Bighole Valley— John Alwin; (C) "Guest" rodeo at the 9 Quarter Circle Ranch— John Alwin; (D) Trumpeter Swan—Ken Reynolds; (E) East meets West, The Rocky Mountain Front West of Augusta—John Alwin; (F) Boulder Falls, Boulder River—Charles Kay

Page 3: (A) St. Ignatius from the South—John Alwin; (B) Bannack— Rick Graetz; (C) Bull of the Woods Pass, Beartooth Mountains— Rick Graetz; (D) Powwow at Elmo—John Alwin; (E) Malcolm Story, Bozeman—John Alwin; (F) Ferns, Glacier Park—Tom Dietrich; (G) Fall color near Helena—Rick Graetz

WESTERN MONTANA: TOWARD A REGIONAL IDENTITY

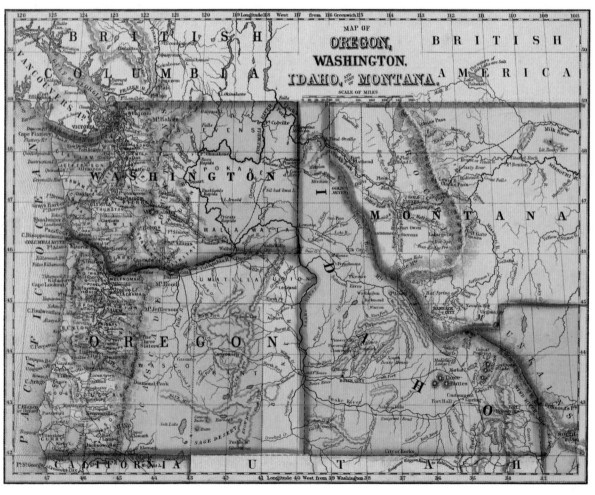

MAP OF OREGON, WASHINGTON, IDAHO, AND PART OF MONTANA.

SCALE OF MILES

Western Montana, first and foremost, is mountains. Grand, spectacular, overpowering and majestic, the kind of stuff meant for big, thick coffee-table books. So overwhelming and pervasive is the natural splendor that it actually is difficult to take a bad landscape picture. The scenic substance is unrivaled, and the thin air of this elevated country somehow seems to sharpen pictures and intensify natural colors. Are there any Western Montanans who haven't taken at least a few scenics they feel merit publication in *National Geographic?*

Western Montana is Rocky Mountain Montana. On the east it begins where the dominantly horizontal dimension of the plains yields to a distinctly three-dimensional mountain world. The contact between east and west, plains and mountains, is usually a gradual one. But to the west beyond this distinctive and diverse foreland belt, a mountainous domain prevails.

First-time visitors to Western Montana often are struck by the diversity of its mountainous landscape. Like many of the early explorers they arrive thinking the Rockies are a single mountain chain, just like the woolly worm so often used to represent the range on aged maps. However, Montana's Rockies are made up of more than two dozen distinct ranges separated by valleys of varying width. In the southwest ranges rise as detached, forested islands from intermontane valleys up to 50 miles across. Farther to the northwest seemingly overlapping ranges leave little room for constricted valleys. The Madison and Gallatin, Whitefish, Cabinet, Pioneer and Tobacco Root ranges — their names are second nature to residents of the region. They would no more call one of them the Rocky Mountains than a resident of Chicago would refer to Lake Michigan as the Great Lakes.

Professor John Crowley, a mountain geographer at the University of Montana, recognizes three distinctive environmental regions within Western Montana that he has named the Columbia Rockies, Broad Valley Rockies, and Yellowstone Rockies.

The Columbia Rockies region is classic mountain landscape. A humid climate, luxuriant and varied natural vegetation, and narrow, forested, valleys are characteristic. Mountains here show considerable variation from the Appalachian-like and rather unimposing Salish Mountains, to the towering, bare peaks of the Lewis Range. Overall, the feel within much of the region is of the Pacific Northwest and it is easy to see why some geographers consider this highland realm to be part of the greater Northwest. A regional economic emphasis on lumbering, tourism and recreation fits its Pacific Northwest setting.

The eastern prong of the Columbia Rockies region claims some of the wildest and most scenic mountain country in Montana and the West. Most Montanans would agree that Glacier National Park, the 1600-square-mile extravaganza of mountains is Western Montana at its scenic best. Park brochures and pamphlets refer to it in phrases like the "Crown of the Continent" and "A Place Touched by Magic." Its complement of towering, glacially sculpted peaks, 50 active glaciers, 200 alpine lakes, mantle of lush vegetation, and its more than 700 miles of trails beckons more than a million visitors annually.

South of Glacier and straddling the crest of the Continental Divide for 100 miles is the nation's second largest and possibly most famous wilderness complex. This is Montana's celebrated Bob Marshall Wilderness and its two recently designated sister wilderness areas, the Scapegoat and Great Bear. Combined, they form a contiguous wilderness of more than 1.5 million acres — 2,400 square miles unviolated by a single mile of road. This wilderness complex combined with Glacier National Park contains the majority of the lower 48 states' remaining grizzly bears. The presence of this backcountry monarch, the undisputed indicator species of the highest quality natural areas, is both a source of pride and a challenge to conservationists nationwide who strive to assure its existence.

To the south and east the unique Broad Valley Rockies environmental region claims more than half of Western Montana. Its basic topographic unity is what geographers call open mountains, a distinctive and rare setting with high, detached mountain ranges separated by broad, smooth-floored valleys. Here intermontane valleys may cover up to 50 percent of an area, whereas in the Columbia Rockies region they generally account for less than 20 percent.

Higher peaks in the major ranges exceed 9,000 feet, comparable to those in the most lofty sections of the Columbia Rockies. At 11,230 feet, Crazy Peak in the Crazy Mountains is the highest in this Broad Valley region, topping Glacier's tallest by almost 800 feet. As in Glacier National Park, ice-scalloped, bare-rock crests of the higher ranges attest to erosion by alpine glaciers during the last Ice Age.

Even the lower Castle, Ruby, and Garnet ranges are high enough to trigger large amounts of orographic, or mountain-induced precipitation. Most receive an average of at least 30 inches a year, with amounts generally increasing with elevation. Some of the highest tracts in the Crazy and Anaconda ranges have an average annual precipitation in excess of 60 inches. These humid conditions support extensive coniferous forests which form a band around each range, extending vertically from an irregular tree line on the top, to the lower flanks where drier conditions gradually rule out continuous tree cover. To the delight of skiers who frequent the region's dozen downhill ski

Opposite page: Western Montana as it was in the late 1800's. Notice the "woolly worm," which always seems to grace historical maps to represent the continental divide.
Above: Western Montana can be divided into three broad environmental regions.

areas, and farmers in the valleys below who rely on irrigation, winter snow pack is commonly measured in hundreds of inches.

These spacious valleys carry the names of the major rivers that drain them — the Bitterroot, Big Hole, Madison, Gallatin, and Smith to name just a few. Valley bottoms generally range between 4,000 and 7,000 feet above sea level (affording residents a chance to use the high altitude baking directions printed on the sides of cake-mix boxes), with large sections of only the Bitterroot and Flathead valleys dropping below 3,500 feet. In contrast to the well-watered highlands, the broad valleys in the rain shadow of the encircling ranges are among the driest places in all of Montana. Sagebrush-covered and peppered with prickly pear cactus, some valley sections are suggestive of regions in the eastern part of the state. In an average year some areas receive even less precipitation than the driest places in Eastern Montana.

Human habitation and economic activity clearly are concentrated in the valley areas where population densities are among the state's highest. Since the gold rush era of the 1860s, residents of the Broad Valleys region have benefited from the complementary relationship of mountains, foothills and valleys. It is

not surprising that this region has developed the most varied economy in the state with well-developed sectors including farming, ranching, lumbering and wood products, mining and refining, tourism and recreation.

Distinct regional identities have evolved in the isolated valley expanses encircled by mountain ranges. People here view themselves as residents of the Bitterroot, Big Hole, Madison or Flathead. The barriers imposed by ranges is striking on a state highway map, which graphically illustrates how main highways avoid cresting mountains wherever possible. Travel tends to be circuitous, paralleling rivers and following nature's thoroughfares. But in such a mountain-studded area crossing mountains is inevitable, and mountain passes are a grudgingly accepted fact of life for residents. Each winter Western Montanans renew their respect for the likes of Homestake Pass (elevation 6,375), MacDonald Pass (elevation 6,325), King's Hill Pass (elevation 7,393), and even innocuous sounding "passettes" like Evaro Hill and Norris Hill, not identified on highway maps.

East of Ennis and south of Bozeman and Big Timber the broad valley landscape abruptly yields to the rugged northernmost extension of an expansive highland centered on Yellowstone National Park. This is Western Montana's Yellowstone Rockies environmental region. It includes all of the Madison Range, most of the Gallatins and the Beartooth Plateau, and the northern end of the Absaroka Range. Combined, these uplands make this the most mountain-dominated of Western Montana's three environmental regions. No section of the state has more extensive areas over 9,000 feet, and the Beartooth Plateau is the only Montana upland where peaks exceed 12,000 feet. More than two dozen rise above that rugged 10,000-foot plateau to elevations in excess of 12,000 feet, including Granite Peak, the state's highest at 12,799 feet.

In this jagged highland, valley floors generally are confined and steep-sided. The only noticeable exception to narrow valley floors is the Yellowstone River's Paradise Valley south of Livingston, which is more similar to the broad valleys to the north and west. Also unlike its sister valleys, the Paradise is unforested except for the sinuous line of riverside cottonwoods that highlight the course of the Yellowstone.

Steep slopes and one of the state's most abbreviated growing seasons severely limit agriculture within the Yellowstone Rockies. Only on the lower, more nearly level and fertile floodplain of the Paradise Valley is there an obvious farming component. Even most livestock operators are confined to the lower valleys and accessible slopes around the periphery of the highlands. Lumbering is present in some areas, but restrictions imposed by accessibility, wilderness areas,

Infrared satellite images from the U.S. Geologic Survey's ERTS/LANDSAT program. At left is shown an area whose corners are approximately Ashley Lake in the northwest, the Rocky Mountain Front in the northeast, the Deer Lodge Valley in the southeast and the wildlands of the Selway-Bitterroot southwest of Missoula. Note the agricultural patterns in the Flathead Valley whose expanse is an exception to narrow, constricted corridors of much of the northwest portion of the region.

Opposite page: This image reveals the very different landscape of southwest Montana, and shows how its broad dry valleys separate distinct mountain ranges. You see here a shot centered over Boulder. Canyon Ferry is the large body of water at the top. Ennis Lake at the bottom. The Berkeley Pit can be seen as a spot of blue.
Please note that infrared images render all greenery in red.

distance from mills and forests that regenerate slowly limit its importance.

Recreation and tourism dominate the economy of most Yellowstone Rockies communities. From the regional metropolis of Red Lodge (population 1,900) on down, economic emphasis is on catering to the visitors who come to enjoy the region's seemingly limitless outdoor recreation potential. Every year thousands are drawn to the area to ski Red Lodge Mountain or take on Sundown run at Big Sky, to hike and fish in the pristine and lofty solitude of the Absaroka-Beartooth Wilderness area's 920,000 acres, to enjoy western hospitality at one of the numerous dude ranches in the area, or to hunt elk in the roadless backcountry. The area also serves as Montana's gateway to Yellowstone National Park with the communities of West Yellowstone, Gardiner, and the curious town of Cooke City functioning as portals to this largest, oldest and perhaps most famous of all national parks.

Mountains not only dominate Western Montana's physical scene, they are just as central to the psyche of its residents. We are a mountain-conscious and mountain-addicted group. Residents who dare move out of the region to less topographically endowed environments, places where mere nubbins on the face of the earth are revered as monuments, find they suffer from what might be described facetiously as a variety of agoraphobia, the abnormal fear of open spaces. The degree of stress varies with individuals, but the symptoms are much the same. These include a critical rejection of the offending flat environment and erratic, sometimes even frantic, searches to ferret out something, anything, that even suggests topographic relief.

The Beartooths, Crazies, Madisons and Gallatins, Bitterroots and Missions exert a strong pull, and invariably former residents suffering terminal agoraphobia arrange for trips back home as often as possible. Most Western Montanans probably know at least a few displaced agoraphobiacs for whom the stress was too much. These are the ones who returned, often abandoning advanced schooling, high paying jobs or promising careers for the privilege once again to call Western Montana home.

It's a love affair, plain and simple. Western Montana has cast its spell on most of its residents and openly flirts with the emotions of many of the hundreds of thousands of tourists whose rendezvous are limited by two-week vacations.

Residents sympathize with tourists who are bewitched by the magic of Western Montana. Completely captivated by the attributes of the region, they may exhibit the signs and symptoms that indicate Paradise Syndrome. Glassy eyes, hyperactivity, and an insatiable desire to learn all there is to know about the region are sure early signs of its onset. In milder cases that may be as far as it goes, but for others this is only the beginning.

In full-blown cases Paradise Syndrome almost always manifests itself in a determination to move to Western Montana: to leave the crime, pollution, congestion, two-hour daily commuting and other maladies of the city and to settle into one of Western Montana's picturesque mountain valleys where life seems to parallel the script of a Disney movie when viewed through the windshield of a Winnebago.

Each summer local chamber of commerce offices throughout Western Montana are flooded by requests about job and business prospects from hopeful tourists. A fortunate few are able to pick up and start again in Montana. However, the prospect of uprooting families, the limited employment opportunities in Western Montana, and other harsh realities shatter the hopes of most of making Montana a permanent home. For these would-be residents Western Montana cabins and condos, or at least annual visits, keep them in touch with this special place.

Geographers once assumed that people living in certain types of natural environments, such as mountains, coasts, deserts or steppes, were putty in the hands of nature to be molded, right down to their very personalities, by their physical setting. This doctrine of environmental determinism, now viewed as embarrassingly naive and simplistic, was widespread among geographers as recently as the early 20th century.

According to environmental determinists, mountain dwellers were expected to be conservative and uncomfortable with change, characteristics acquired from the rugged configuration of the surrounding landscape. Inwardly focused on their own region, they were expected to have little time or concern for the goings-on in adjacent plains regions. A suspicion toward strangers, extreme sensitivity to criticism, superstition, strong religious feelings, and an intense love of home and family were other presumed traits among mountain folks. The difficulty of life in such a rugged setting meant that residents naturally would be industrious, frugal, provident, and peculiarly honest and endowed with strong muscles, unjaded nerves, iron purpose, and disinterest in luxury. These qualities may characterize some Western Montanans, but few today would suggest they are directly and solely attributable to the mountainous setting.

As a group we Western Montanans are a varied lot, but we do seem to share some traits that make us different from, say, the residents of southern Michigan, Florida, or metropolitan New York. Here residents still seem to have time for the sort of old-fashioned neighborliness that has long since disappeared in

rapid-paced sections of the country. Visitors to Western Montana comment on the informality and friendliness of its citizens. Two strangers passing on a sidewalk are as likely as not to acknowledge each other with a smile and a "Howdy." Each late summer and early fall virtually every daily newspaper in the region prints letters to the editor from grateful tourists back home in Des Moines or Seattle or Cleveland thanking individuals, and sometimes entire communities, for help beyond the call of duty extended to them during some crisis while vacationing in Western Montana.

Titles, by themselves, don't seem to mean much to most Western Montanans, who prefer to accept others as equals. Even "Mr." and "Mrs." are usually abandoned here and most direct people-to-people contacts are on a first-name basis. In some sections of the nation a family name and what one's parents did have a profound bearing on political, economic and social acceptance and success. Here there is an obvious disdain for such blue-blooded stratification. When Western Montanans hear reference to "breeding" they are more inclined to think of black white-face cattle!

There isn't much of a market for Yves St. Laurent or Christian Dior evening gowns in Butte or Belgrade, Melrose and Moiese. Dress here tends to be just as casual as the residents. If anything, an Eddie Bauer look is the norm. Levis and substantial, Vibram-sole hiking boots capable of scaling Mt. Everest are standard apparel in any season. We tend more toward the practical and durable.

It's not that Western Montanans don't dress up. Some businessmen, for example, wear three-piece suits to work every day. But chances are in most settings they wouldn't stand out if they didn't. Even when well-turned-out, a Western Montanan isn't bedecked in the latest Paris or New York fashion. Our tastes for styles seem to run a little behind many other parts of the country. Certainly other Western Montanans have sensed that they aren't quite up to date when they step off a plane at Denver's Stapleton International or Seattle's SeaTac and feel as if they have just passed through some sort of fashion time-warp.

That residents of the region are not especially citified should not be surprising since half are rural dwellers. According to 1980 figures almost half of Western Montana's counties are 100-percent rural and the region lacks a single Bureau-of-the-Census-defined metropolitan area. With a population of 33,388, Missoula is the region's major city. Even if those in the outlying areas are added, the total population of 65,476 would rank it as only a modest-size suburb around many major U.S. cities. Most common in Western Montana are towns in which population is less than the community's elevation in feet. This holds true even for some of the mid-size towns like Dillon (pop. 3,976 and elev. 5,406 feet), Philipsburg (pop. 1,138 and elev. 5,250 feet), and Hamilton (pop. 2,661 and elev. 3,524 feet).

The total lack of merging megalopolitan complexes isn't missed by most Western Montanans. From Missoula on down, communities retain a human and livable scale. In many, residents know just which house you're talking about if in conversation you say, for example, "you know that pink house in the 400 block of South 5th . . ." Without exception a cross-town excursion can be accomplished by auto in just a matter of minutes. And even though Bozemanites might curse the three or four minutes they are held up each morning and evening rush hour by the light at 7th and Main, and Missoulians dread the five to six minutes lost at their infamous "malfunction junction," they quickly regain perspective after visits to Seattle or Denver, Los Angeles or Chicago. Even for Missoulians the day is far in the future when tuning to a local radio station's live helicopter traffic report will become a regular rush-hour routine.

Skiing some of the best powder the West has to offer only a half-hour from home; trying that new fly in a crystal clear, Blue Ribbon trout stream; a leisurely Sunday-afternoon drive through the vivid fall colors of Glacier; the anticipation of sunrise on opening day of big-game season in your favorite drainage; calling up Sid for last-minute, weekend cross-country ski reservations at the Izaak Walton Inn; heading into the Bob with a string of horses; or just parking your camper at Hyalite Reservoir for the weekend or launching your 17-footer into Canyon Ferry Lake at the Silos — how much more could we outdoor-oriented Western Montanans want! Perhaps we should pinch ourselves each week just to make sure this is reality. For what to others is only a dream, or at best, a too-short Montana vacation, is available to us 52 weeks a year.

The quality-of-life revolution that swept this country beginning in the 1960s has permanently changed Western Montana. Pulled here by the promise of life in an ecotopian environment and pushed out by seemingly insurmountable environmental, economic and social problems back home, countless refugees from Colorado, displaced Californians, and escapees from New Jersey have made Western Montana their home in the last 20 years. Many arrived convinced that they weren't going to let Montana become another Colorado or Bozeman another Boulder. Once linked up with numerous native Montanans who shared their concern for preservation of the natural environment, Western Montana quickly evolved into the undisputed center of the state's vocal and influential environmentalist community. Working through groups like the Montana Wilderness Association, the Environmental Information Center, and more regional organizations such as the Madison-Gallatin Alliance or Save the Kootenai River Association, these conservationists lobby religiously and strive to keep the public informed on critical environmental issues.

Not all Western Montanans are avid conservationists, but within the region there is a prevailing concern for environmental quality. The siting of high-voltage transmission lines, the damming of Kootenai Falls, wilderness designations, the plight of the grizzly, or even a coal mine in British Columbia that could adversely impact the water quality of the Flathead drainage, are major public issues.

Rocky Mountain Montana may account for only the western one-third of the state, but that third encompasses an area of approximately 50,000 square miles. That's larger than many states, including New York or Pennsylvania. By eastern U.S. standards distances here are immense. The 564 highway miles from Red Lodge in the southeast to Yaak in the northwest is equivalent to driving Interstate 95 from Boston, Massachusetts to Richmond, Virginia and enroute passing through Rhode Island, Connecticut, New York, New Jersey, Delaware and Maryland! You'd have to be waiting at the door when the Red Lodge Cafe opens at 6:00 a.m. to eat breakfast there and have any hope of driving to Yaak the same day with enough time for a few leisurely aperitifs before your midnight snack at Yaak's rustic Dirty Shame Saloon.

With a regional population of about 400,000, approximately half of the state total, Western Montana is the most populated section of the American Rockies. Nowhere else have people moved in and occupied a section of the Rockies as they have in Montana. In each of the other Rocky Mountain states only a small percentage of residents live within the mountain section, even when that portion accounts for over half their state's area. A mere 30 percent of Idaho's population is scattered through the Rocky Mountain two-thirds of the state, and even in Colorado only 300,000 people, less than 15 percent, can call the mountainous western 60 percent of the state home. For most residents of the other Rocky Mountain states the Rockies are a sparsely populated neighboring area, an impractical permanent home, a place to which they retreat solely for recreation. For Western Montanans the mountains are home, a place where you cover your tomatoes in July and have not yet put away your snow shovel when your downlander neighbors already are tuning up their lawn mowers.

Montana's population core has been centered far to the west since the 1860s when the rush of hopeful miners and other frontiersmen began to fill western valleys. By the 1870s well over 90 percent of Montana's census population was clustered within a relatively small section of the territory's southwestern corner. This was the state's historic core, the nucleus around which the state we know today was built. Montana is still the only state or province that has its capital, its two major universities, many of its largest cities (six of the nine biggest), and much of its manufacturing within the Rocky Mountains.

Western Montanans like to think people are talking about their third of the state when they hear others refer to Montana as a "state of mind" or as a "symphony." Residents just assumed Governor Schwinden was referring to Western Montana when he commented that Montana was "the last of the best" on the occasion of his inauguration speech in 1980. Western Montanans are rightfully proud of their section of the Big Sky Country — both its people and the place are essential elements of the Montana mystique.

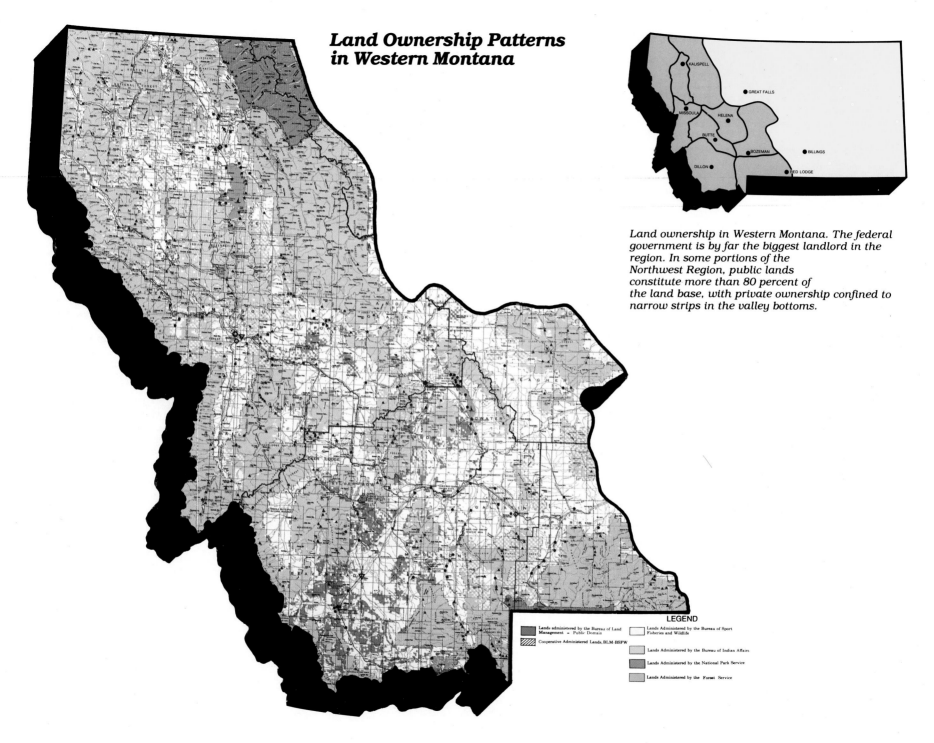

Land Ownership Patterns in Western Montana

Land ownership in Western Montana. The federal government is by far the biggest landlord in the region. In some portions of the Northwest Region, public lands constitute more than 80 percent of the land base, with private ownership confined to narrow strips in the valley bottoms.

LEGEND

Lands administered by the Bureau of Land Management – Public Domain

Cooperative Administered Lands, BLM-BSFW

Lands Administered by the Bureau of Sport Fisheries and Wildlife

Lands Administered by the Bureau of Indian Affairs

Lands Administered by the National Park Service

Lands Administered by the Forest Service

9

WESTERN MONTANA: THE PHYSICAL BASE

GEOLOGY: ROCKY MOUNTAIN GENESIS

Over the Mission Mountains, Grey Wolf Peak in the center, the Swan Range in the distance. Rick Graetz photo.

The complexity of Western Montana's geologic evolution is apparent on a wall-size geologic map of the state. It shows each major rock unit with a different color or pattern and uses heavy black lines to indicate faults. In Great Plains Montana the pattern is rather simple with sections thousands of square miles in area shown with the same color or shading. This indicates extensive tracts covered by the same rock unit, still lying flat and undisturbed right where it was deposited tens of millions of years ago. In Western Montana the pattern is anything but simple. On the map the region is a jumble of colors and irregular shapes. Rather than lying in nice flat layers covering large areas, these rocks have been severely folded, faulted, thrusted and intruded by molten rock from below. The result is a complex regional geology on which geologists thrive. To them it is a 10,000-piece jigsaw puzzle made even more challenging by a third dimension. Investigations to unravel the region's complex geologic evolution have resulted in more than a thousand published reports and articles.

Even at a general level, the story of Western Montana's geologic evolution is a fascinating one that at times sounds a bit like Ripley's *"Believe It or Not."* Ideas on the evolution of Montana and all of North America have changed dramatically over the last 20 years as notions previously laughed at are gaining acceptance. Contemporary theories refer to things like splitting and drifting continents and spreading sea floors, all of which may have a direct bearing on the geologic history of Western Montana.

Precambrian

We can pick up our brief overview of the region's geologic development about one and a half billion years ago during the Precambrian geologic period, the time span that includes rocks older than 600 million years.

It now is assumed that the earth's outer shell, its crust, and the upper layer of the mantle immediately below, consist of a number of rigid plates. The number, as well as the size and shape of plates evidently has changed through geologic time, but now totals about twelve. These plates are in constant, imperceptible motion, drifting and carrying the continents along with them. They sometimes split or collide with one another generating forces that can produce mountain ranges and volcanic activity. Deep in the distant past of the mid-Precambrian, the micro-plate of which Montana was a part, split in two. Most of Montana was just to the east of the line along which the plate separated, and became a part of the eastern fragment. The two plates drifted apart allowing the sea floor of the Pacific Ocean and a new plate to form in the widening space between them. The section that pulled away from Montana may now be a part of the Siberian section of the Soviet Union. The plate of which Montana was a part drifted in the opposite direction for eons until about 290 million years ago when it collided and merged with other drifting continents to form the gigantic land mass of Pangaea which itself split and separated into our present continents.

There was no Idaho or Washington one and a half billion years ago and Montana was located on what was then the west coast. This Precambrian sea reached deep into Montana, submerging everything west of its shoreline, which ran approximately through Browning, Choteau, Lewistown, Roundup, Three Forks, and Dillon. Rivers emptying into the sea deposited sand, silt, and mud in near shore areas, and carbonates precipitated out of the ocean waters. As these bottom sediments accumulated just off the edge of the new continent, the floor of the marginal sea evidently subsided, thereby permitting an extra thick accumulation. In what is now far western Montana and was then a belt 120 miles out at sea, the subsidence was greatest and accumulation thickest.

Since deposition, these water-lain sediments have lithified into rocks including sandstones, shales, mudstones and impure limestones and in many areas have been compacted further and altered into harder forms, especially quartzite (previously sandstone) and argillite (previously shale). Abundant fossil mud cracks, ripple marks, raindrop impressions, and casts of salt crystals suggest this depositional environment definitely was not a deep ocean. More likely it was a shallow sea or perhaps even a tidal flat that was alternately wet and dry. Its limestone rocks now contain fossils of primitive blue-green algae (stromatolites) that attest to the presence of organisms that must have been exposed to the air much of the time during their growth, possibly in slimy green algal mats on mud flats more than a billion years ago.

These Precambrian-age sedimentary rocks are referred to collectively as the Belt Series. Nearly all of Montana west of Drummond and Glacier National Park is underlain by them. These usually somber colored rocks of reddish-purple, gray, brown, and green are easily recognizable on mountain sides and in road cuts throughout the region. With a possible thickness of several miles in the far western fringe of the state, it is easy to see why they so dominate the landscape. In fact, some of the region's mountain ranges including the Purcell, Cabinet, Mission and Sapphire ranges are composed almost entirely of these rocks.

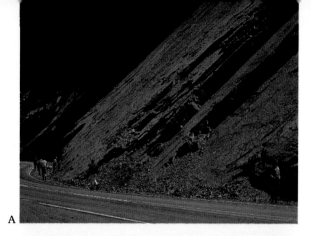

Right: (A) An exposure of Belt rock showing in a road cut near Phillipsburg. (B) Stromatolite — fossils formed from some of the earth's earliest life forms, primitive algae. (C) Mud cracks and (D) ripple marks formed in ancient mud and solidified into Belt rock of the Flint Creek hills. John Alwin photos.

Prairie Reef and its geologic cousin, the Chinese Wall, in the Bob Marshall Wilderness are exposed reefs of limestone formed more than 225 million years ago. Pat O'Hara photo.

Paleozoic

During the Paleozoic Era, which includes the time from the end of the Precambrian some 600 million years ago up to 225 million years before the present, Western Montana was probably rather low, flat and featureless. Mountains were not yet a part of the landscape. Rocks dating from this span of time tell of a region over which seas repeatedly advanced and retreated — what geologists call transgressions and regressions. Sometimes all of Western Montana was submerged and at other times only parts were below water. At least 25 different Paleozoic rock units are recognized and named. They now have a combined thickness of from 5,000 to 10,000 feet. Limestone deposited under these seas is the most abundant rock type. It can be seen as thick layers of light gray cliffs on many of the mountains from southwestern Montana north to the Sawtooth Range. The popular and bold Chinese Wall in the remote backcountry of the Bob Marshall Wilderness is made up of these limestones.

Farther to the south the gray cap of the Bridgers is also Paleozoic limestone. This same 330 million-year-old formation towers as gray cliffs on both sides of the narrow gap through which I-90 passes just west of Bozeman Pass. In addition to limestone, Western Montana's Paleozoic rock includes thick layers of sandstone and shale. Geologists especially are interested in these rocks because most oil and gas discovered in Montana has been associated with them.

On the eve of the Paleozoic, Western Montana was left as a land area except in the far southwest where a sea extended northward. It was a curious sea that contained an exceptionally high concentration of phosphate, which precipitated out in layers several feet thick. This Phosphoria formation has been mined commercially at several sites in the southwest and once supplied Stauffer Chemical's phosphorus plant west of Butte.

Mesozoic

Relatively peaceful conditions of leisurely transgressions and regressions of Paleozoic seas were shattered by dramatic developments in the subsequent Mesozoic Era, between 225 and 65 million years ago. The face of Western Montana underwent a monumental transformation. Forces of unbelievable strength left the previously flat-lying layers of Belt and Paleozoic rocks folded, contorted, and actually standing on end. Huge slabs of these rocks miles in thickness were moved about like toy cars and slid distances of 80 miles and more. Molten material from deep within the earth punched its way up from below, and belching and spewing volcanoes added to the drama.

It was a collision, of sorts that terminated the geologic tranquility of Western Montana. The first rumblings of change date from approximately 170 million years ago when the Paleo-Pacific plate and the North American plate converged just to the west of Montana. Since the crustal material of the oceanic plate was more dense, it buckled under the western, continental edge of the North American plate. Like the front end of an automobile after a head-on collision, the edge of the overriding continental plate was shortened, crumpled and lifted upward. This marked the beginning of the formation of Montana's first Rockies.

It has been estimated that the compression generated by this collision shortened the blanket of sedimentary rocks in Western Montana from west to east by no less than 75 to 100 miles. Previously flat sedimentary rock layers buckled into folds up to 25 miles wide and originally up to 5 miles high. These crinkled and inclined layers of rocks can be seen throughout Western Montana. In places, previously horizontal rocks now stand vertically and others have been completely overturned.

Compressive forces also deformed rocks by faulting. The most impressive of these were the large overthrust faults that fractured weak or brittle buried rock layers and shoved large sheets up and over onto adjacent rocks. Western Montana's most celebrated is the Lewis Overthrust which carried a huge 1,000-plus-square-mile sheet of layered rock at least six miles thick eastward, perhaps from as far away as northern Idaho, to where it eventually came to rest atop what is now Glacier National Park. This gigantic thrust sheet originally included Belt rocks at the bottom mantled by progressively younger Paleozoic and Mesozoic sediments. Erosion has long since stripped away the fairly thin covering of Paleozoic and Mesozoic rocks from the top of this displaced slab and have cut deeply into the older and harder Belt rocks below, etching out the peaks that now tower above the Park. Conspicuous and resistant 9,056-foot Chief Mountain on the northeastern edge of the Park is a large island mass of Belt rock. It was once part of the thrust sheet and was stranded when erosion removed the inter-connecting Belt rock.

Overthrusting of rocks occurred in a broad section of Western Montana north of a line extending south from just east of Glacier National Park through White Sulphur Springs, the northern end of the Bridgers, Whitehall and Dillon. Nowhere within this region has overthrusting produced a more unique mountainous landscape than in the Sawtooth Range south of Glacier. High north-south trending ridges and parallel intervening valley troughs give the natural landscape a wave-like appearance. This topography results from once horizontal and layered slabs of rocks which have been faulted into relatively short slabs and then thrusted up or slid over those to the east. The rock formations now stand up at a high angle, stacked sideways like a tilted deck of cards. Each linear ridge and valley marks the upturned edge of a rock unit, ridges corresponding with resistant rocks (often limestone) and valleys with more easily eroded strata (often shale).

Hiking east-west through this area over ridges and valleys one crosses the same sequence of rock units time and time again. This can be explained by the fact that previously adjacent and horizontal rock units were faulted into short sections as they were thrust and stacked sideways.

Upward migrations and intrusion of molten material from deep within the earth, and even Mount St. Helens-like volcanoes played a part in the evolution of the region's first, or Ancestral Rockies. To understand their presence we have to return to the collision of the Paleo-Pacific and North American plates. You may remember that while the lighter continental edge of North America rode over the oceanic plate and was

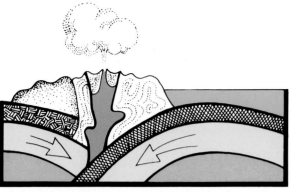

Above: When the earth's plates collide, one usually buckles downward, causing uplift and crumpling of the overriding plate. Convergence of plates is associated with mountain building, deep-sea trenches, volcanoes and earthquakes.

Left: This rock garden is the result of superheated liquid rock or magma being squirted between rock formations above it and then revealed by erosion. Western Montana has one very large such formation called the Boulder Batholith, seen here east of Butte. John Alwin photo.

uplifted, compressed and crumpled, the heavier oceanic plate buckled down and descended into the earth's mantle. Rocks drawn down in this subduction zone eventually began to melt as they moved deeper into the earth. High temperatures and pressure altered the oceanic plate as though it were in a gigantic pressure cooker. Some rock melted and produced molten rock, or magma. Because it was lighter than its enclosing rock, this magma rose, but not all of the molten material reached the surface. Some cooled and solidified into granite thousands of feet below ground forming large bodies called batholiths. This happened under a large area between Butte and Helena 70 to 80 million years ago. Erosion has stripped away overlying rock and exposed the 60- by 30-mile Boulder Batholith. Its now irregular landscape of boulders and spires (the result of much more recent erosion) dominates the mountainous terrain between these two towns and is easily visible along Interstate 90 on Homestake Pass east of Butte.

Batholiths and smaller intrusions pushed up under other sections of Western Montana and have been exhumed. These include the Tobacco Root Batholith in the north end of the Tobacco Root Mountains, the Philipsburg Batholith, those in the Pioneer and Castle mountains and many smaller intrusives in the Little Belts and other ranges. It is no coincidence that most of Western Montana's ghost towns and present-day mining districts are near these intrusives. Most of the metal-bearing ore deposits in Western Montana owe their existence to these intrusives. As great masses of molten material pushed upward they cracked and fissured the enclosing host rock through which they moved. Superheated "juices" with high mineral concentrations produced by cooling and crystallization of these deeply buried bodies were squeezed into the fissures. There they deposited the ores as vein fillings which have yielded billions of dollars worth of gold, silver, copper and lead.

In places molten material reached the surface where some flowed or blew out through volcanoes. During the emplacement of the Boulder Batholith, a field of large volcanoes developed on the surface. Erosion has long since destroyed the outline of perhaps once classic volcanic cones, but lava that poured from them still blankets sections of the area with up to 10,000 feet of basalt. These volcanoes spewed ash that drifted far to the east and can be identified in 70 million-year-old rock as far away as extreme southeastern Montana.

Above: Mountain building forces have left these once horizontal rocks standing on end at Devil's Slide near Gardiner. William Koenig photo.

Tertiary

The initial compression and associated folding and thrust faulting that began 170 million years ago was only the prelude to a protracted period of intense geologic activity within Western Montana. This mountain building episode continued into the subsequent Tertiary Period (65 to 3 million years ago) and probably continued in fits and starts until at least 50 million years before the present.

Volcanoes developed in areas including the Madison Range where peaks like Lone Mountain (11,166 feet), Fan Mountain (10,304 feet), and Sphinx Mountain (10,876 feet) are all remnants of the subsurface plumbing that once fed volcanoes. Farther east a large complex of volcanoes produced a highland, the remnants of which we now call the Crazy Mountains. To the northwest volcanoes also spewed out the thick pile of volcanic rocks that form the 300-square-mile Adel Mountains between Craig and Cascade.

One of the most intriguing legacies of this volcanic activity is the petrified forests of Montana's Gallatin Range. These and associated "forests" of Yellowstone National Park contain some of the world's most spectacular deposits of fossilized plants. They are entombed in sediments that William Fritz, geologist at the University of Montana, thinks are derived primarily from mud flows and deposits of rivers that drained slopes of towering volcanoes some 50 million years ago, near the close of this initial phase of intense geologic activity. Some trees were buried where they stood and today remain as upright, petrified stumps still seemingly supported in solid rock by now fossilized roots. More commonly they remain as petrified trunks, stripped of branches and roots (probably while being carried downhill) and lying horizontally in the enclosing rock. Volcanoes that spawned these mudflows may have reached elevations of 10,000 feet above adjacent valleys. This would explain the mixture of cool-temperate trees like spruce and fir found along with much more tropical species like fig, magnolia, and avocado. Mud flows must have carried down stumps of trees from temperate zones to areas where they were mixed with species of the tropical lowlands. The 6,000 feet of volcanic rocks that now sit atop the Gallatin Range and the volcanic pile on the Absaroka also came from these same volcanoes.

In south-central Montana the collision of the plates mentioned earlier cracked the earth's crust and squeezed upward large blocks with their mantle of

sedimentary rocks. One large block defined at the edges by faults pushed upward beginning 50 to 60 million years ago forming today's Absaroka and Beartooth ranges. Since this entire highland between Highway 89 on the west and Red Lodge on the east is one large block of the earth's crust, geologists refer to the entire elevated tract as the Beartooth Range. Most has been stripped of its previous veneer of younger rocks and now only a few remnants sit atop the north portion of the Beartooth Plateau. Rocks on the surface are exposed sections of the earth's crust and are

The Indiana University Geologic Field Camp conducted each summer since the 1940s from a base in the Tobacco Root Mountains enjoys a national reputation and enrolls students from about 50 major universities. Intended as a "capstone" to an undergraduate degree, the program is the largest of its kind in the nation, having instructed more than 2,000 students. John Alwin photos.

A

B

C

(A) Some of the oldest exposed rocks in the world are found high in the Beartooth Plateau. Mt. Rosebud is in the background. Wayne Scherr photo.

(B) Evidence of volcanic activity can be seen in these columnar rocks in the Absarokas just above Gardiner. John Alwin photo.

(C) These sawtooth ridges in the Rocky Mountain Front are the leading edge of rock layers overthrust onto the prairie. Rick Graetz photo.

among the oldest rocks discovered in the world. When scientists working for NASA wanted extremely old rocks for their planetary and early crustal genesis studies they came to the western part of this uplifted and exposed chunk of the crust. In the Absaroka Range geologists found granite-type rock that dated at 3.5 billion years — only 200 million years younger than the world's oldest known rock.

Although Western Montanans think of the Madison and Gallatin ranges as separate highlands, they are part of the same crustal block that was pushed upward like the Beartooth block to the east. Geologic evidence suggests they and the Beartooth were part of the same large block during at least the initial period of uplift. A fault along the east side of the Paradise Valley apparently developed later, separating the block and allowing the eastern portion of the Madison-Gallatin block to tilt downward, forming the Paradise Valley. This tilting may help explain why the lava flows of 50 million years ago piled up to such depth over the Gallatins — they simply filled in a lower area.

Between about 50 to 20 million years ago Western Montana experienced a period of relative geologic tranquility. Major processes during that span were erosional, as nature worked at reducing the Ancestral Rockies. Material eroded from highlands was carried by rivers and deposited into adjacent lowlands. As highlands were worn down and valleys filled in, the natural landscape was subdued and may have resulted in a rather flat and featureless Western Montana by 20 million years ago.

The mountains and ranges Western Montanans know today probably started taking shape about 20 million years ago when, instead of being compressed as was the case in the forming of the Ancestral Rockies, the region was quite literally pulled apart in an east-west direction. A likely explanation for this is an exceptionally high heat flow below the earth's crust directly under the area. This would have caused the overlying crust to rise and stretch. By at least 20 million years ago crustal extensions evidently reached the point where north-south running tensional, or "pull-apart," faults developed in the crust, breaking it into numerous large blocks. Even though the entire region rose, some blocks rose higher than adjacent ones. Those that rose the most became fault-block mountains while the others became high inter-montane valleys. In some places new pull-apart forces reactivated existing faults and some former highlands experienced renewed uplift.

Block faulting produced the Second Rockies, the ones we see today in Western Montana. The nature of these fault-block mountains is most apparent in the more linear ranges like the Mission and Bridger. Both ridge-like highlands correspond to the most elevated western edge of elongate and tilted fault blocks. Vertical movement was most pronounced along north-south faults on their west sides and today their west faces are the most dramatic, rising abruptly above flat valleys to the west. Certainly one of the most impressive sights in Montana greets travelers heading north on Highway 93 as they crest the hill just north of Ravalli. From this vantage point the mile-high west face of the snow-covered Missions seems larger than life.

Some geologists think that the rivers of southwestern Montana used to drain out of the state to the south prior to the formation of the Second Rockies. Uplifting associated with the evolution of today's mountains closed former channels and backed water into large lakes which flooded intermontane valleys. Valleys like the Bitterroot, Deer Lodge, Madison and Gallatin are blanketed with up to several thousand feet of light-colored, Tertiary-age lake beds. They are composed of the sand, silt and gravel eroded off adjacent highlands and deposited by rivers on the floor of the ancient lakes into which they drained. Lake beds are seen most easily in road cuts or along steep river banks where their generally light color and loose and soft nature make them easy to spot.

Material in these sediments tells us much about late Tertiary time. An abundance of ash attests to continued violent and explosive volcanic activity. Fossil remains of animals like camels, four-tusked elephants, and three-toed primitive horses not only help date the block faulting that produced the lake beds in which they are found, but also tell us that Western Montana was then a much drier, even desert-like place.

After millions of years with their southern outlets blocked by high mountain ranges, new northward flowing drainage channels were cut across lower divides. The new escape channels that allowed water to drain to the north were cut as steep canyons and gorges through the solid rock of former divides. The narrow canyon of the Madison River through the Beartrap area north of Ennis, the constricted Jefferson River Canyon east of Whitehall, and the "Gates of the Mountains" through which the Missouri passes north of Helena also may have originated in this manner. Although the lakes have long since drained, their horizontal layers of lake sediments have left Western Montana's large intermontane valleys with consistently flat floors.

We should be careful not to refer to the Second Rockies in the past tense, since they evidently still are forming. Movement along faults of these great blocks, with valleys dropping down relative to rising highlands, continued through the Tertiary and still is occurring today. This movement generates the earthquakes that periodically shake Western Montana and makes this region one of the most earthquake prone in the nation, only slightly behind California.

Above: Geologic memorial to the 19 campers who died under the slide caused by the huge earthquake at Hebgen Lake, Aug. 17, 1959. Tom Dietrich.
Below: The reservoir backed up by the slide is now known as Quake Lake. Tom Dietrich.

Quakes

Western Montana's two major mountain-building episodes since the Precambrian have left the earth's crust and overlying rocks fractured and faulted. Movement along these fractures continues today, especially at contacts between the large crustal blocks formed during the most recent and on-going mountain-building period. Gigantic blocks corresponding to intermontane valleys are still settling relative to adjacent highland blocks. Rather than constant slipping taking place, faults hold and rock along the fault is deformed by stresses. As the rock is strained, elastic energy is stored in it just like a watch spring. Initially, friction is sufficient to lock the two blocks together, but stresses eventually may build to the point where the blocks suddenly slip, releasing the pent-up stress and causing an earthquake. The same results can and do occur when movement along a fault is lateral instead of up and down.

Sections of Western Montana lie at the northern end of the Intermountain Seismic Belt, a north-northwest trending earthquake zone that begins in the south around Las Vegas, Nevada. The Belt enters southwest Montana along a more than 150-mile front centered on the Hebgen Lake area, and narrows to about 100 miles as it swings to the northwest through Bozeman, Butte, Helena, and on to just beyond Kalispell. According to Mike Stickney, Director of the Earthquake Studies Office at the Montana Bureau of Mines and Geology, earthquakes in this zone rank Montana as the nation's fourth most seismically active state. Most of the state's recorded quakes have been within this swath, with most notable concentrations in the Big Arm Bay area just southwest of Flathead Lake, the Helena Valley, the region between Townsend and Three Forks, and the territory from the southern Gravelly Range eastward to Hebgen Lake. The Hebgen Lake area is the most seismically active.

Each year this section of Western Montana experiences hundreds to thousands of quakes and averages about 150 per month. Most are small and detectable only by sensitive seismographs, but some usually qualify as at least modest quakes capable of startling residents in nearby areas. Montana's first major earthquake occurred in 1925 north of Three Forks. Its two most famous and destructive quakes were those at Helena in 1935 and Hebgen Lake in 1959.

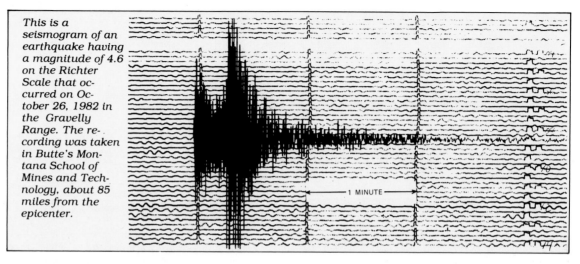

This is a seismogram of an earthquake having a magnitude of 4.6 on the Richter Scale that occurred on October 26, 1982 in the Gravelly Range. The recording was taken in Butte's Montana School of Mines and Technology, about 85 miles from the epicenter.

1 MINUTE

According to a 1983 publication by the Montana Bureau of Mines and Geology, Helena is the only major city in the state that is known to lie near an active fault capable of causing large earthquakes. The community also has the unenviable distinction of claiming the state's first reported quake, on May 22, 1869. Since the 1920s when systematic efforts were made to record quakes, Helena generally has experienced at least several principal quakes yearly. The strongest and most destructive series was the swarm that beset the city in 1935. They began in early October and continued sporadically until November. In all, the community was shaken by more than 2,000 quakes, including some large ones. Several people lost their lives and property damage was estimated at up to $4½ million. The series of quakes toppled the clock tower atop the Northern Pacific Railroad depot and virtually destroyed the newly completed high school. All totaled, more than half of Helena's buildings were damaged. Signs of this destructive series of tremors still can be seen in many masonry structures.

The most powerful earthquake yet recorded in Montana occurred at 11:37 P.M. on the night of August 17, 1959 in the Hebgen Lake area. On average, only about ten quakes of this magnitude (7.1 on the Richter scale) occur in the world each year. Since there were no foreshocks, the major tremor took everyone by surprise late that August night. The quake was strong enough to tilt and drop the block corresponding to the Madison

Valley in the Hebgen Lake area. The north shore of the lake dropped up to 20 feet, causing three sections of Highway 287 to slide into the lake, and innundated shoreline buildings. The jolt created giant waves large enough to overflow Hebgen Dam, an earthfill structure that dropped more than nine feet.

Within 30 seconds the shaking ground also triggered the huge Madison Canyon rockslide. Forty million cubic yards of rock broke loose from high on the south side of the Madison Canyon and slide downhill with such velocity that its leading edge and huge boulders, some larger than houses, were carried 300 feet up the north side of the valley, burying 19 campers — all within a minute. The mile-long tongue of debris up to 225 feet thick blocked the Madison River and formed Earthquake (Quake) Lake.

This giant of Montana earthquakes was felt over a 600,000-square-mile area. Montana newspaper accounts record that in Anaconda thousands ran into the streets, at Cardwell the ground shook so violently it was difficult to stand and the air was hazy with dust, chickens fell off their roosts in Judith Gap, plaster cracked in Helena, and people were awakened and objects shifted around in scores of other communities. The ground shook as far away as Rapid City, South Dakota and Salt Lake City, Utah where the upper floors of tall buildings swayed, and Colfax, in Eastern Washington, where some water pipes snapped.

The popular Hyalite Canyon seen here from the top of Hyalite Peak is a classic U-shaped valley, the result of glacial sculpting. John Reddy photo.

Artistry of the Ice

Western Montana's geologic evolution has continued through the Pleistocene Epoch, which covers most of the last three million years. This was a time of major developments in the evolution of the region's physical landscape. A continued uplift of mountain blocks added elevation to their summits, and accelerated stream erosion may have removed hundreds of cubic miles of Tertiary sediments from intermontane valleys, adding even more relief. In this epoch one of the most interesting geological processes to help shape the landscape of large sections of Western Montana was multiple Pleistocene glaciation.

Both continental and alpine glaciation altered Western Montana. Continental glaciers were gigantic sheets of ice thousands of feet thick covering hundreds of thousands of square miles. The sheet that invaded sections of Western Montana during Pleistocene ice ages is known as the Cordilleran Sheet. It formed in the Rockies and Cascade ranges of Canada and spread southward into northwestern Montana, northern Idaho and northern Washington with each glacial period. At its maximum extent in Western Montana, portions, or lobes, of that ice sheet reached to just south of Flathead Lake in the Mission Valley and as far down the Swan River Valley as Clearwater Junction. Alpine glaciation was more of a home-grown phenomenon. Rather than ice invading the state from Canada, alpine glaciers originated within Montana's own mountains, sometimes spreading into adjacent valley areas.

Geologists still are working out the sequence and chronology of continental and alpine glaciation in Western Montana. It has been assumed that continental glaciers may have advanced into the region four times and that highlands experienced at least as many periods of Pleistocene alpine glaciation. Whatever

Alpine Glacial Landforms

Although both depositional and erosional features remain once alpine glaciers recede from an area, those formed by glacial erosion are usually the most striking and easiest to identify.

One of the most common erosional features left by mountain glaciers is the **cirque.** This is a steep-sided, half-bowl shaped depression cut into the side of a mountain by erosion beneath and around the head of a glacier. It is here that snow and ice initially accumulate to sufficient depth to form a glacier and from which it may begin a slow movement down an associated valley. Devoid of ice, these incised basins high on the flanks of mountain peaks are commonly the site of small lakes called **tarns.** Where the heads of several glaciers have scooped out adjacent cirques around the same peak, it may be left as a sharp angular summit, called a **horn,** once glaciation has ended.

Other conspicuous and distinctive remnants of alpine glaciation are **"U"-shaped valleys.** Glaciers rarely cut their own valleys, preferring to move down those already begun by rivers. As a large glacier fills and creeps downhill through such a valley it commonly is met by smaller tributary glaciers which flow in from the sides. Once ice melts, the awesome erosive power of the recently retreated glaciers is obvious. Valleys are dramatically altered, with what might have been a winding course replaced by one much straighter. Ridges that formerly extended farther out into the valley are lopped off and left as **truncated spurs.** Narrow river valleys previously "V"-shaped in cross section are replaced by "U"-shaped troughs with much wider floors and steep side walls. Since smaller tributary glaciers lack the erosive power of their much larger counterpart in the main valley below, their narrow and less deeply eroded troughs are left as **hanging valleys,** which empty into the main valley high up on side walls. Rivers cascading from these hanging valleys produce some of the Rockies' most scenic falls.

Sharp, serrated ridges are another common and striking landform in glaciated mountains. These sawtooth ridges, called **aretes,** are formed when erosion by ice in adjacent cirques or valleys wears away and sharpens the intervening divide, just like a rasp hones the blade of an axe.

As they move down valleys, glaciers pick up and push along debris. A pile of material often

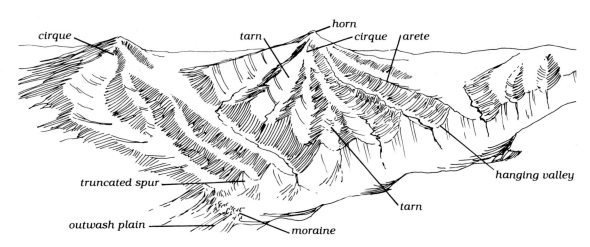

Evolution of the glaciated landscape.

accumulates in front of the leading edge of the advancing glacier, as it does in front of a bulldozer. Once the glacier reaches its maximum length and starts to melt back, the debris, combined with other material that is deposited by meltwater at the edge of the glacier, are left as a ridge called an **end moraine.** As the ice retreats it leaves behind material that has been deposited below the ice forming an irregular surface of low relief called **ground moraine.**

Looking north from the National Bison Range in the Mission Valley. This is kettle and kame topography--potholes left on a glacier-scoured plain by blocks of melting ice. Charles Kay photo.

the number, interglacial periods separated each glaciation. These were probably times when the climate was warmer and wetter than today and during which glaciers melted. The last Ice Age in the region may have begun about 25,000 years ago and ended as recently as 10,000 years ago — only yesterday in terms of geologic time.

The last ice of the Cordilleran Sheet retreated across the Canadian border at least 10,000 years ago. Alpine glaciers now are gone except for small remnants in high recesses in Glacier National Park and the summits of a few other lofty Western Montana ranges. Erosion and deposition by these Ice Age glaciers was so recent that young glacial features are still common-place in many of the region's mountains and in the valley areas of the state's northwest corner. The jagged sculpted peaks of mountains from Glacier south to the Crazies and Absarokas, the smoothed landscape of the Tobacco Plains in the Eureka area, water bodies from giant Flathead to spectacular Lake McDonald, popular Seeley Lake and the numerous ponds at Ninepipe National Wildlife Refuge, and even the hill rising immediately south of Polson for which truckers heading south on Highway 93 must downshift, are all legacies of this age of ice.

Geologists now think that average temperatures during recent ice ages may have been only marginally cooler. More critical was a much heavier winter snowfall and conditions that allowed accumulation to exceed melting. Thus, snowfields persisted and grew from year to year.

As high mountain snowfields thickened, melting, recrystallization, and compaction resulted in a metamorphosis of the snow with increasing depth. Freshly fallen, fluffy snow on the surface of the snowfield is underlain by a more compact and granular snow glaciologists call *firn* or *neve*. This is the same kind of granular snow that can be seen in old drifts at the end of winter. At greater depth, compaction further compressed the granular snow until it eventually became glacial ice. When overlying firn and ice reached sufficient thickness, probably at least 90 feet, the bottom layer of ice underwent further deformation and began to spread laterally under its own ponderous weight. Movement down valleys eroded them into troughs and sometimes carried glaciers out into adjacent lowlands to a point where a warmer climate thwarted further advance and eventually forced the ice to retreat.

During the last Ice Age, and presumably earlier ones, snowfields and, eventually, glaciers developed over many Western Montana highlands. The largest ice-covered area was the sprawling 60- by 150-mile-long tract in Montana's high and rugged north divide country. At its maximum extent this ice cap blanketed the territory from the Whitefish and Swan ranges on the west to the foothills of the Rockies on the east, and from the Canadian border south to the Blackfoot River. In this area that now includes Glacier National Park and the Bob Marshall Wilderness complex only higher peaks and ridges in the northern section reached above a sea of engulfing mountain glaciers, which spread down into valleys for distances up to 90 miles. At that time this part of Western Montana must have looked much like sections of Canada's ice-covered high Arctic islands.

Portions of at least two dozen other Western Montana highlands also supported glaciers. The largest of these was the complex which covered the higher sections of the Absaroka and Gallatin ranges and the entire Beartooth, spilling over the edges into adjacent valleys. Most other Western Montana highlands supported much smaller glacial ice masses with some of the more extensive of these found on the Cabinet, Crazy, Madison, Tobacco Root, and Anaconda-Flint Creek ranges.

The action of these recent alpine glaciers and ice caps added the dramatic scenic sculpting to highlands. Erosion by alpine glaciers sharpens mountain terrain imparting angular landforms on previously rounded hills. Glaciated Western Montana mountains exhibit all the classical alpine glacial features including cirques, horns, aretes, U-shaped and hanging valleys, and moraines. Glacier National Park is unrivaled as a place to view the spectacular artistry of now gone mountain glaciers, but other Western Montana ranges also display less extensive areas with many of the same features.

While alpine glaciers and ice caps covered many of Western Montana's loftier highlands, a continental ice sheet up to a mile thick invaded Montana's northwest corner, filling valleys and smothering all but the highest summits of the Purcell and Salish mountains.

In the last Ice Age the first probing finger-like extension, or lobe, of the Cordilleran Ice Sheet probably inched south into Montana via the Kootenai River Valley just north of Eureka. At that point the Kootenai flows along the bottom of a section of a gigantic steep-sided valley known as the Rocky Mountain Trench. Extending for 800 miles from the Yukon south to Flathead Lake, the trench marks a linear belt under which the earth's crust sank during the formation of the Rockies. The lowland presented the southward spreading ice with its path of least resistance and tended to funnel ice into northwestern Montana.

Glacier Park is a showcase of glacial features. Above is
the ice carved wall above Iceberg Lake in the
the Swiftcurrent Valley. Notice the notch in the rocky skyline.

Above right: The photographer climbed into the notch to shoot Iceberg Lake
looking back east to the valley. Rick Graetz photos.

Right: Only an infant compared to glaciers of the past, but a glacier
nonetheless, is Grasshopper Glacier in the Beartooth Mountains. Charles Kay
photo.

As the ice lobe pushed southward it subdued the landscape over which it passed. Low areas were filled with debris carried along by the ice, and ridges and other high points on the valley floor were smoothed. One distinctive landform left by the advancing ice can be seen in the Tobacco Plains. These are the streamlined drumlins visible around Eureka and north toward the Canadian line. They formed beneath the advancing ice when its movement piled up and molded underlying glacial debris into elongate ridges shaped like the inverted bowl of a spoon. Ideally, drumlins trend parallel to the movement of the ice and have their steepest slope pointing in the direction from which the ice came. In the Tobacco Plains country a north-south orientation and steepest faces on the north confirm that ice moved into this area from that direction.

When the ice lobe reached about as far south as Rexford, it evidently split. A small portion continued up the Kootenai and the main body, called the Flathead Glacier or Flathead Lobe, continued down the Rocky Mountain Trench, passing through the lowland between the Salish Mountains on the west and the Whitefish Range to the east. Glacial striae, or grooves gouged in underlying bedrock by harder rocks as they were pushed and dragged along by the overriding glacier, tell us that the main tongue of ice moved in a southeasterly direction paralleling the route of today's Highway 93 and passing over the sites of communities of Trego to Stryker and south through the Olney area enroute to the Flathead Valley. As the front advanced

southward, even thicker parts of the Cordilleran Sheet followed, crowding the adjacent mountain slopes and eventually lapping onto them. Numerous local mountain glaciers heading in the Whitefish Range to the east flowed down from the highland to join the great Flathead Glacier.

The lumbering Flathead Lobe pushed southward, eventually reaching to just south of Polson where warmer conditions ended a journey that had begun hundreds of miles to the north. Now at its maximum extent, the Flathead Glacier may have had a thickness of 5,000 feet at the Canadian border, and buried the site of the city of Kalispell under 2,500 feet of ice and the south end of Flathead Lake with 850 to 1,000 feet.

Top: Giant ripple marks are discernible from Markle Pass near Hot Springs.

Bottom: Ancient shorelines of Glacial Lake Missoula are a familiar sight to Missoula-area residents. These appear on the hills of the Bison Range. John Alwin photos.

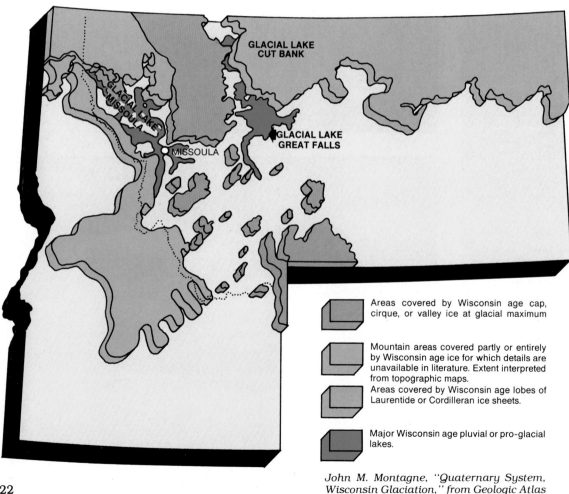

GLACIAL LAKE CUT BANK

GLACIAL LAKE MISSOULA

GLACIAL LAKE GREAT FALLS

MISSOULA

Areas covered by Wisconsin age cap, cirque, or valley ice at glacial maximum

Mountain areas covered partly or entirely by Wisconsin age ice for which details are unavailable in literature. Extent interpreted from topographic maps.
Areas covered by Wisconsin age lobes of Laurentide or Cordilleran ice sheets.

Major Wisconsin age pluvial or pro-glacial lakes.

John M. Montagne, "Quaternary System, Wisconsin Glaciation," from Geologic Atlas of the Rocky Mountain Region, 1972.

The southernmost extent of this ice is marked by the Polson Moraine, a definite ridge rising 500-600 feet above Polson. This is the pile of debris the ice had pushed along its advancing front and left where it came to rest once ice began its retreat. The moraine now serves as a natural dam, holding back the waters of Flathead Lake, which probably occupies a pre-existing, but glacially deepened basin. Dr. Dave Alt, professor of geology at the University of Montana, thinks the lake fills a basin that marks where a large block of stagnant ice survived for centuries after the end of the last Ice Age. He points to a general lack of other moraines north of here as evidence that the glacier probably withdrew rather quickly, perhaps within a couple of thousand years.

Glacial deposits farther south in the valley tell us that a lobe of ice during the preceding Ice Age may have reached even deeper into Flathead country. Glacial striae just east of the National Bison Range and glacial debris verify that ice reached south to the Jocko River where the thin leading front of the glacier almost encircled the Bison Range, leaving it an island in a sea of ice. Instead of retreating to the north at a steady pace, this glacier evidently backed up haltingly, depositing a series of moraines south of Ronan, collectively called the Mission or Ninepipe Moraine. These are much lower and less well-developed than the younger Polson Moraine to the north and constitute a modestly higher belt with an irregular surface of swells and swales, pock-marked by ponds. Each of these small ponds in the Ninepipe National Wildlife Refuge marks a place where a chunk of buried ice in the moraine melted, creating a depression which has filled with water.

Sometime before its final withdrawal from the Flathead, the glacier spawned several major sublobes which moved into adjacent lowlands as finger-like extensions. One reached up Ashley Creek along which Highway 2 now passes west of Kalispell. The moraine that dams the south end of Ashley Lake probably was left by a portion of that glacier. Farther south a short arm of ice buried Wild Horse Island and pushed west into and beyond the Big Arm of Flathead Lake. One extension from this lobe pushed ice to the northwest where it deposited a moraine, which now holds Lake Mary Ronan, and another reached at least five miles to the southwest up the valley from the small lakeside community of Big Arm.

Another more major extension split from the Flathead Glacier at the north end of the Mission Range and proceeded up the Swan Valley. The north end of the Missions, in the apex of these two glaciers, was buried by ice approximately as far south as Ronan. This explains why the north end of the range is much less jagged than the southern portion, which was sharpened by alpine glaciers. The Swan branch of the Flathead Glacier reached south to Clearwater Junction (intersection of Highways 82 and 200). Cabin owners and other recreationists who retreat to the tranquil string of Swan Valley lakes like Salmon, Seeley, Inez, and Alva can thank this glacier for scalloping out the basins they occupy and depositing the glacial debris which holds back the water in many.

While the Flathead Lobe pushed south down the Rocky Mountain Trench other great lobes farther to the west carried the Cordilleran Ice Sheet deep into Montana's northwest corner. The Thompson River Lobe pushed up the Kootenai River Valley, continuing beyond its great bend to south of where Highway 2 now crosses. The numerous small lakes around Happy's Inn are water-filled depressions left in its moraine and the Thompson Lakes may be the remnants of a much larger lake that developed along the glacier's margin. A Bull River Lobe spread south along Montana's far western border area, reaching as far into the state as Bull Lake and perhaps almost to the Clark Fork River.

At its maximum extent this flood of Canadian ice into northwest Montana reached such a thickness that the Thompson River and Bull River lobes coalesced, smothering all but the highest peaks under ice and linking up with the Flathead Glacier to the east. Glacial striae are etched in the flanks of the northern Purcells up to elevations of 7,100 feet and there are suggestions that ice may have covered everything lower than 7,300 feet above sea level at the Canadian line. At that time, even the highest peaks in the border area like Robinson Mountain (7,539 feet) and Northwest Peak (7,705 feet) reached only a few hundred feet above the ice. Thickness decreased to the south, but not dramatically, and the site of Libby may have lain frozen under 4,000 feet of ice. The dendritic crest of the Cabinets remained as the only extensive area left standing above the Cordilleran Sheet in Montana's far northwest. But even this crest was not free of ice. Sharpened peaks with their associated cirques and "U"-shaped valleys tell us that although not covered by continental ice, the Cabinets were mantled by alpine glaciers that flowed down to meet the ice sheet which lapped high up on its flanks on all sides but the south.

The Bull River Lobe may not have reached as far south as the Clark Fork River during the last Ice Age, but there is abundant proof that the glacier immediately to the west did. The Lake Pend Oreille Lobe not only reached the river, but evidently flowed across its narrow valley in the Idaho-Montana border area forming a 2,000-foot-high ice dam. With the river plugged by ice, impounded water from the Clark Fork-Flathead drainage basin backed up, forming a giant natural reservoir called Lake Missoula. Ice-dammed lakes developed in other parts of Montana during the last glaciation, but Lake Missoula is the most famous. The lake's periodic drainage and associated catastrophic floods are of special interest to geologists.

Lake Missoula reached an elevation of almost 4,200 feet above sea level and had a volume of 500 cubic miles. Since its shape was controlled by the pattern of the Clark Fork drainage, its outline was irregular, with arms extending up tributary valleys. The innundated area eventually totalled 2,900 square miles and included all of the Montana section of the Clark Fork Valley to as far east as Drummond, the Bitterroot south to Darby, the Blackfoot to Clearwater Junction, the St. Regis to the Idaho line, as well as the Camas Prairie, Little Bitterroot and Jocko valleys. The Mission Valley also was covered with water lapping up against the southern edge of the Flathead Glacier. The top 700 feet of the National Bison Range was an island in this section of the lake.

If you look carefully on the slope of the Bison Range you can see faint horizontal lines which mark former shorelines of Lake Missoula. They can be detected on the west sides of Mount Jumbo and Mount Sentinel, especially when they are emphasized by a dusting of half-melted snow. Lightly colored silt settled to the bottom of the lake and accumulated in thick deposits that still can be seen on hillsides and in road cuts. One of the best exposures is right along Highway 93, on the east side about halfway between Ravalli and Arlee.

The presence of multiple shore lines and layered sequences of lake silts tells geologists that Lake Missoula filled and emptied at least 36 times. A gradual melting back of the Lake Pend Oreille Lobe might have allowed water to flow out slowly, while a rupturing of the ice dam would produce a rush of escaping water. One, and probably many more, of these emptyings was swift and dramatic and produced landscape features that suggest a flood of catastrophic proportion.

Perhaps the most impressive evidence for a catastrophic flood is the giant ripple marks that can be seen in some areas formerly submerged by the lake. Instead of standing an inch or two high like ripples one might see on the sandy bottom of a river, some of these are made of much coarser gravel and cobble-size material and reach heights of 30 feet! The speed and volume of flows necessary to produce such giant ripples is mind boggling. One of the best vantage points to see giant ripple marks is from atop Markle Pass, four miles south of the Hot Springs turn-off on Highway 382. When the ice dam burst, water filling the Little Bitterroot Valley to the north rushed through this pass into the Camas Prairie Basin. Looking down on this several square miles of giant ripples at the north end of the Prairie one can begin to appreciate the volume and speed of water as it raced toward the new outlet.

WEATHERWISE

Western Montana, like all of the state, has a national reputation for extremely cold weather. When Johnny Carson refers to a frigid state in a joke, there seems to be a better than even chance that state is Montana. Of late, we even seem to be beating our more deserving neighbor to the east. A check of long-term climatic data shows that our cold weather notoriety isn't completely justified, especially if considering only Western Montana. Rather than a characteristically uniform and frigid climate, Western Montana weather ranges from admittedly brisk to a quite moderate Pacific Northwest clime. Striking variation from place to place, not pervasive cold, is the dominant feature.

Rocky Mountain Montana falls within a broad transition zone between more nearly maritime climates to the west and profoundly continental climates to the east. The former area is greatly influenced by proximity to the ocean, which heats and cools more slowly than the adjacent land and therefore experiences more moderate temperatures. Winters generally don't get as cold nor summers as hot as places farther inland. In contrast, continental, or land controlled climates, are far removed from the moderating effect of the ocean waters and the less extreme airstreams that originate over them. In the continental interior dramatic seasonal shifts in temperatures between character-istically cold winters and hot summers are the norm.

Seattle, Washington is a classic example of a city with a maritime climate. Its January average temperature of 40°F and July average of 65 mean a difference of only 25 degrees between the coldest and warmest months. Climatically, no place in Montana is as maritime as Seattle, but the maritime influence in the far west is apparent when stations there are compared with those in the state's eastern fringe. Thompson Falls' 42 degree differential (January average of 26.5 and July average of 68.5) is markedly less than the 63.8 degree variation (January, 5.7 and July , 69.5) at Westby, near the North Dakota line.

As temperatures at these two Montana stations suggest, the maritime : continental contrast between west and east in Montana is most pronounced during winter months. It is then that frigid continental Arctic and polar air spreads south out of Canada. While this bone-chilling cold blankets Eastern Montana, Western Montana often is basking in milder Pacific air. This explains why overnight lows in Eastern Montana communities like Glasgow and Miles City might be 30 below or less, while temperatures in Missoula or Kalispell might not fall lower than a balmy 20 degrees above.

It isn't that Western Montana is never invaded by frigid Arctic air, it's just that it happens less frequently than on the plains to the east. Higher elevation and the blocking effect of the mountains aren't always enough to deflect and keep out the invasions of Arctic air, and periodically it builds to sufficient thickness to spill through mountain passes into valleys.

Dramatic drops in temperature often accompany these invasions: Helena experienced a 79-degree drop in a 24-hour period during a cold wave earlier this century. Differences between the high pressure associated with Arctic air and lower pressures of the Pacific systems to the west, may result in steep pressure gradients and high winds as more moderate Pacific air is displaced by cold Canadian air. It is these wintery blasts of icy, easterly winds that Western Montanans most dread. Their arrival not only is accompanied by plummeting temperatures and skyrocketing heat bills, but also by the strong easterly gusts that invariably produce the season's worst drifting. To minimize the impact of these blasts, farm shelter belts in many of Western Montana's larger valleys are planted on the east sides of buildings, not on the north as might be expected. Even Missoula, which is considered more of a Pacific Northwest community, has its dignity affronted periodically when so-called Hellgate winds funnel frigid Arctic air into the Missoula Valley via the defile of the Clark Fork River (Hellgate Canyon). Similar winds issuing from the narrow gorge of the Flathead River Canyon just east of Columbia Falls have topped 80 miles per hour at Glacier Park International Airport to the southwest.

When the entire state is in the wintery grip of Arctic air, overnight low temperatures in Western Montana valleys may approach or even exceed those of plains towns to the east. Virtually all of its communities have record daily low January temperatures of minus 20 or less. Butte's all-time record low is minus 52, Bozeman's minus 43, Helena's minus 42, Missoula's minus 33, and Kalispell's minus 38.

The state chamber of commerce doesn't brag about it in promotional brochures, but Montana has the dubious distinction of holding the low monthly temperature record in the conterminous United States for six months of the year; January at minus 70, February at minus 66, August at an embarrassing plus 5, September at minus 9, November at minus 53, and December at minus 59. Contrary to what even most Montanans might assume, these low temperature records weren't set in places like Cut Bank or Glasgow in Eastern Montana; they all belong to stations in Western Montana. The minus 70 observed at the 5,470-foot level of Rogers Pass east of Lincoln on January 20, 1954, still stands as the coldest temperature ever recorded in the lower 48 states. The other five record-setting monthly lows were set at stations in high mountain valleys, with three claimed by the same Riverside Ranger Station between 1924 and 1933. Located just east of West Yellowstone along the Madison River at 6,700-feet elevation this station might have set the other nine monthly records if it hadn't been abandoned in the 1930s.

The extremely low overnight winter temperatures in Western Montana valleys are explained partly by elevation and topography. Temperatures in the lower atmosphere generally decrease with increasing elevation at a rate of approximately 3½ degrees for every 1,000-foot rise. With many valley floors averaging 5,000 to 7,000 feet above sea level, it shouldn't be surprising that they experience low winter temperatures.

Already-cold, overnight readings in high mountain valleys sometimes are accentuated by topography. On still, cold nights even more frigid air from higher up on adjacent mountains may settle into valleys. Cold air drainage, as it is called, occurs because colder air is heavier, and like water, it moves downhill. This phenomenon, coupled with high elevation, helps explain why such extremely low temperature records are held by Western Montana valley stations. Without exception, Western Montana communities with the lowest January averages are situated in high, mountain-enclosed basins. Third-ranking Cooke City, hemmed in a narrow valley at 7,600 feet elevation and with mountains rising above 10,000 feet to the north and south, manages only a 13.5-degree January average; Wisdom sitting at 6,100 feet in the bottom of the Big Hole Valley has an average of 12.7, ranking it

Western Montana by the seasons.

Right: Lolo Pass in January. Charles Kay photo.

Far right: Balsam Root in bloom. George Wuerthner photo.

Below: The west face of the Swan Range in the Holland Lake area. Mark Thompson photo.

Below right: A summer storm passes through the White Sulphur Springs area. The Belt Mountains and Mt. Edith in the distance. Rick Graetz photo.

The land of extremes. In the Beartooth Mountains in summer, left, and, right, the Pebble Creek area of the Beartooths in winter. Tom Kaiserski photos.

second coldest, and blue-ribbon winner West Yellowstone, at 6,600 feet in the bottom of a high basin in the upper Madison Valley, checks in with the coldest January average at 11.4 degrees. Residents of the Sun Belt must think the Ice Age still lingers in Western Montana when, day after day, the national weather report lists West Yellowstone as the nation's cold spot with temperatures bordering on the ridiculous.

Once cold air fills high mountain basins or less elevated and larger lowlands like the Helena and Missoula valleys, it sometimes obstinately lingers for days. Occasionally, even after milder Pacific air has spread over the state and brought warming as far east

as the North Dakota line, residents of these western lowlands may have to suffer through several more days of cold. Chillier air remains in valley areas because it quite literally is trapped, held in by warmer overriding air.

In sparsely populated areas inversions have little consequence other than prolonging cold weather, but in more densely populated valleys they can cause serious air pollution problems. Along with the cold air, other pollutants including car exhaust, particulates and wood smoke, are trapped below the inversion and too often reach levels that can be health hazards. With its relatively small size in proportion to population, the

Missoula Valley has one of the state's most serious air pollution problems. Continued population growth and the widespread use of wood burning stoves are adding to pollution levels in other Western Montana valleys as well.

Temperature inversions and the attendant air pollution problems may develop while the whole region is under the influence of Arctic air. Cold air drainage may fill valley bottoms with air cooler than overlying air (temperature inversion) and the high barometric pressure that accompanies Arctic air intensifies the problem. High pressure systems mean heavy, subsiding air movement which increases the likelihood and

26

persistence of cold air drainage. High pressure systems also usually mean weak pressure gradients and little chance of the winds and turbulence that are necessary to mix air and flush out valleys.

Most Western Montanans don't have to endure the same rigorous winter temperatures as the 735 residents of West Yellowstone or the 100 year-round citizens of Cooke City. Some live in communities with January averages that don't even sound very Montana-ish. Big Timber's January average of 26.8 is the state's warmest and neighboring Livingston isn't too far behind at 25.7. Farther west in the lower valleys, Januarys are nearly as moderate. Bitterroot communities like Hamilton (24.8) and Darby (25.8) have helped earn that valley the unofficial title of Montana's Banana Belt. To the north in the Mission and Flathead valleys and west down the Clark Fork, towns have relatively high winter averages by Montana standards. Januarys in St. Ignatius (24.8), Bigfork (26.1), Superior (24.8) and Thompson Falls (26.5) are all as warm or warmer than in Des Moines, Iowa; Lincoln, Nebraska; Madison, Wisconsin; Chicago, Illinois; Detroit, Michigan; or Albany, New York.

Western Montana is at its climatic best during summer months. Few places can rival it for its nearly ideal combination of warm days, cool nights, gentle mountain breezes, and low humidity. Most residents live in valleys where July averages are in the mid-60s. High temperatures typically reach into the 70s and 80s and then drop into the 40s or low 50s at night. Even when daytime temperatures occasionally rise into the 90s, the heat is much more bearable than in the Midwest or on the East Coast where high humidity wilts even the most faithful sun worshippers.

Higher average elevation and a location less influenced by continental air systems help assure that Western Montana normally does not experience the same hot daytime temperatures as on the plains to the east. Certainly one of the most prized climatic traits of these western valleys is their cool summer nights and comfortable sleeping temperatures. A well-known summer visitor of more than 170 years ago commented on this daily temperature disparity while in the Jefferson River Valley in early August, 1805. He wrote: ". . . while we in the valley are nearly suffocated with intense heat of the mid-day sun; the nights are so cold that two blankets are not more than sufficient covering." Today's summer visitors quickly learn why motels make sure guests have extra blankets and that the T-shirt that was fine for daytime outings has to be augmented with a sweatshirt, sweater, or spring coat if venturing out after sunset.

Western Montana's large valleys are among the state's driest places. This prevailing semi-arid climate

Above: A snow telemetry site in summer showing the snow pillow, foreground, which takes measurements of snow pack from the bottom.

At right is a modernized survey house with solar panels to charge batteries for instruments that send year-round data to researchers. U.S. Soil Conservation Service Snow Survey photos.

SNOTEL

In Western Montana the U.S. Soil Conservation Service (SCS) is charged with monitoring mountain snow and projecting stream flows and water supply for farmers, municipalities, power generators and others who depend on these waters. High-country winter recreationists are familiar with the diagonal "Snow Course Marker" signs that indicate more than 200 snow-data measuring sites in Western Montana's mountain watersheds. Most of these are monitored manually and have to be visited monthly by snow surveyors who measure the snow depth and water content, and make other meteorological observations.

By the winter of 1982-83, some 65 of these sites were equipped as SNOTEL (SNOw TELemetry) stations. These innovative and fully automatic installations update measurements of up to 16 parameters every 15 minutes and store data until a master control station hundreds of miles away

radios for its transmission. Master stations in Boise and Ogden send instructions to SNOTEL sites via radio signals bounced off short-lived ionized trails that form behind sand-sized meteorites passing through the atmosphere 50 to 75 miles above the earth. The reflected signal triggers an on-site transmitter that sends back the requested data via the same route. A complete transaction takes only one-tenth of a second. Most sites are contacted once or twice daily for data. Since SNOTEL units are self-contained and batteries are kept charged by solar panels, they need be visited only once a year to provide maintenance and to recharge the precipitation gauge. This eliminates the need for frequent, costly, and sometimes dangerous visits by snow surveyors as is still required at remaining "manual" sites. An obvious additional advantage is the up-to-the-minute data and its availability during heavy storm periods.

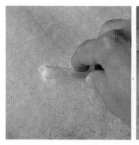

Testing snow melt water for PH. Phil Farnes photos.

Acid Snowfall

Winter recreationists revel at the wild and remote beauty of the high mountain country of southwest Montana. There, far from civilization about the only pollution you might not be surprised to see would be an occasional pull tab from a pop can or a discarded candy wrapper. However, recent preliminary research shows that what appears to be pristine snow blanketing this high country harbors invisible pollutants.

Montanans have heard about the acid rain problems in eastern sections of the United States and Canada downwind from major industrial centers. There now is a proven link between acid precipitation and smoke from manufacturing and utility plants, and auto emissions. Acid precipitation occurs when sulphur dioxide and nitrogen oxides from these sources rise into the air, oxidize and then combine with cloud moisture to form mild solutions of sulphuric and nitric acids. Winds can carry these emissions hundreds of miles from their source before they fall as acid precipitation.

Snow sampling by the U.S. Soil Conservation Service at more than 200 mountain stations in Western Montana during the winters of 1980-81 to 1982-83 showed that snow in sections of southwestern Montana is excessively acidic. Clean, "pure" snow has a slightly acidic pH of 5.6, but some tested on the Montana side of the Bitterroot Range showed a pH of a much more acidic 4.0 (when the pH drops one whole point, acidity increases tenfold). A pH of less than 4.8 represents a potentially serious problem. The area of snow with a pH of less than 5 varied somewhat in the three winters, but in all years covered about

a 5,000-square-mile area just east of the Idaho line. Other ranges commonly showing a snow pH of less than five included the Pioneer, Tobacco Root, Sapphire, and Beaverhead mountains.

Acid precipitation is of greatest concern because of its ability to kill lakes. This is well documented in the Adirondack Mountains of upstate New York where acid precipitation from industrial areas to the west has virtually destroyed animal and plant life in scores of lakes. Areas underlain by granitic or basaltic rocks are low in natural buffers like carbonates, which neutralize the acid, and are especially susceptible to acidification. In those lakes as pH levels of water decrease, the first victims are eggs of amphibians and fish. As waters grow more acidic, frogs die and bacteria disappears, disrupting the lake's natural cycle. Last to go are the adult fish which absorb lethal doses of heavy metals, like mercury, that are leached out of rocks by the progressively more acidic waters.

Impact can reach beyond the aquatic habitat. Evidence suggests that forest productivity may be reduced if trees are subjected to acid precipitation for extended periods. Also, the same heavy metals (including mercury) that are leached by the acid waters may find their way into domestic water supplies.

Investigations of acid snowfall in Western Montana are still in the early stages, but some general observations may not be premature. Phil Farnes, SCS Snow Survey Supervisor in Bozeman, believes that acid pollution probably is entering Montana from the southwest, but admits "we don't have a fix yet on where it's coming from." Any attempt to pinpoint specific pollution sources is little more than guesswork now, but he said he wouldn't be surprised if the pollutants are emanating from as far away as southern California and being added to by smoke and emissions from San Francisco and the Salt Lake City area. It is not impossible that some pollution may be originating on other continents and riding wind currents into southwestern Montana.

Farnes doesn't think that acid precipitation is yet a serious problem except perhaps as a threat to a few isolated high mountain lakes. Still, he is convinced that the situation needs to be monitored. Any weakening of current national air pollution standards and increased pollution levels in metro areas hundreds of miles away may have serious implications for our high-mountain lakes in areas like the Beartooth, Tobacco Root and Bitterroot.

helps explain the extra-cool summertime nights. Once the summer sun sets, the ground begins to radiate heat accumulated during the day. Because of the prevailing dryness of the atmosphere over valleys there is little moisture in the air to absorb this heat and re-radiate it back to the surface. Semi-arid conditions also mean that night skies are often clear, with no clouds to help insulate and hold back the heat of the day. This radiational cooling of valleys begins shortly after sunset and often is accompanied by light breezes of cooler air that drain surrounding mountain slopes and flow in to lift the warmer valley air. Almost like clockwork light winds begin around 9 or 10 p.m. and provide westerners with a natural air conditioner. These cool to cold summer nights mean that backyard gardeners often are unable to grow corn to maturity, and green tomato recipes are sought-after items in higher valleys.

Variation in average annual precipitation in Western Montana is nothing less than amazing. The region claims the state's driest place — Dillon at 9.55 inches and its wettest — the higher reaches of Glacier National Park at more than 120 inches per year.

Topography explains precipitation and the dramatic variations encountered over quite short distances. Most of the moisture-producing weather systems pass through the region from the west. Pacific air masses moving over Western Montana are forced to rise over the Rockies. As they lift, they cool, and their ability to hold moisture decreases. If they rise and cool sufficiently, air masses reach a level where they no longer can retain all their moisture, and condensation and eventually, precipitation may follow. Such mountain-induced moisture is called orographic precipitation.

Precipitation generally increases with elevation on the windward side of the mountains and reaches its maximum along crests. As air masses move down the east side of the Rockies they warm and are able to hold more moisture. Subsiding and warming air is not conducive to precipitation and, not surprisingly, lower lee sides of mountains and adjacent valleys, in the rainshadow region, are predictably dry. Since the Northern Rockies are not just a single ridge, but are made of a series of ranges, the pattern of heavy orographic precipitation over highlands and dry valleys lying in their rainshadow is repeated many times in Western Montana.

The large intermontane valleys of the southwest are among the driest places in the state. In an average year Dillon (9.55 inches) in the Beaverhead Valley, Helena (10.21 inches) in the Helena Valley, Ennis (11.55 inches) in the Madison Valley, and Three Forks (11.7 inches) in the Gallatin Valley each receive less precipitation than Eastern Montana communities like Ekalaka, Miles City, and Glendive.

Western Montana valleys tend to be driest in their western half where the rainshadow effect of the blocking mountain ranges to the west is most pronounced. Precipitation totals increase in an easterly direction where even modest rises in elevation trigger progressively higher amounts of orographic precipitation. This can be seen in the saucer-shaped Gallatin Valley along a 35-mile-long northwest-southeast transect beginning at one of the lowest points in the valley and running up onto the lower flanks of the Bridger and Gallatin ranges. At Three Forks (elevation 4,080 feet) in the western section of the valley where the rainshadow effect is most pronounced, annual precipitation averages a dry 11.7 inches. Eleven miles to the southeast in Manhattan (elevation 4,300 feet) precipitation totals 12.8 inches; at Belgrade (elevation 4,500 feet) nine miles farther up the transect, 13.9 inches falls in an average year; ten miles away at the Montana State University campus in Bozeman (elevation 4,900 feet) the figure is 18.6 inches; and Fort Ellis (elevation 5,200 feet) at the lower slope of the Gallatin Range receives approximately 25 inches per year. In 35 miles the environment changes from a semi-arid sage-brush and cactus-riddled landscape to a nearly sub-humid world of moss and pine trees. On the nearby 9,000- to 10,000-foot crest of the Gallatins, precipitation climbs to more than 50 inches per year.

Except in the far west, most moisture falls in the April-through-September, six-month period, with May and June the wettest months. Still, orographic winter precipitation is sufficient to pile deep snowpacks on highlands. Winter snowfall in southwestern mountains like the Crazies, Beartooths, Bridgers and Tobacco Roots ranges between 300 to 500 inches. To the west and northwest these figures rise to more than 800 inches in the Montana portion of the Bitterroot Range and to more than 1,000 inches (more than 80 *feet*) in higher sections of the Missions and Glacier National Park.

Deep winter snowpacks provide Western Montanans with excellent skiing at the region's downhill ski areas. Cross-country skiers and snowmobilers are assured deep snows in the high country even in the driest of winters. More important economically is the role this snowpack has in providing the life-giving waters to irrigated farming in the semi-arid valleys below. Each year, spring and summer snow melt in the high country helps to fill mountain and valley reservoirs and the streams from which farmers and ranchers draw their allotted supply of this critical resource. Statewide, almost 75 percent of spring and summer stream flow comes from melting snowpack.

Montanans take the good with the bad.

Top: Cold. Monida Pass area. Rick Graetz photo.

Above: This is what an inversion looks like-- Missoula. February of 1983. John Alwin photo.

Left: Bridger Bowl, one of Western Montana's excellent local ski areas without lines. Robin Brown photo.

29

THE WATERS WITHIN

At 7,937 feet, Triple Divide Peak in the southcentral section of Glacier National Park isn't the Park's most impressive summit, but it might be one of the most distinctive on the entire continent. This is the only place in the United States, and one of only two places in North America, where divides of three continental drainage basins meet.

Montana is the only state to contribute water to Hudson Bay, the Gulf of Mexico-Atlantic Ocean, and the Pacific. Water on the summit's southwest begins its trip to the Columbia River and the Pacific via appropriately named Pacific Creek. Little Atlantic Creek collects water from the southeast flank and directs it on a more than 3,000-mile journey to the Mississippi Delta and the Gulf of Mexico. The north side drains to Hudson Bay Creek, headwaters for the one-percent of Montana that empties into frigid Hudson Bay via the Saskatchewan-Nelson River system.

Pacific Drainage Basin

The Montana section of the Pacific Ocean drainage basin falls entirely within our Western Montana region. Although it covers only 17 percent of the state, it provides 58 percent of Montana's total stream flow. The drainage receives heavy precipitation, much of it orographic, and has a large water surplus. This simply means that in most areas the amount of precipitation normally greatly exceeds what might be lost to evaporation and transpiration by plants. Much of the abundant moisture finds its way into the region's two major river systems — Flathead-Clark Fork and Kootenai.

The Flathead River system is dominantly Montanan. It drains an area of just over 9,000 square miles, all but 450 miles of which lie within the state. Its North, Middle and South forks collect most of its waters as runoff from the wet, west side of Montana's remote north-divide country, notably from Glacier National Park and the Bob Marshall complex. The average annual flow of the Flathead River at its mouth is greater than the Missouri as it pulls out of Montana, even though the latter's drainage basin is ten times larger.

Waterfall, Glacier Park. Tom Dietrich photo.

The few privileged residents and the army of annual visitors to the upper Flathead almost universally are impressed by the beauty of bank-full, white-water rivers that cascade off the highlands. Hydraulic engineers might be equally awed by the beauty, but looking at the same scene, they also are likely to see a "hydroelectric landscape." As in most of Western Montana's Columbia Rockies region, the upper Flathead has the three prime prerequisites for hydropower generation. First is an abundant supply of water and generous stream flows. It is water passing through turbines that generates electricity at hydro dams — the greater the volume of available water the greater the potential power output. Steep stream gradients are another regional plus from a power perspective. A river's drop in feet per mile represents "head" and has a direct bearing on its power potential. Finally, a mountainous terrain with narrow valleys and gorges usually means more sites suitable for dams.

Given the nearly ideal hydroelectric landscape in the upper Flathead watershed it is somewhat surprising that only one major power dam has been built. Federally owned Hungry Horse Dam on the South Fork of the Flathead is one of the state's giants. When built in the early 1950s it was the world's fourth highest and third largest dam. The 564-foot-tall concrete structure holds 34-mile-long and 3½-mile-wide Hungry Horse Reservoir.

Although primarily for onsite power generation, Hungry Horse is a classic example of a multipurpose dam. By harnessing the river and retaining flow that is released when desired, the dam also enhances downstream navigation, flood control and irrigation, and provides water recreation on its picturesque reservoir. As a headwaters dam within the Columbia Basin, it also provides power storage. During the spring and early summer heavy runoff season, the dam is able to hold back up to 3½ million acre feet of water, enough to

North Fork of the Flathead near Polebridge. George Wuerthner photo.

flood one million football fields under 3½ feet of water. Every gallon eventually passes through the turbines of 20 major power dams in Montana, Idaho, and Washington before it reaches the mouth of the Columbia. Rather than producing a huge surge and surplus of power at these dams during the peak-flow period, upstream storage and controlled release allows for more uniform power generation during the entire year.

The combined waters of the Flathead's three forks enter the broad Flathead Valley east of Columbia Falls through the constriction of Bad Rock Canyon. Here a lazy, island-dotted river meanders across the flat valley enroute to its delta at the northern end of Flathead Lake. Numerous oxbow-shaped lakes southeast of Kalispell like Egan and Church Slough trace abandoned courses. One used to empty into the lake farther to the west, where it deposited a delta that connected high offshore islands and formed the site on which Somers

is built. The old waterways covered the valley with the fertile alluvial, or river-derived, soils so prized by farmers, and now equally sought after by housing developers.

Flathead Lake, this nearly 200-square-mile remnant of the last Ice Age, is the nation's largest freshwater lake west of the Mississippi. Although a natural water body, its level is now somewhat regulated (over a range of ten feet) by Kerr Dam, five miles below the lake on the Flathead River. The sign in nearby Polson beckons travelers to venture off the beaten path and "See magnificent Kerr Dam — Higher than Niagara." But viewed from the vista point just to its southwest, this Montana Power Company structure plugging the gorge of the Flathead is dwarfed by the towering cliffs that rise hundreds of feet above its gates. Kerr is primarily a power generating and power storage project.

Construction of additional dams in the upper Flathead drainage has been discouraged by

Snow Seeding

In the early 1970s near record-low water levels on the Columbia River threatened Pacific Northwest power supplies to the alarm of the federal Bonneville Power Administration (BPA). Power generation in the Columbia drainage is so dependent on runoff and storage within the upper watershed, it is understandable why they looked to the upper Flathead for an answer to their water shortfall.

Hoping to make up for a projected seven percent deficit in 1974, the BPA proposed a very controversial snow seeding program in the Flathead drainage above Hungry Horse Dam. Using silver iodide crystals to "seed" orographic storm clouds in the Swan Valley area, BPA officials projected they would be able to increase snowfall and thus runoff by ten percent over the target area in the mountains to the east, which included sections of the Bob Marshall Wilderness.

Technically, this probably would have been possible. The BPA already had experimented with snow seeding in the area in the 1960s and projects by Montana State University researchers in the Bridgers, and by Montana Power Company in the upper Madison drainage, had shown that winter cloud seeding could increase snowfall by 15 to 23 percent. The project never was carried out even though the Montana Board of Natural Resources gave the go ahead despite widespread opposition. The National Park Service and U.S. Forest Service were against the seeding and vocal opposition also came from outfitters, hikers, and local residents concerned with the practical problems of deeper snow. Environmentalists worried about the affect of silver iodide on fish and wildlife and the appropriateness of so impacting a federally designated wilderness area. Others suggested the projected power shortage might be dealt with by turning off some of the neon signs in major downstream load centers like Spokane, Seattle, and Portland.

Along the Clark Fork River near Milltown. Jeff Gnass photo.

Montana's Blue Ribbon Trout Streams

The term Blue Ribbon trout stream is a Montana original. In 1959 a committee of four state and federal biologists devised a classification scheme for the state's fishing streams. The end product was a map on which each class of stream was highlighted by a different color. They adopted county fair ribbon colors, awarding a blue shading to their Class 1 rivers or streams of national as well as statewide value. Even though the committee did not use the term blue ribbon, it eventually became common usage.

Providing residents and tourists with a guide map to the state's best fishing was not the intention of the committee. The primary objectives were public education and stream preservation. By the late 1950s Montana had long boasted of its 32,000 miles of well-stocked fishing streams. Committee members felt such a widespread notion was dangerously misleading and likely to encourage a false sense of security and complacency. If the state actually had that many miles of high-class fishing streams, what difference would it really make if "just" 20 or 50 miles were lost a year. The committee's objective was to devise a ranking and to convey, for the first time, the relative value of the state's recreational stream fisheries.

Since this resource does not lend itself well to dollar-value assessment, there had been a tendency for it to be undervalued in the planning process. The stream map identified and gave long-overdue recognition to the state's most prized fishing streams, and showed the public, administrators, and planners that even though Montana may have 32,000 miles of "well-stocked streams," only 410 miles were of the highest Class 1 variety. Armed with this information, residents were better able to seek the protection these waters merited.

The original 1959 classification was based on a quantitative and qualitative assessment of four factors: availability/access, aesthetics, fishing pressure, and stream productivity. Seven segments of six southwestern rivers (Big Hole, Madison, Missouri, Rock Creek, West Gallatin, and Yellowstone) totalling 410 miles were designated Class 1 and shown with blue on the stream map. The revised 1965 map showed Class 1 stream mileage had increased to 452 miles, with the inclusion of 51 miles of the Flathead River north of Flathead Lake the only major change.

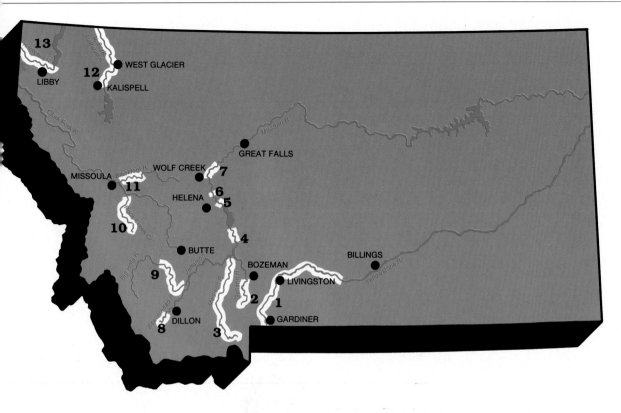

In 1980 the Montana Department of Fish, Wildlife and Parks classified state streams in a less subjective, computer assisted program. The Sport Fishery Potential component of this newer classification ranked four factors very similar to those in the original 1959 study. Fish abundance was based on the combination of weight and number of trout and other desirable non-trout game or sport fish per 1,000 feet of stream. Ingress, or accessibility, to streams was ranked in terms of adjacent land ownership (public versus private). Assignment of an aesthetic grade was based on an admittedly subjective assessment of natural beauty, with obvious detractions including pollution, dewatering, channelization, riprap (especially cars, old washers and dryers), mine tailings, and busy nearby highways. Finally, use was based on actual or estimated fishermen-days per unit length of stream.

According to George Holton, Assistant Fisheries Division Administrator (and a member of the 1959 and 1965 Stream Classification committees), trout streams with a rating of 1 in sport fisheries potential are considered Blue Ribbon trout streams. This newer classification identifies 551 miles of Class 1 sport fishery (Blue Ribbon) trout streams. Sections of some previously identified Blue Ribbon streams don't show up in this assessment, but several new streams and other reaches on previously identified rivers show up as Class 1.

Segments:

Includes all trout river segments with a "1" (Highest) rating for "Sport fishing potential."

1. Yellowstone	Yellowstone Park to Columbus
2. Gallatin	Spanish Cr. to Gallatin Gateway
3. Madison	Yellowstone Park to mouth
4. Missouri	Toston Dam to Canyon Ferry Res.
5. Missouri	Canyon Ferry Res. to below Canyon Ferry
6. Missouri	Hauser Dam to Cochran Gulch
7. Missouri	Holter Dam to Sheep Cr.
8. Beaverhead	Clark Canyon Res. to Grasshopper Cr.
9. Big Hole	Wise River to mouth
10. Rock Creek	Forks at Rock Cr. to mouth
11. Blackfoot	Clearwater River to mouth
12. Flathead (North & Main)	Canadian Border to Foys Bend
13. Kootenai	Libby Dam to Kootenai Falls

Information mapped from Montana Dept. of Fish, Wildlife and Parks stream fishery evaluation Sept. 5, 1980.

The fabled Rock Creek, a Blue Ribbon stream. Tom Dietrich photo.

designation of portions of the North, Middle, and South forks as Wild, Scenic, and Recreational rivers in 1976. This special federal protection should deter major impoundments. The river below Flathead Lake lacks such protection and several sites on the Flathead Indian Reservation have been considered by the U.S. Army Corps of Engineers for possible dam construction.

For now, the aquamarine Flathead is a scenic, free-flowing river between Kerr Dam and its confluence with the Clark Fork of the Columbia. But if all five potential dams were built, the Flathead River between Kerr Dam and just east of its mouth would be converted into a stair-stepped series of reservoirs, obliterating rapids, flooding productive agricultural land and impacting fish and waterfowl habitat. This is not the first time a dam has been considered for the lower Flathead and certainly it will not be the last. Dam proposals have a way of resurfacing.

Just above Paradise the Flathead swings north to merge with the muddy waters of the Clark Fork of the Columbia. The river was named for the celebrated explorer of the Lewis and Clark Expedition, but the name did not come into common usage along most portions until more than 100 years later. Captain Lewis actually christened what is today's Bitterroot as "Clark's River" as they approached it in the early fall of 1805. But in his detailed 1814 map of the expedition's route, Clark referred to the Bitterroot as the "Main Fork" and to the waters connecting it to the Columbia as Clark's River. Presumably, the name also applied to the eastern branch above the mouth of the Bitterroot.

Later settlers largely ignored the name, adopting more localized names for their segments. Between its headwaters and the mouth of the Flathead, various reaches were known as Silver Bow Creek, Deer Lodge River, Hellgate River, and Missoula River. The section between the mouth of the Flathead and Pend Oreille Lake in north Idaho was the only one along which the original name stuck. Even the final leg of the river that drains the lake and flows to meet the Columbia just north of the Canadian line took on another name. The Pend Oreille still drains the lake of the same name, and Silver Bow Creek is still the headwaters stream, but in between the name, Clark Fork, has been restored. Despite its checkered nomenclature, the Clark Fork of

One of the far northwest's lovely waters, the Yaak River. Rick Graetz photo.

the Columbia has been more true to history than Lewis' Fork, which is now known as the Snake for its entire length.

Waters in the 6,115-square-mile upper Clark Fork basin above Montana Power Company's small Milltown Dam just east of Missoula run the gamut from some of the best to some of the worst water quality in the state. Rock Creek, for example, is considered one of Montana's Blue Ribbon trout streams. The long history of metals mining and processing in the Butte-Anaconda section of the upper drainage has made Silver Bow Creek one of the state's most polluted waterways.

As recently as the early 1970s the upper Clark Fork looked more like Detroit's Rouge River or Cleveland's infamous Cuyahoga, befouled and stained rusty red by pollutants. Trout populations declined to as few as four catachable fish per mile, and those pathetic creatures were not considered edible because of toxic levels of heavy-metal residues (lead, cadmium, copper, zinc, arsenic, and mercury) in their systems. Settling pond spills at the Anaconda Minerals Company smelter in Anaconda in the 1960s wiped out fish on the upper reach and caused fish kills as far as Missoula, 120 miles downstream.

Pollution control programs by the Anaconda Company and others beginning in the 1970s have improved water quality in the upper basin. Trout have returned to the river in great numbers and had increased to an average of almost 1,000 catchable fish per mile by the late 1970s. Fishermen were lured back to the river as fish populations increased. In December, 1982, joint tests by the company and the state Department of Health and Environmental Sciences and the Department of Fish, Wildlife and Parks showed that brown trout are now safe to eat, although there are still some water-quality problems.

Given their close proximity to Missoula and their natural attractions, it is not surprising that the Clark Fork and its Blackfoot and Bitterroot tributaries are among the state's most heavily used by floaters and other river recreationists. Few Missoula high school students or undergrads at the University of Montana are not aware of the "variety" of outdoor recreation opportunities along the lower reach of the Blackfoot. Use is enhanced by a progressive, cooperative river-management zone formed by state and local agencies along with private landowners and Champion International, which owns extensive tracts in the drainage.

Beyond the mouth of the Blackfoot and below Milltown Dam (another popular floaters reach), the Clark Fork takes on the waters of the Bitterroot just west of Missoula and acquires the stature of a major Western Montana river. Here its valley is quite broad and its course lined with cottonwoods as it flows westward. Just below Alberton the Clark Fork enters narrow, ten-mile-long Alberton (or Fish Creek) Gorge where the stately river is tossed and thrown about in a stretch of rapids and high waves. This is no section for neophyte floaters. One particularly big rapid is known by the well-deserved title of The Boateater.

Large river flow, steep stream gradient, and a narrow gorge, the trilogy of the hydroelectric landscape, are present in the Alberton Gorge and so, of course, is the proposal for a hydroelectric dam. For now, the major hydro dams are much farther downriver, below the mouth of the Flathead. Montana Power Company's Thompson Falls Dam near the town of the same name is a run-of-river dam. It lacks a major reservoir like that upriver from Washington Water Power Company's Noxon Rapids Dam just south of Noxon.

Tucked up in the remote and wet corner of Montana, north and west of the Flathead-Clark Fork drainage, is the state's section of the Kootenai watershed. The river heads some 130 miles north of the Montana-British Columbia line, high in the Canadian Rockies and flows south toward the international border as the Kootenay. South of the border its spelling changes as it continues southward for another 50 miles before swinging sharply to the west. Its course carries it diagonally across the extreme northeastern Idaho panhandle, on to its junction with the Columbia River about 25 miles north of the Washington border, and back to the same Canadian province where it began its more than 480-mile journey.

Like all other major rivers in the Pacific Northwest, the Kootenai is now a harnessed and tamed river. The Corps of Engineers' Libby Dam, completed in the mid-'70s, has converted half the Montana reach into a slack-water reservoir. Mud-lined Lake Koocanusa (KOOtenai-CANada-USA) also extends for an additional 40 or 50 miles northward into British Columbia, replacing 91 miles of once wild and free-flowing water.

Power interests don't believe that the river has given enough. The Corps of Engineers has plans for a reregulating dam farther downriver that would cost an additional ten miles. At another site 11 miles west of Libby an even more ambitious project has been proposed by a consortium of Western Montana and North Idaho electric co-ops. It calls for the construction of a 30-foot-high concrete and steel dam at scenic and historic Kootenai Falls. This hotly contested power project would destroy the last free-flowing waterfall on a major river in the Pacific Northwest.

Even though not one of Montana's longer rivers, the Kootenai leaves the state as its second largest in terms of average annual flow, surpassing the Missouri and Yellowstone and second only to its sister river, the Clark Fork. As trivia buffs undoubtedly know, and as the official state highway map proclaims, the 1,820-foot elevation of the Kootenai just before it crosses the Idaho line is the lowest point in Montana.

Atlantic Drainage Basin

The Clark Fork, Kootenai, Flathead and other Pacific-slope waterways have interesting histories, but they have not received the notoriety of some of their counterparts east of the Continental Divide. Mere mention of the Missouri or Yellowstone conjures up images of yesterday's fierce Blackfeet war parties, Lewis and Clark, buckskinned fur traders, and the riverboats that once plied their waters. Today, the names Madison, Gallatin, Beaverhead and Big Hole are known by trout fishermen the world over. The streams and rivers of Western Montana's Missouri Basin are truly among Montana's most prized multipurpose, renewable resources.

Top: The Red Rock Lakes, namesake of a national wildlife refuge, played a critical role in the preservation of the Trumpeter Swan, top right. Photos by George Wuerthner, Joe Case.

Above: Trout fishermen the world over dream of such sunny days on the Madison River. This is the West Fork, Madison Range in the background. George Wuerthner photo.

The multifaceted role of these rivers and waters probably nowhere is better illustrated than along the Missouri and its headwater streams in southwestern Montana. Let's take the Red Rock-Beaverhead-Jefferson to show the multiuse aspect of these headwater rivers, although others would be just as appropriate. It and its cousin streams benefit wildlife, farmers, floaters and boaters, fishermen, municipalities and power generators.

Red Rock River begins in the peaks of the Centennial Mountains west of Yellowstone National Park and flows northward into the broad Centennial Valley. The towering Centennials on the south and the more broken highlands of the Gravelly Range to the north provide a dramatic backdrop and water catchment area for additional streams that feed extensive marshes and lakes in this unique valley. Accessible only by graveled roads (of the "local inquiry may save time" variety) and far from major population centers, this is one of Montana's most remote valleys. Its abundant aquatic habitat and isolation make it an ideal location for 32,000-acre Red Rock Lakes National Wildlife Refuge. This exceptional, high altitude (6,600 feet) marsh provides habitat and sanctuary for thousands of waterfowl, big game animals and a varied complement of other wildlife. The trumpeter swan is easily the Red Rock's most famous celebrity. In fact, the refuge was critical to saving this largest of North American waterfowl from extinction earlier this century.

Less than 15 miles below Lower Red Rock Lake and the wildlife refuge, the flow of the meandering river is held back by Lima Dam. Like many other Missouri headwater reservoirs this one is used primarily for local irrigation. The 84,000 acre feet of storage makes irrigated farming possible on thousands of acres on the dry valley floor downstream.

Extensive irrigated agriculture in the Dillon area depends on Red Rock River water in the even larger Clark Canyon Reservoir south of town. Clark Canyon Dam and Barretts Diversion Dam farther downstream, which directs water into 44-mile-long East Bench Canal, were completed in the mid-1960s. The East Bench Unit, as the entire project was called, provided an economic shot-in-the-arm to the Dillon economy. It made possible irrigated farming on 22,000 acres of rangeland and provided supplemental irrigation waters to another 28,000 acres. This is cattle country, and it is not surprising that most of the new lands were planted in hay. Additional acreage and a lengthened irrigation season, which sometimes permits three hay crops, has expanded the local feed base and permitted sizable additions to Beaverhead County's already large cattle herd. The county now ranks first in the state with more than 175,000 head, 21 times the number of people!

Clark Canyon Reservoir's 5,900 acres also helps minimize downstream flooding, provides fish and wildlife habitat, and attracts water recreationists. Public campgrounds and boat launching ramps enhance access to the reservoir's trophy trout waters.

Far left: A proper presentation of the fly on the Madison. George Wuerthner photo.

Left: West Fork of the Sun River, one of the "wilderness" rivers emanating from the Bob Marshall country. Pat O'Hara photo.

Below the dam the river becomes the Beaverhead, and for 12.7 miles between the dam's tailrace and the mouth of Grasshopper Creek is considered a Blue Ribbon trout stream. Internationally renowned, as are other Missouri headwater rivers, this stretch consistently rewards fishermen with their limits of sizable brown and rainbow trout. Good rafting, excellent float fishing, and professional outfitter services help assure this reach heavy use.

Diversion of water into the East Bench Canal often results in dewatering along the winding lower course of the Beaverhead north of Barretts Dam. Dewatering for summer irrigation is a serious problem on the Beaverhead as well as other Missouri headwater trout streams. Fishermen and the state Department of Fish, Wildlife, and Parks are concerned about a situation which results in sections of some rivers drying up completely. One solution being pursued is water reservations to preserve adequate in-stream flow on the Beaverhead, Gallatin, Madison, Jefferson and Big Hole.

North of Dillon the river winds its way past 150-foot-tall Beaverhead Rock, a historic and prominent riverside sentinel resembling a beaver. Ascending the river in August of 1805 Captain Clark commented both on the "Beaver's Head" and the "crooked" nature of the river. With the exception of a few diversion dams and some barbed wire stretched across the river by ranchers, a similar twisting and wildlife-rich, bushy-banked river greets today's floaters.

Two miles south of Twin Bridges, the Ruby, dubbed the Philanthropy by Captain Lewis to honor one of President Jefferson's cardinal virtues, enters as a major tributary. Lewis most likely would have disapproved of the name "Stinking Water River" it bore during the early settlement period, but probably would have been a bit more comfortable with its present name. Just downriver from Twin Bridges the Beaverhead joins with the Big Hole, originally named the Wisdom by Captain Lewis for a second presidential virtue, to form the Jefferson River.

The "Jeff", as it is called by some who know it best, lends its name to the broad valley which carries it around the north end of the Tobacco Roots. Beyond Twin Bridges the river hugs the steeper west side,

flowing across the foot of the parched, sage-clad eastern foothills of the Highland Mountains. This verdant waterway must have seemed a veritable oasis to the droves of miners who once worked the mines like the Cricket, Galena, Aurora and Victoria that dot the Ironrod Hills and dry gulches west of Silver Star. To the east, beyond the valley bottom, a much smoother slope rises to the treeline of the majestic Tobacco Roots.

Hayland and livestock now dominate the valley floor. Two main lateral ditches, the Creeklyn and Parrot, and scores of smaller ones with intriguing names like Old Dutch and Panama, direct water to a mosaic of productive irrigated fields that parallel the river to beyond Whitehall. The braided and meandering river flows through an even wider valley as it approaches

Top: The Jefferson River. Rick Graetz photo.

Above: Canoeing the Missouri River's Canyon Ferry Reservoir. Rick Graetz photo.
Below: Mystic Lake has been significantly raised by a dam. Leon Odegaard photo.

Waterloo and retains a generous floodplain east to La Hood and the mouth of the Jefferson Canyon. Despite encroachment and impact by man, this valley remains a rich wildlife habitat. Mule deer and whitetails, moose, black bear and even occasional elk from the high country share this riparian meadow environment with smaller mammals and varied birdlife. Passing through this section in August 1805, the Corps of Discovery recorded a "beautiful valley from six to eight miles wide" and a river "about 90 yards wide . . . crooked and crowded with islands; its low grounds wide and fertile; though covered with fine grass from nine inches to two feet high, they possess but a small proportion of timber, and that consists almost entirely of a few narrow-leaved cottonwoods distributed along the verge of the river. The soil of the plain is tolerably fertile . . ."

Although this general description of the river and its valley is still surprisingly accurate more than 175 years later, the actual course is probably not the same as it was that summer of 1805. The Jefferson has altered its course innumerable times since then and the process continues today. These changes are obvious when recent photo-revised U.S. Geological Survey topographic maps are compared with earlier ones. They show that channels have been abandoned and new ones built, and new islands have appeared, while previous ones took on different sizes and shapes or disappeared entirely.

East of La Hood the river squeezes into narrow and steep-sided Jefferson Canyon, temporarily leaving farmland and cottonwood groves behind. This is a very different 12-mile reach of the river and one not seen by most travelers who now opt for the much speedier Interstate 90 route just to the north. Locals still use narrow and winding Highway 10 through the canyon, but chances are tourists don't venture this way unless headed for Lewis and Clark Caverns, Montana's first and best known state park. Even though these popular caves carry their names, the explorers evidently passed them, unaware of their existence. Downstream from the caverns, the Jeff breaks out of the London Hill's limestone walls through a narrow gap east of Sappington. Once again the river spreads over a broad floodplain as it continues its circuitous course to the Three Forks of the Missouri.

Near the Three Forks one can climb to the top of the same limestone cliff Captain Lewis scaled on July 27, 1805 and saw the Missouri's three forks — from the southwest the Jefferson, named to honor the president and "projector of the enterprise;" the middle branch, christened the Madison after James Madison, Secretary of State; and the southeast fork, called the Gallatin after Secretary of the Treasury, Albert Gallatin. The historic juncture is now protected as Missouri Headwaters State Park. This is the site of the annual

Colter Run, a challenging cross-country and cross-river affair that commemorates the legend of John Colter's 1808 run for his life and escape from the Indians. Nearby Bozemanites know this as a place where the snow disappears quickly in the spring and where warm, sunny skies make it an ideal place for that first-of-the-season, pre-mosquitoes picnic.

Between the Three Forks and the Toston Diversion Dam near Lombard, the Missouri knifes its way through canyons and the dry plains of the Clarkston Valley. The concrete structure at Toston backs up the river for several miles and diverts copious quantities of water into the West Side and East Side canals. The latter transports water across the river through a less-than-attractive, 84-inch steel pipe almost 700 feet long. Some 50 miles of canals direct these waters to the more than 15,000 acres they irrigate south and east of Canyon Ferry Lake. The Montana Water Development Association estimates this acreage could be doubled.

Lewis and Clark would scarcely recognize the reach of the Missouri from the site of Townsend north to the Adel Mountains where it flows out of our Western Montana region. Three large dams (Canyon Ferry, Hauser and Holter) now plug the river creating a string of reservoirs. A short Blue Ribbon stretch between Hauser Dam and Holter Reservoir is all that remains of this once free-flowing reach. As with any project of this magnitude there has been a trade-off between major costs and benefits. Harnessing the wild river meant the innundation of thousands of acres of wildlife habitat and productive farmland. On the benefits side, the dams generate power, enhance downstream navigation and irrigation, help minimize flooding, and provide Montanans with one of their most popular recreation complexes.

Canyon Ferry Lake, 25 miles long and covering 55 square miles, is the giant among these main-stem reservoirs. Centrally located among the dry Montana cities of Great Falls, Helena, Butte, and Bozeman, it is a mecca for water recreationists. More than 400,000 people visit each year, and that number grows annually. Locals have their favorite boat launching sites (Silos, White Earth, or maybe Cove Bay), and their own secret fishing spots and secluded bays where they tie up and camp for the night.

Although farmland was lost under the reservoirs, their water made crop production possible in some adjacent areas. Just below Canyon Ferry Dam, the 2.7-mile-long Helena Valley Tunnel carries water through the north end of the Spokane Hills and into the semi-arid Helena Valley, one of the state's driest. Completed in the late 1950s, this project irrigates at least 15,000 acres.

Downstream from Hauser Lake and Dam, visitors can board an excursion boat on Upper Hauser Lake

The Yellowstone River in the Paradise Valley, and the Absaroka Range beyond. The Yellowstone is Montana's last undammed major river. Tom Dietrich photo.

and cruise through the 1,200-foot-deep Gates of the Mountains gorge first described and named by Lewis and Clark. The spectacular canyon is accessible by water or trail only and remains much as it was at the time of the Expedition. Once beyond Holter Dam, the Missouri passes through yet another defile, through the Adel Mountains north of Craig, before it opens into the Chestnut Valley and leaves our Western Montana region. Water it collects from the western mountains carries the river across Eastern Montana where it gains little additional flow. Just beyond the Montana-North Dakota border it joins with the Yellowstone, another major river that also acquires much of its flow as runoff from the highlands of southwestern Montana.

Though part of the Missouri Basin, it is common to recognize the Yellowstone drainage as a distinct watershed within Montana. This sister river to the Missouri originates in the highlands of northwest Wyoming, but not at Yellowstone Lake as many assume. The river begins its journey of some 670 miles to the Missouri southeast of Yellowstone National Park on the flanks of 12,000-foot peaks in the south Absaroka Range. Flowing in a northwesterly direction it enters the Park and then Yellowstone Lake. Below the lake, it has carved a tortuous path through the Park's colorful layers of volcanic rock and makes the remarkable Upper and Lower Yellowstone Falls and the awesome Grand Canyon of the Yellowstone. It is probably the

yellow walls of this gorge to which the river, originally named the Roche Jaune, owes its name.

The Yellowstone enters Montana at Gardiner already a good-size river. From the Wyoming line to Columbus, a distance of 148 miles, it is classified a Blue Ribbon trout stream. This is one of the state's most prolific fisheries with a well deserved international reputation. For its initial 17 Montana miles, to the north end of Yankee Jim Canyon, the Yellowstone is wide, shallow and swift as it flows through a constricted valley floor. This constriction tightens and white water increases as the waters pass through four- to five-mile-long Yankee Jim Canyon, named after an enterprising, late-19th-century miner who built a toll road through this narrow gorge.

Once through Yankee Jim the river enters appropriately named Paradise Valley where it takes on

Montana's Water — Use It or Lose It?

The headlines read: "Struggle coming over Montana's Water," "State could thirst for water supply in future," and "Is state water eyed for refilling Kansas wells." The news is that Montana's water is being eyed fondly by many out-of-state interests. This prospect has implications for almost all Montanans since water is the lifeblood of our major industries — agriculture, tourism, mining, and energy. There is a mounting concern here that all water flowing out of the state soon may be claimed by downstream states, other water deficit areas, or even the federal government. Given the population and political clout of these states, not to mention the federal government, Montana could find it difficult to defend its water rights.

Interbasin water transfers, or piping water out of one watershed and over a drainage divide into another, is not new to Montana. In fact, the state has two ongoing diversions. The oldest is owned and operated by the Butte Water Company. In 1899 the company completed a pumping station on the Big Hole River at Divide and the next year began pumping water over the Continental Divide (a rise of more than 800 feet) and into Butte, more than 20 miles north. The system has been expanded since the turn of the century, but even in 1982 sections of the original redwood stave

pipe still transported almost two billion gallons of Big Hole River water. The state's other interbasin diversion is the 29-mile-long Saint Mary Canal near the Canadian border northeast of Glacier National Park. It conveys an average seasonal flow of 175,000 acre feet from the Saint Mary River across the Hudson Bay Divide and into the North Fork of the Milk River. This additional flow in the Milk helps provide for the extensive irrigation downstream between Havre and Glasgow.

Since these two diversions merely redistribute water within Montana, they have not been as controversial as proposals to transfer water out of the state. Some proposed schemes have been nothing less than grandiose. The Yellowstone-Snake-Green Project would have diverted water from the Upper Yellowstone River over the Continental Divide and into the Snake River of southeastern Idaho. From there it was to be pumped across another divide and into Wyoming's Green River, a Colorado tributary. As the only major river in the nation's driest quarter, the Colorado's precious water has been fully apportioned among states in its watershed. In lower basin areas like southern California and Arizona water is in especially short supply and has even placed limits on continued population growth and economic development. Montanans probably would have gained little solace from knowing that the projected two million acre feet a year diverted from the Yellowstone (about one-

fourth the river's annual flow) would have helped fill backyard swimming pools in Los Angeles.

Other diversions also have surfaced, but none even approach the magnitude and ambition of the North American Water and Power Alliance (NAWAPA) scheme. It was proposed by a Los Angeles firm in the 1960s as a panacea for most of the continent's water problems. The massive project had an estimated cost of at least 100 billion dollars. The basic concept was to collect the flow of major northern rivers in giant reservoirs and then redistribute this water southward to other parts of the continent. The plan called for the diversion of water from as far away as the Yukon River in Alaska and the Peace and Athabaska rivers in the Canadian Northwest. These waters, along with more captured from the Columbia, Kootenay and Fraser rivers, would be diverted into the Rocky Mountain Trench, forming a 500-mile-long reservoir that would be held back by a Canadian dam three times as high as Grand Coulee just north of Eureka, Montana. It was planned that water from this reservoir would be carried by canal southward across Montana's far west and pumped over the Bitterroot Range south of Thompson Falls enroute to its destination in the arid Southwest and northern Mexico.

The likelihood of such a scheme being carried out seems remote, but smaller diversion proposals involving Montana water already are upon us. Serious consideration has been given to using Montana water to help recharge the Ogallala Aquifer in five mid-continent states. Some experts think this underground reservoir in Colorado, Kansas, Oklahoma, Nebraska and Texas could be pumped dry within 15 years, crippling irrigated agriculture in those states. Montana officials estimate it would take 10 to 40 million acre feet of water to recharge the Ogallala.

Another potential diversion is outlined in the Yellowstone Pipeline Company's application to divert 250,000 acre feet per year from the

Yellowstone River. Their plan calls for withdrawal near Terry via a 108-inch-diameter, 230-mile-long pipeline terminating southwest of Sheridan, Wyoming. The company's application to the state of Montana mentions coal-fired steam generation, coal gasification, coal liquefaction and coal slurry as possible uses for diverted water. A coal slurry pipeline would mean diversion out of the Yellowstone Basin.

Like all other western states, Montana has constitutional provisions that claim proprietary ownership to water in the state. Montana also has a statutory provision prohibiting the export of state waters without consent of the legislature. But it is not difficult to imagine situations which could lead to the exercise of a historically little-used Congressional power to apportion interstate water.

In the face of actual and potential assaults on Montana water from within and outside the state, Montana finally set about sorting out water rights and working toward a state water plan. The 1970s witnessed new legislation that called for development of a uniform, statewide permit system for appropriation and use of water, a centralized record keeping system for all water rights, and a procedure to determine and adjudicate water rights. Legislation for the first time also permitted public agencies to file for instream water reservations and made fish, wildlife and recreation beneficial uses of water. Previously, only consumptive uses were considered beneficial and water had to be diverted out of the river channel to establish a valid water right.

Montanans eventually could see the constitutionality of their water reservation system challenged in the courts. Downstream states that long since have lost abundant wildlife and clean rivers may not understand how strongly Montanans feel about their rivers. Who do those snaildarter-types up there in Montana think they are, reserving more than 60 percent of the Yellowstone River for instream flow to benefit fish, wildlife, and stream morphology, recreation and water quality?

Montana's only hope to protect its water lies in its ability to convince others that the flow of its rivers is already legally spoken for. It could someday come down to a use it or lose it proposition. The trick may be to convince out-of-state interests that all claims are valid and based on established use.

a gentler character. The valley widens markedly here and a lazier, sometimes meandering and braided river continues its sinuous journey northward. Paradise Valley, shaped like a trough and cradled between the Gallatin Range to the west and the rugged Absaroka Range to the east is undeniably one of Montana's most picturesque settings. It is easy to see why this area has drawn such a variety of people, from fourth generation ranchers to fly-fishing enthusiasts, 1960s vintage hippies, a sprinkling of Hollywood stars and starlets, artists and authors, and the recently arrived Church Universal and Triumphant.

At the north end of the valley, just 2½ miles south of Livingston, the Yellowstone squeezes through an

It doesn't take an engineer to see the potential for building a dam at the controversial Allen Spur site on the Yellowstone. John Alwin photo.

hourglass-shaped constriction. A large flow, decent head, and a narrow rock gorge strategically situated at the lower end of a generous valley make the Allenspur site — guess what — one of the most highly rated among the more than 20 potential dam sites on the Yellowstone River system. Dam builders especially are impressed by the project's massive water-storage potential. Because the river is still free-flowing and receives most of its flow as mountain runoff from snow melt, it has a profoundly seasonal flow. Near Livingston, the river has an average annual flow of about 3,800 cubic feet per second, but varies from a low monthly average of 1,200 in January to almost 14,000 in June. Advocates argue for a structure that could hold back some of this peak flow and release it in a more controlled manner to the benefit of downstream agricultural, municipal, industrial and flood-control purposes.

One plan called for a 380-foot dam across that narrow gap and a reservoir stretching out of sight

some 31 miles to the south, with a maximum width of four miles. Such a reservoir would be able to hold four million acre feet and provide downstream users with 1.5 million acre feet annually.

The impact of such a dam and reservoir on the Yellowstone would be massive. Above the dam a free-flowing and productive trout stream would be replaced by a constantly fluctuating reservoir. The 380-foot dam would have a maximum draw down of 72 feet, sufficient to guarantee an unsightly mud flat between high and low water levels, and associated dust problems. The reservoir would innundate productive agricultural land and homesites and destroy wildlife habitat. Geologic problems at the potential dam site include unstable slopes, porous underlying rocks, and an active history of faults and seismic activity that concerns many of the residents of Livingston who would live just below this wall of water. Below the dam, modified flows would change stream morphology and alter aquatic ecosystems.

An Allenspur Dam has been an on-again, off-again proposition for more than 80 years. Each renewal of the proposal meets with a resounding NO from a loud chorus of opponents. In 1974 even the Montana legislature decreed, in Senate Joint Resolution 42, that an Allenspur Dam would be inconsistent with the state's goals and objectives. During the late 1970s and early 1980s the issue has waned, but Montanans are almost certain to hear again about Allenspur in the years ahead. Whether Montanans like it or not, their rivers are being eyed as a source of water by out-of-state users. Their demands coupled with those of downstream users in Montana could lead to a renewal of pressure to build a dam that could even out river flow.

THE VEGETATIVE MOSAIC

Fragile alpine tundra high in the Beartooths; misty giant cedar groves on the flanks of the Cabinets; parched sage and cactus plains in broad southwest valleys; the Bitterroot River's sinuous cottonwood groves; backwater swamps in the north shore area of Flathead Lake; a lush mantle of mixed conifers on the slopes of the Little Belts; and the Big Hole's fertile sub-irrigated meadows — these are just some of the elements in Western Montana's surprisingly mixed vegetative mosaic.

Although the Montana Rockies generally are thought of as a forested environment dominated by coniferous trees, less than half the region is forest covered. The satellite image on the back cover of this volume shows the general pattern of Western Montana's vegetation. Although the image does not show natural tones, the color has been enhanced in a way that clearly differentiates major vegetation types. The dark green of forests is easily distinguished from the valley stringers of green paralleling rivers and identifying large irrigation projects. White areas correspond with elevated tracts above treeline, some tundra covered. Finally, grasslands and sage covered valleys, plains and foothills show up as tan or cream colored.

The vegetative scheme appears chaotic even at this general scale, but the pattern begins to make sense when the factors of topography and elevation are considered. In mountainous areas plant communities, as well as climate and soils, are arranged in altitudinal zones, each adapted to progressively cooler, windier and more humid conditions that usually prevail with increasing altitude. Contacts between these layers or zones may be sharp and abrupt, but more commonly they are graduated.

The lowest zone is the semi-arid steppe, characteristically treeless except for riparian hardwoods (cottonwood and willow) along stream courses. Western Montana's steppe areas are found in rainshadow settings where annual precipitation may be as low as 12 inches or less. Cactus can be found in places, although various grasses and sagebrush dominate.

East of the Divide, in southwestern Montana, steppe is more extensive than forest. Tucked up in the rainshadow of the main crest of the Rockies and with

A

B

Opposite page: The forest texture. Ron Glovan photo.

(A) The Paradise Valley from the air. Wayne Scherr photo.

(B) Cottonwoods along the Yellowstone River. Jeff Gnass photo.

(C) Larch, also called Tamarack, is the one conifer whose needles change color and drop each fall. Jack Tuholske photo.

(D) Alpine wildflowers near Medicine Mountain in the Beartooths. George Wuerthner photo.

D

C

43

(A) In the Ross Creek Cedars Scenic Area. John Alwin photo. (B) Bitterroot, Montana's state flower. Wayne Scherr photo. (C) A forest fire billows smoke into the sky over Yellowstone Park. Rick Graetz photo. (D) Some of the forest landscape ends up in lumber mill log decks such as this one at Columbia Falls. John Alwin photo.

along Highway 287 west of Ennis as just one place that might even be able to support some type of tree cover if it were not for overgrazing.

The subhumid prairie parkland lies immediately above the semi-arid steppe. Its presence is explained by progressively wetter conditions up the flanks of valleys. Vegetatively this is a transition zone from sparse grasses and even some sage at lower levels to more-lush grass and park-like clumps of forest on higher sites, often on shady, north-facing slopes. West of the Continental Divide forest groves are commonly of ponderosa pine, but east of the Divide within our region extreme winter climate rules out ponderosa, and Douglas fir occupies the same niche. Thousands of years of periodic burning of valleys by Indians caused these fire intolerant stands to retreat. Strict controls on burning and fire suppression over the last 100 years have eliminated this check on forest expansion and stands now are reappearing as wet years encourage trees to take root on lower slopes. Flathead Pass in the northern Bridgers is just one place where century-old Douglas fir now are well-established on former grassland. Western Montana's subhumid prairie-parkland zone provides some of the state's best non-irrigated grazing. The best of these bench lands also are suitable for crop production and some have been broken and planted in grain.

Tree cover becomes much more extensive in the next highest, montane forest altitudinal zone. The tree species present in this zone vary geographically and in accord with logging and fire history. The west's montane forest is nowhere more lush and varied than on the wet intermediate slopes of the Columbia Rockies. This is the only place in Montana with commercial stands of moisture-loving trees such as larch, cedar, hemlock, and grand fir. Cedar and hemlock cover most humid sites, grand fir occupy intermediate locations, and Douglas fir and ponderosa pine thrive in the least humid areas.

The Yellowstone Rockies' and Broad Valley Rockies' montane forestland is less varied and not as lush as that of Montana's far west. Douglas fir is the climax, or naturally regenerating species, although many sites have been replaced by lodgepole pine. Lodgepole has a serotinous cone held closed by a resinous bond that is freed only when subjected to temperatures of at least 113 degrees. The species therefore is well adapted to seeding itself over newly burned areas. It often comes up as the only tree variety on a burned site and quickly establishes such dense cover that other species can't get started. The extensive and almost pure stands of fire maintained lodgepole forests in the mountains of southwest Montana undoubtedly are linked to the region's fire history.

some places also situated behind local blocking ranges, this corner is one of the state's driest regions. Most sections receive less than 12 inches of precipitation a year, with the driest areas receiving less than 10 inches.

Sagebrush is more common here than anywhere else in Western Montana and even more abundant than in many sections of Eastern Montana. Not all range experts agree on how extensive sagebrush was in these southwest valleys before the arrival of white settlers, but most acknowledge that overgrazing has led to a heavy invasion by the plant. Present livestock grazing

practices perpetuate this condition, but the alteration may predate the arrival of livestock in the region. According to Jack Taylor, Associate Professor of Range Management at Montana State University, "grazing here may have been excessive since the end of the last Ice Age and probably at no time since has this been lush grassland." Large numbers of bison, elk, deer and other grazing and foraging animals must have been lured into these generous, protected valleys with their light to non-existent snow cover. They may have begun a process that has been taken over by cattle and sheep. Taylor points to the sage-covered Virginia City Hill

Western Montana's highest forestland falls within a subalpine zone. Englemann spruce and subalpine fir dominate this cool and wet world. Where logging or fire has removed this forest, lodgepole pine, as well as western larch in the Columbia Rockies, has moved in to occupy modified sites.

Above the treeline, a harsh environment of wind, cold and frozen ground rules out the growth of trees except as gnarled and dwarfed individuals in a scattering of protected sites. Here, high elevation creates an Arctic climate and vegetation. This is the alpine tundra zone where slopes are covered by alpine grasses, low shrubs and a surprising display of summer wildflowers — all very similar to those on the vast tundra plains of northern Canada and Alaska.

Forestlands may not cover even half of Western Montana, but they are basic to the economy and as much a part of the regional identity as the mountains. Surprisingly few residents actually live "in the trees," with large communities like Missoula, Kalispell, Butte, Helena and Bozeman located in the semi-arid steppe and subhumid prairie parkland. Nearby forested areas are highly regarded by residents, some of whom are willing to commute long distances to and from work each day for the privilege of living in, or at least adjacent to, the trees of the montane forest or parklands just below. To them a natural, wood-look home in the pines is a Western Montana ideal. Bridger Canyon is popular among Bozemanites, as is Pattee Canyon for Missoulians. The forested hills adjacent to Interstate 15 in the Prickly Pear Valley south of Helena have attracted a flood of capital-city workers and given Jefferson County one of the highest growth rates in the state. Even residents who don't live in Western Montana's "Forest Parks," "Mountain Views" and "Blue Sky Heights" are within sight and scent of the region's extensive coniferous forest estate.

With a combined area of about 16 million acres, Western Montana's 11 national forests take in the majority of the region's forestlands. In the heavily vegetated northwest corner only a small percentage of Lincoln and Mineral counties is not national forest. Across the region, forest names like Flathead, Deerlodge, Helena and Gallatin are part of the vocabulary of almost every resident.

Passage of the 1960 Multiple Use Sustained Yield Act provided the legal basis for the multiple use of Western Montana's and the nation's national forests. Officials must now manage these federal lands for a wide range of often conflicting uses. Timber, water, wildlife, recreation, grazing and minerals must be weighed in forest planning. There probably isn't a single national forest in the region where there aren't ongoing conflicts between timber interests and hikers, snowmobilers and cross-country skiers, or livestock grazers and big-game hunters. Public review and comment are integral elements of the national forest planning process, but that doesn't mean that final management decisions please all.

For much of their history Western Montana's national forests have been most closely associated with timber production. They now supply about half the timber used in Western Montana's wood products industry, with most of the remainder coming from giant timberlands owned by Burlington Northern, Champion International and St. Regis. Commercially, the montane and lower levels of the subalpine zones are most desirable. Douglas fir is the most important species, followed by ponderosa pine, western larch, Englemann spruce and lodgepole pine.

Thousands of jobs depend on timber supplied by these federal forests. It is difficult to find a town or city without a sawmill or houselog plant, or at least a post and pole mill. Sawmills are most ubiquitous and range from one-family, John Walton-type operations up to huge corporate complexes. A pulp and paper mill and several particle board and plywood plants add to the region's product mix.

Between 1950 and the early 1970s, wood products was *the* growth industry in the region, accounting for the overwhelming majority of new jobs in manufacturing. Expansion was accompanied by a significant increase in the amount of timber cut on national forest land. By 1969 this had ballooned to 72 percent of the harvest. Public concern mounted that timber production was taking precedence over other forest use. Residents worried about the forests' ability to sustain such high production levels and were aghast at some environmentally destructive logging practices.

In the 1960s national attention was focused on the management practices of the Bitterroot National Forest south of Missoula. There, allegations of overcutting, improper use of clearcutting (where all trees are cut down over an area) and excessive terracing and road building forced a reassessment of harvesting practices. Pressure from an increasingly ecologically-minded and outdoor-recreation-oriented public there and elsewhere helped lead to a reduction in percentage of the cut on Forest Service land and a greater emphasis on environmental and scenic elements. Visually, one major change has been smaller clearcuts which are blended into the landscape, mimicking natural openings in the forest.

In this era of computer generated simulation models in forest planning and management it is even more interesting that those charged with managing our national forests are reconsidering the role of fire, one of nature's own management tools. Nearly all forests in Western Montana were propagated or have been changed greatly by natural fires. It is estimated that sites were burned on the average of once every 150 years prior to modern forest-fire suppression. Some trees have evolved genetic traits in response to fires. These include the heat release cone of lodgepole, mentioned earlier, thick and fire-resistant bark that allows trees to live long enough to cast their seeds over a burned area, and species like Englemann spruce and western larch with light, wind-carried seeds that are blown long distances.

Large Western Montana fires occurring just after the turn of the century, especially during the infamous summer of 1910, have resulted in relatively large areas vegetated by even-aged stands of lodgepole pine. Where a single species dominates over expansive and continuous areas, insects that feed on that tree are more likely to spread unchecked and reach epidemic proportions. This is the case today as the mountain pine beetle ravages across Western Montana. Trees attacked by the beetle look as if someone had gone after them with a power drill. Once inside the trees, beetles lay eggs that produce larvae which feed on tissue just below the bark. A fungus carried by the larvae kills the trees, leaving them the rusty red and brown tone now so common in national forests from the Gallatin to the Flathead. Over time this standing and fallen dead timber creates a major source of fuel to feed yet another catastrophic fire. If fire had been allowed to assume its natural role over the last 70 years, local and regional burns would have resulted in more of a forest mosaic made up of a mix of tree species and different age stands. In this way nature helps ensure that both insect epidemics and large-scale fires are minimized.

Generally, fires also benefit wildlife. For a number of years after forest burns, grasses, forbs and shrubs thrive and provide wildlife with abundant food and cover until trees once again occupy the site. The seed of one important browse species for deer and elk, the redstem ceanothus, can lie dormant in forest soil for up to 200 years until stimulated to grow by fire.

Some designated wilderness areas already have fire management plans which permit lightning-caused fires to burn under prescribed conditions. Promising results in trial areas on some Western Montana national forests are leading the way to a time when all Montana national forests will have fire-management plans. This does not mean that all fires will be allowed to run rampant. Plans will call for their immediate suppression in some areas or under specified conditions, but others will be allowed to burn. Even if in designated areas, fires will be assessed on an individual basis to assure protection of public safety and private property, minimize impact on air quality and chances of escape beyond designated burn areas, and to comply with a long list of manageability criteria.

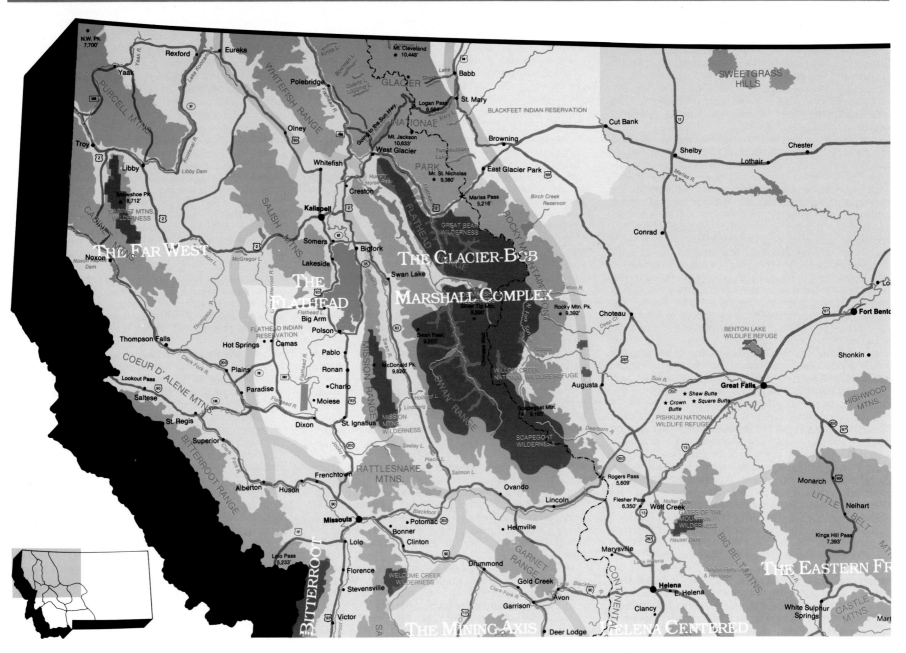

N.W. Pk. 7,700'
Rexford
Eureka
Yaak
Yaak R.
Lake Koocanusa
PURCELL MTNS.
WHITEFISH RANGE
Polebridge
Kintla L.
Bowman L.
Quartz L.
Logging L.
GLACIER
Mt. Cleveland 10,448'
Lake Sherburne
Babb
Olney
Logan Pass 6,664'
St. Mary
Lake St. Mary
BLACKFEET INDIAN RESERVATION
Cut Bank
Troy
Kootenai R.
NATIONAL
Going to the Sun Hwy.
Mt. Jackson 10,633'
West Glacier
Browning
Shelby
Chester
Libby
Libby Dam
Whitefish
PARK
Mr. St. Nicholas 9,380'
East Glacier Park
Lothair
Marias R.
Snowshoe Pk. 8,712'
Creston
Hungry Horse Res.
Two Medicine Lake
Conrad
CABINET MTNS. WILDERNESS
SALISH MTNS.
Kalispell
Marias Pass 5,216'
Birch Creek Reservoir
Marias R.
CABINET MTNS.
Somers
GREAT BEAR WILDERNESS
THE FAR WEST
Bigfork
THE GLACIER-BOB
FLATHEAD RANGE
Noxon
McGregor L.
Lakeside
ROCKY MOUNTAIN FRONT
Teton R.
Lo
Noxon Rapids Dam
Swan Lake
MARSHALL COMPLEX
THE FLATHEAD
Rocky Mtn. Pk. 9,392'
Choteau
Deep Cr.
Fort Bento
Thompson R.
Silver Tip Mtn. 8,890'
Flathead L.
Big Arm
FLATHEAD INDIAN RESERVATION
Polson
Swan Peak 9,255'
Chinese Wall
N. Fork Sun R.
Sun R.
BENTON LAKE WILDLIFE REFUGE
Thompson Falls
Hot Springs
Camas
MISSION RANGE
Pablo
Gibson Res.
Augusta
Great Falls
Shonkin
COEUR D'ALENE MTNS.
Clark Fork R.
Plains
Ronan
McDonald Pk. 9,820'
WILLOW CREEK NATIONAL WILDLIFE REFUGE
Shaw Butte
Lookout Pass
Charlo
Crown Butte
Square Butte
Saltese
Paradise
Moiese
SWAN RANGE
Holland L.
Lindbergh L.
Scapegoat Mtn. 9,185'
PISHKUN NATIONAL WILDLIFE REFUGE
HIGHWOOD MTNS.
St. Regis
Flathead R.
Dixon
St. Ignatius
MISSION MTNS. WILDERNESS
SCAPEGOAT WILDERNESS
Dearborn R.
Clark Fork R.
Superior
Seeley L.
Placid L.
Salmon L.
RATTLESNAKE MTNS.
Jocko R.
Rogers Pass 5,609'
Monarch
Frenchtown
Ovando
Lincoln
Flesher Pass 6,350'
Wolf Creek
LITTLE
Alberton
Huson
Neihart
Holter Dam
GATES OF THE MOUNTAIN WILDERNESS
Blackfoot R.
Missoula
Potomac
Helmville
Hauser Dam
BIG BELT MTNS.
Kings Hill Pass 7,393'
Bonner
Marysville
Lake Helena
Lolo
Clinton
GARNET RANGE
Canyon Ferry Lake & Reservoir
THE EASTERN FR
Lolo Pass 5,233'
Drummond
Little Blackfoot R.
CONTINENTAL
Florence
Clark Fork R.
Gold Creek
Helena
BITTERROOT
Stevensville
WELCOME CREEK WILDERNESS
Avon
E. Helena
Clancy
White Sulphur Springs
CASTLE MTNS.
Victor
Garrison
THE MINING AXIS
Deer Lodge
HELENA CENTERED
Mart

THE SOUTHWEST

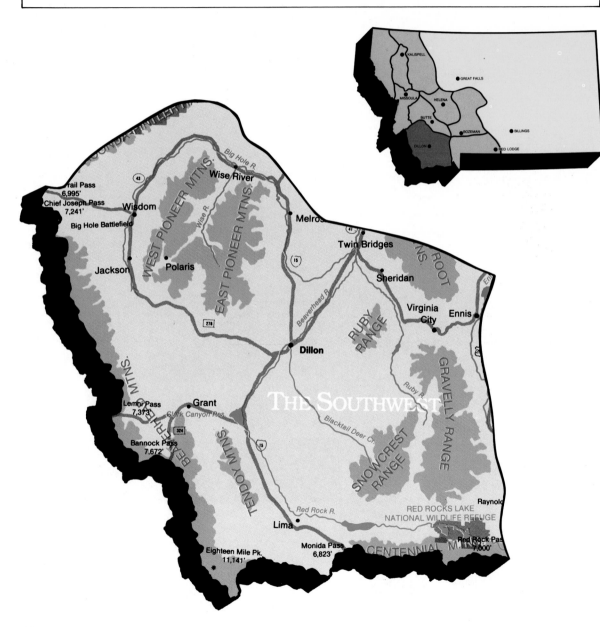

Southwest Montana is a spacious land of generous, often sage covered, dry valleys separated by islands of forested mountain ranges. This is classic Broad Valley Rockies where vistas stretch to distances of 50 miles or more. Life for residents is dominantly rural and centered within intermontane valleys. Population is sparse and towns small, even by Montana standards. Dillon, with less than 4,000 citizens, is the undisputed regional capital. The remaining 7,000 residents are sprinkled thinly over the area's more than 8,000 square miles and are served by towns ranging from second-ranking Ennis (population 660) to Wisdom (154) and Cameron (10).

Economically, ranching dominates the Southwest. This is cattle country and has been for generations: it dominates the regional identity and personality. The ranching lifestyle is firmly ingrained in residents and apparent on the landscape. Even strangers quickly traversing the region via Interstate 15 can't help but notice the numerous ranches, hayfields and haystacks, jack fences and loading chutes, and the ubiquitous cattle that outnumber residents by more than ten to one.

Stockgrowing got a surprisingly early start in these high mountain valleys, and actually predates the more celebrated arrival of gold seekers to many of the same gulches. During the 1850s and 1860s the Southwest developed as one of Montana's earliest and most important livestock producing areas and claimed some of its first ranches. These were strictly open-range outfits, relying on the free and unfenced range. Sensing the opportunity for hefty profits in the 1850s, former Hudson Bay Company trader Richard Grant and his family were among the earliest to use this nutrient-rich rangeland to winter-over and fatten cattle. In the spring they drove their herd south to the Oregon Trail where westward-bound pioneers were eager to replace their trail-worn and emaciated stock on terms quite favorable to the Grants. Word of the suitability of southwestern Montana valleys for stockgrowing spread and in the '50s and '60s others drove in herds from places as far away as Oregon and California.

The day of the open range is gone now in the Beaverhead, Madison, Big Hole and other livestock valleys of the Southwest. But like their earliest counterparts of more than a century ago, today's stockmen still depend on native range and they still produce cattle for shipment out of the region. Most ranches are cow-calf operations that supply young animals to out-of-state feedlots, especially in Corn Belt states.

Carrying capacity and suitability of range for livestock is as variable as the region's topography and precipitation. Some higher and wetter benches provide excellent grazing, but as Madison County Extension Agent Merle Lyda points out, some of the driest sections are "so darn poor they're not even worth messing with," since even one head would have to forage over too large an area. More than one cattleman blames overgrazing by excessive numbers of sheep around the turn of the century for the poor condition of some range. They point to sheepmen who took advantage of government grazing leases, using them as excuses to continually trail their flocks up and down, back and forth over land between the base ranch and high country, grubbing off grass with each pass, eventually leaving the range in a "sheeped" condition.

Grazing on federal lands is widespread in the Southwest, where government land greatly exceeds private holdings. Over 500,000 acres within Beaverhead National Forest and approximately 800,000 acres of Bureau of Land Management (BLM) holdings are critical to livestock operations. Each year the cost of grazing leases is assessed and adjusted to reflect a rancher's cost of operation, fair-market value of grazing land and numerous other variables. Even though ranchers periodically might grumble about fees, most would admit that rates are quite reasonable, especially when compared to state leases which are based on highest bid and are considerably more expensive. With a feeding period of six months, ranchers are thankful to be able to subsidize their operations with cheaper grazing available on federal leases.

Forest Service allotments are outside valley areas on mountain slopes. If you've traveled the highways and backroads of this area in late June to mid-July, you've undoubtedly encountered plodding herds being trailed to summer pasture and had to gingerly inch your car through a sea of bellowing bovines. Some more distant ranchers trail for up to a week to reach their summer pasture. The seasonal shift of herds from valley areas to higher mountain pastures in summer and back down in the fall, is common practice in mountain areas worldwide, and geographers call it transhumance.

When livestock can be "turned out" to their allotment is strictly controlled by the Forest Service. Crossfencing, water systems and rotation between pastures are standard on many leases. Gone are the days when ranchers could turn their animals loose and forget about them until snow forced them out of the high country. Permittees may complain about the added work of moving cattle from pasture to pasture, but most agree that strict grazing management promotes better forage, and animals come off summer range in better shape. Most livestock is trailed back to valley areas by middle to late October. Cattlemen are eager to have their herds out of the mountains before the start of big-game season.

Above is the Big Hole Valley showing storm over the Beaverhead Mountains. Below are the East Pioneer Mountains in the Sawtooth Creek area. Photos by Tom Dietrich, George Wuerthner.

Except for the Ruby Range, which lacks National Forest land and is BLM administered, bureau lands characteristically begin at the lower treeline and extend to foothills, benches, and even reach into some valley bottoms. These are lands that have never left federal ownership and for various reasons were not acquired by homesteaders or others. Unlike Eastern Montana and most other sections of the state where BLM lands are fragmented and scattered, here they form more continuous and blocky units. This distribution adds to the importance of these federal lands in the regional ranching economy, especially within Beaverhead County. Sections of BLM land are considered integral components of many ranches, which are usually described as having a size of so many deeded acres and so many leased acres. Allotments almost automatically are tied to a specific ranch and stay with it when sold.

With its large cattle population it is not surprising that hay is the region's dominant crop. Approximately 80 percent of all harvested cropland in the area is in irrigated hay. With a high protein content of up to 19 percent, some even finds its way into dairies in the Flathead Valley, Washington and Idaho. Big Hole Valley hay once had a national reputation and was shipped as far away as the East Coast where it was highly regarded by race-horse owners. Most hay, though, is consumed by local beef cattle. Putting up winter feed for brood cows is essential for area ranchers. Many ranchers run 700 to more than 1,000 head and at two tons per animal per winter, huge volumes must be baled or stacked every summer. Long before extensive mechanization of haying, two inventive Big Hole ranchers developed the unique Beaverslide to facilitate field stacking large amounts of hay.

Marketing is the weakest link in ranching for many operators. Most still depend on "order buyers" or "commission buyers" who visit their ranch in the fall to make an offer on their calves. Others routinely truck young animals and send cull cows "down the road" to auction yards in Butte or Bozeman, where they hope competitive bidding might result in a higher price. A new, still somewhat experimental method of video-taping herds on the ranch and then showing tapes to prospective bidders has been tried at the Butte Livestock Auction. A few enterprising ranchers, eager to cut out middlemen, have joined to set up their own marketing associations. One large group has been shipping calves directly to Columbus, Nebraska for 20 years. In 1982 they shipped 10,000 head. Other smaller groups of ranchers have sent their own agent to the Corn Belt states to establish direct contact with feedlot operators.

Greater diversification and larger ranches are two obvious trends among Southwest livestock operators.

For example Lynn Owens, who ranches up the North Meadow Creek west of McAllister, runs 300 head of cows, who yield just about that many calves. He also earns income by keeping 60 calves to yearlings and runs 100 sheep. More ranchers are augmenting cash flow with supplemental yearling operations.

According to Beaverhead County Extension Agent John Maki, sprinkler irrigation is growing in popularity. Where possible operators have expanded barley acreage and worked it into their hay : grain crop rotation scheme. This high altitude region produces excellent malting barley, much of which is grown under contract to brewers including Coors and Anheuser-Busch. Ranchers typically grow wheat or barley for two to three years in a field and then plant alfalfa hay for five to six years. As Maki points out, they seem to want their land back in hay as soon as possible.

Economics have worked against small "starvation units" and in the last decade most Southwest ranchers have either expanded or gone out of business. Like others, Jay Barnowsky, who runs a 700-cow operation adjacent to the Ruby River west of Sheridan, has had to double the size of his cattle operation over the last ten years "just to maintain the same kind of living." Existing farm debt coupled with high interest rates and lack of available land have all but ruled out further expansion for many.

In some sections the rancher's plight is made worse by the proliferation of rural subdivisions and second-home developments which occupy land that might otherwise have passed to land-hungry ranchers. This is a serious problem in the upper Madison River Valley above McAllister. At first, most large ranches passed to usually wealthy and often absentee owners who simply wanted a Western Montana ranch to which they could retreat each summer. These were operated by managers, but making a profit wasn't too important since tax write-offs and real estate values assured owners a more than generous return on investment. Many of these ranches have changed hands several times and have been divided into large chunks which have since been subdivided into "ranchettes" — parcels ten acres or so in size, large enough to gobble up vast areas of former agricultural land, but too small to be of any agrarian benefit.

Speculators realized there were plenty of out-of-staters and Montana residents who could be sold on the recreation and/or profit potential of such acreage. In slick brochures, lots sounded like a little bit of heaven — situated in the picturesque Madison Valley at the base of the towering Madison Range, located adjacent to one of the world's most famous Blue Ribbon trout streams and less than an hour from Yellowstone National Park. Couple these amenities with low interest rates and easy monthly payments

over long terms and it is understandable why there are few owner-operated ranches in the upper Madison Valley.

Rancher Lynn Owens has watched this metamorphosis of the rural landscape with great concern and admits he had sympathy for the individual who recently was arrested for chopping down a billboard advertising one of the largest developments. "We've got a pretty area and a few too many people have found out about it," he laments. Owens hates to see what is happening and views each new home as "a nail in the coffin of the rancher." "Subdivisions place a false sense of value on the land," he points out. Prices escalate to levels beyond the reach of those who would buy and pay for acreage on the basis of agriculture. Land necessary to the continued expansion and survival of ranchers is thus removed from the market.

While ranchers are forced to accept what seems inevitable change in the Madison, others rejoice at prospects of expanded recreation and tourism. Real estate agents, restaurateurs, innkeepers, shop owners, guides and outfitters all benefit from revenues generated by increasing numbers of residents and tourists. Symbolically, Ennis lost its last farm implement dealership in the 1960s, and has evolved into primarily a tourist town that springs to life each summer.

Ennis realtor Jess Armitage, a native son, has calculated that 35,000 acres in the Madison Valley between Norris Hill and Raynolds Pass have been subdivided into parcels of less than 20 acres. Madison River frontage commands the highest price. While land has yet to be sold by the square foot, that time may be just around the corner. In 1982 Armitage sold 1.3 acres on a dry cactus bench fronting the river just south of town for $30,000.

High prices and a quest for privacy no longer available along all reaches of the Madison have led to a leapfrogging of developments into the upper Ruby. Armitage recalls that a few years ago he couldn't persuade clients to travel the short distance to view lots in that valley. The filling in of the Madison and the discovery that the Ruby is an excellent trout stream in its own right have led to a mini-land rush into that drainage.

Fly fishing for rainbows and browns is one of the major recreational lures of southwest Montana. The Madison, Beaverhead and Big Hole are among the most highly regarded trout streams in the nation, if not the world. Fly rods have been named after them, innumerable articles and ads in publications like *Field and Stream* and *Fly Fisherman* have extolled their virtues, and more than passing mention in books on the world's great trout fisheries have imparted a magic ring to their names among fishermen worldwide.

A

B

D

C

(A) The Centennial Mountains near the Red Rock Lakes. Rick Graetz photo.

(B) The Little Sheep Creek area with the Tendoy Mountains in the background. George Wuerthner photos.

(C) Sheep herder in the Beaverhead Mountains. George Wuerthner photo.

(D) Staple of the southwest economy--cattle. Phil Farnes photo.

51

The beaverslide, a landmark of "loose stack" haying, was invented in the Southwest Region. Charles Kay photo. The historical shot is of haying on the C-D Ranch, in the Big Hole. Montana Historical Society photo.

Montana's Beaverslide Haystacker

One of the most distinctive sights in some of the western valleys of Montana is the Beaverslide, a strange looking, 30-foot-tall haystacking implement towering over fields. They are most common in the Big Hole Valley, but probably are seen by most just north of Deer Lodge where they easily are visible from Interstate 90.

The prototype of the Beaverslide was built in 1907-08 by Big Hole ranchers David J. Stephens and Herbert S. Armitage. Experimentation led to refinements and the pair applied for and received a patent on their unique sliding stacker in 1910. The name Beaverslide came later. Most people familiar with the stacker, including the ranchers who use it, assume the name has something to do with beavers and a slide they might use down a steep bank, but evidently it is linked to the county of its origin. Once known as the Beaverhead

County Slide Stacker, the name eventually was shortened to Beaverslide.

A Beaverslide is a derrick-like structure with a slide along which a hay basket is lifted. Baskets are counter-balanced, so that when resting at the base of the slide their tines fall back and provide a slightly inclined loading platform onto which hay is dumped. Once filled, it is pulled by cables attached to its two ends and strung through pulleys mounted on the top of the stacker. Cables used to be attached to two- or three-horse teams that lifted the basket as they moved at a right angle away from the stacker. Today, power winches quickly pull the basket to the top of the glide surface where hay falls into the stack through an opening in the frame.

With this device, haystacks of 20 tons standing almost 30 feet were commonplace. Ranchers took pride in producing perfectly rectangular stacks. It was the job of those arranging fork loads on top to see that the pile was well formed. They were the specialists and usually the highest paid members of a haying crew. Stackmen also had to be skilled at dodging the rattlesnakes that often accompanied the basket loads of hay.

Rows of loose hay are scooped up by "buck rakes" and heaved by the "derrick man" up the beaverslide and onto the stack. John Alwin photos.

The Beaverslide was an inexpensive, homemade implement that could quickly stack large amounts of hay. This was important in sections of the West, especially in areas with extensive and often rough wild-hay meadows, where large tonnages had to be stacked as feed for brood cows. With its advantages over most commercially available stackers, use of the folk implement spread, or diffused, from its area of origin in the Big Hole into other Western Montana valleys and the states of Idaho, Wyoming, Nebraska, South Dakota, Colorado, Nevada, California, Washington and Oregon, as well as the Canadian provinces of British Columbia and Alberta.

Diffusion of the stacker's use can be attributed to at least two major factors. Perhaps of greatest importance were Big Hole residents who traveled to areas both within and outside of Montana specifically to build Beaverslides. David Hirschy built approximately 500 stackers in six western states plus British Columbia between 1940 and 1970 and might be considered the "Johnny Appleseed" of Beaverslides. Diffusion also was linked to seasonal laborers who worked on Big Hole ranches during summer haying seasons. They came from throughout Montana and adjacent states, attracted by word-of-mouth or by newspaper advertisements. Miners from nearby Butte also routinely timed their vacations so they could work in the valley's hayfields. Laborers usually were provided with room and board and could look forward to good home-cooked food since wives of ranchers gave the Big Hole "a reputation all over the northwest for feeding its haymen" as was advertised in a 1919 Jordan, Montana newspaper. Haymen gained firsthand knowledge by working with the stacker, but did not have to trust their memories for construction details. Those planning to build their own could return home with postcards showing detailed pictures of the stacker in use. Once introduced, new areas became potential centers for further diffusion.

Only modest changes distinguish today's Beaverslides from their predecessors. When haying crews began replacing horses with gasoline power in the 1930s and 1940s the basket size was increased. Soon, baskets ranged up to 25 feet across, 8 feet wider than the patented version. The most obvious modification was the addition of attached side wings. Appearing in the 1950s, these features and a detached backstop help to hold and shape the haystack.

Associated implements also have changed. Motor driven mowers, dumprakes and sweeprakes have been standard for decades. Gone, too, are horse buckrakes that picked up hay from the field and carried it to the stacker. Custom-built power buckrakes often are constructed using ¾-ton truck frames on which the rear axle is removed and reinstalled in an inverted position, thereby providing multiple "reverse" speeds which then become forward speeds. A rake and simple elevator device are attached to the new front and steering is adapted to allow the driver to face toward the rake. The result is a more maneuverable vehicle capable of quick turns in a short radius. Once a stack is completed, side wings are folded back and the slide is dragged to a new stacking yard using a small tractor.

Recent decades have witnessed a decline in Beaverslide usage throughout most of its former use areas. In many places, slides now sit abandoned in fields, remnants of an earlier time. In most of these areas newer, commercial, large capacity haying systems like loaf stackers or large round or rectangular balers have displaced the Beaverslide. Yet, the stacker continues to be the standard implement for field stacking hay in Big Hole country, still known as the "land of 10,000 haystacks," and in several other Western Montana valleys including the Flint Creek and Little Blackfoot around Avon.

Where still used, the Beaverslide continues to provide the same advantages it has for decades. Ranchers cite its speed in stacking hay, less spoilage from larger stacks which have a smaller surface to volume ratio, suitability in areas of rugged and wet ground where more modern machinery breaks down, advantages in areas of light hay where more mechanized equipment can't be justified economically, and relatively small initial investment when compared to commercial big package haying systems.

Not only is the Beaverslide holding its own in the Big Hole, but new slides are being built in other Western Montana valleys. Improvements continue to be made. In the mid-1970s two Big Hole service station owners began building metal Beaverslides of essentially the same design and size as wooden versions. They cost almost $10,000, about five times as much as wooden models, but it is expected that they will last several times as long as the wooden variety. The willingness of ranchers to make such an investment shows their commitment to the time-proven Beaverslide.

The Southwest Region claims much of the waters of the famed Madison River. George Wuerthner photo.

Those who have donned waders to test their skills in these waters include the likes of presidents Hoover and Eisenhower and national figures such as Wallace Beery and Bing Crosby. Many a mere mortal in the region has come face to face with the great and near great on these rivers and found himself engaged in conversation on the salmon fly hatch or the appropriateness of a muddler versus a woolly worm.

Stunning mountain settings are part of the lure of these rivers, but more critical to the reputation of each is its high fertility. One key contributing factor is widespread limestone and dolomite rock deposited by oceans more than 60 million years ago. Rivers and their tributaries passing over these rocks pick up calcium, magnesium, and carbonate. This makes rivers highly alkaline, a chemical condition that encourages phytoplankton, minute, floating aquatic plants that form the base of the food chain for river life. Additional nutrients include phosphorus and nitrogen washed in as by-products of agriculture and leached from the rich soils of grassy meadows contributing more "fertilizer." The net result is an extremely fertile water capable of supporting an abundance of aquatic insects on which trout subsist. Fish thrive like cattle in a feedlot, and some eat their way to record size. Modest stream velocities, favorable pool to riffle ratios, streambank cover and suitable water temperature further enhance the sport fishery potential of many reaches.

With approximately 3,500 trout per mile the Madison is one of the state's most heavily fished rivers. For fishermen there are really two Madison Rivers, an upper reach above Ennis Lake and the 35-mile stretch below. Summer fishing pressure is heavy on the upper river and 80 percent of it is from nonresidents. The trout fishing fraternity, however, avoids summer fishing on the lower Madison, which now seems more popular among rafters and inner-tube floaters.

Fishermen avoid the lowest 35 miles because of thermopollution. Thermal problems date back to 1900 when the Madison dam was built across the river seven miles downriver from Ennis to provide hydroelectric power to the Southwest. Water impounded by the structure filled a basin and formed Ennis Lake, also known as Meadow Lake or Madison Reservoir. The naturally shallow basin and more than 80 years of sedimentation have produced a reservoir with an average depth of only about nine feet. Less than one percent of the lake is deeper than 16 feet. With its shallow depth and relatively large surface area of 640 acres, the reservoir acts like a giant solar collector. During its 20-day passage through the reservoir water is unnaturally heated during the summer before it leaves the reservoir. This seasonal warming of Ennis Lake causes the lower river near Norris to average 7½ degrees warmer than the section just above Ennis. Water temperatures on the lower reach have climbed to 82 degrees.

Bathtub temperatures that are a delight to inner tubers are a disaster for fish. Dick Vincent, regional fisheries biologist for the state Department of Fish, Wildlife and Parks, points out that 58 degrees is the optimal temperature for trout. Even a few degrees one way or the other impacts growth and reproduction. At 64 degrees, not uncommon in the lower Madison, growth rate drops by 75 percent according to Vincent. Slowed feeding means that fishermen are less likely to catch fish, and that is the typical situation on the lower Madison from late June through September. River temperatures already have come dangerously close to the 84 to 85 degree range which could lead to wholesale die-offs. A prolonged heat spell of several weeks in the 90s could raise water to killing temperatures.

Several solutions to the Madison River thermal problem have been proposed. One calls for elimination of the small Montana Power dam, returning the lake to a river system. A 1983 study by Blue Ribbons of Montana, a Madison-Gallatin planning organization, suggested building a dike system that would create a water channel to move water quickly through the lake.

To the west on the Beaverhead, it's not thermopollution, but access that presents the greatest problems for fishermen. Devotees of the Madison are surprised to hear that the Beaverhead has at least 50

Top: Battle Mountain on the site of the Big Hole Battlefield where troops and civilian irregulars encountered Chief Joseph and his Nez Perce in 1877. Jeff Gnass photo.

Left: Clark Canyon Reservoir south of Dillon. George Wuerthner photo.

Above: Ennis Lake on the Madison. Rick Graetz photo.

Top: Virginia City, 1866. Montana Historical Society photo.

Above left: Outlaw Rock near Bannack, a popular spot for bushwhacking unsuspecting travelers. Rick Graetz photo.

Above: The other side of social order, the Methodist church at Bannack. Tom Dietrich photo.

percent more pounds of trout per mile than its sister river (3,200 lbs. versus 2,000 lbs.). Its super rich water places it in a class by itself in terms of number of monster trout. According to Vincent, the Madison averages three trout over 20 inches in length per mile, while the Beaverhead claims a phenomenal 180 of these gargantuans for each mile segment.

The Southwest attracts tourists and recreationists for a myriad of outdoor activities in addition to fishing. Almost two million acres of Forest Service land provide the essentials for some of the best big-game hunting in Montana. White-tailed and mule deer, elk, moose, black bear, bighorn sheep, and mountain goats are bagged for wall trophies or home freezers. These hunters share hundreds of miles of trails with hikers and others armed only with cameras. Camping ranges from remote backcountry tenting among alpine lakes to tamer outings in the scores of public and private developed campgrounds throughout the region.

Visitors to the Southwest find themselves in one of Montana's longest settled and most historic quarters. This is where white civilization took root in Montana and is a region sometimes referred to as the cradle of Montana history. The area claims some of the state's oldest towns including its first two territorial capitals. Settlement in the American Far West did not advance in a wave-like fashion along a single broad front as it

55

(A) The Lima Peaks. Rick Graetz photo.

(B) The Tobacco Root Mountains from the air. Mark Thompson photo.

(C) Inside a school room at Bannack. Charles Kay photo.

(D) Overview of Virginia City today. Wayne Scherr photo.

had in the East and Midwest. Instead outposts of civilization first were established in widely scattered pockets and then settlement pushed outward from each. In this sense, the Southwest was part of the nucleus around which Montana grew.

Gold drew the initial rush of settlers into the dry gulches. Colors were struck along Grasshopper Creek in the summer of 1862. Gold previously had been discovered in other Western Montana gulches, but none promising enough to generate a true town. By that first autumn in 1862, Bannack may have had 500 residents and by year's end ballooned to some 1,500. That year mining activity and population shifted to the east and the even richer placer deposits discovered along Alder Gulch. The pace of development at the new diggings was frantic. Within a year a string of communities sprouted along a ten-mile segment of the gulch.

The rapid growth was recorded in the diary of one miner on November 12, 1864, when he wrote: "It surprises me to see how rapidly this country improves. First two miles below here is Virginia City, a thriving village with many business houses; then one mile farther down is Central City, not Quite so large; then in another mile you enter Nevada, as large as Virginia City; then about a mile and a half further brings you to Junction City. The road connecting these "cities" is bordered with dwellings on both sides all along. I shouldn't have the patience to count the business places, but can say that the market is so well stocked that all necessaries and many luxuries can be obtained in the stores. Recalling that only eighteen months ago this was a 'howling wilderness,' or rather a howling desert . . ."

Virginia City's *Montana Post,* Montana's first newspaper, reported almost 100 buildings were being erected in Virginia City and environs by mid-1864. Population in the gulch may have reached 10,000 within the first year, but declined almost as quickly as it blossomed. As easily worked deposits were exhausted and new, more promising strikes were made in other western gulches, transient miners pulled up stakes and moved on. The exodus already was under way in 1870 when the census tallied only 867 in Virginia City and 381 in Bannack.

This was a colorful era of bawdy mining camps with their interesting amalgam of brothels and literary guilds, quick riches and dashed dreams. Some of the characters would fit right into a Louis L'Amour novel. None was more infamous than Bannack's debonair sheriff, Henry Plummer, leader of a notorious gang of outlaws. The legend of the mining camps' secretive vigilantes and their mysterious "3-7-77" symbol lives on today with this sequence of numbers still adorning state highway patrol decals.

The look and feel of this frontier time still can be experienced. The ghost town of Bannack is a popular tourist attraction that draws 35,000 visitors a year despite its remote location and gravel-road access. The town is dominated by its large two-story brick courthouse erected in 1875-76 as seat of government for Beaverhead County. During the Nez Perce War of 1877, when Chief Joseph and his warriors were camped just outside of town, this masonry building functioned as military headquarters and safe refuge for women and children awaiting an attack that never came. Wood-frame and log homes, shops and two jails still stand. Even Skinners Saloon has survived, one of the few buildings dating back to the community's first two years. Enough of the town remains to make history believable and to allow visitors to become immersed in that past.

Virginia City is an even more popular stop for those seeking links with the region's mining past. Unlike Bannack, Virginia City was never a ghost town. Buildings on the west end of the main drag have been saved and restored in such a way that if not for all the campers and cars parked along the street, you might think you were back in the 1860s. The east end is more functional and has a mix of old and new. The heavily worn stone step at the entrance to the historic Post Office building reflects its long service to the community. Just up the road west of town Nevada City has been recreated by transplanting original buildings from other Montana mining camps.

One of the most satisfying ways to capture the feel of the mining west is to head into the hills in search of less publicized remnants. An especially good area is west of Melrose in the Pioneer Mountains where back roads reward the inquisitive with ghost towns, smelters, rows of beehive-shaped charcoal kilns and a plethora of mine shafts and prospect pits.

Recent rises in the price of gold have lured modern prospectors back to the hills, but most miners in the Southwest now are employed at less glamorous talc mines. Large open pit operations in the Ruby Range and on the east flank of the Gravelly Range make this one of the world's premier talc producing regions. Southwest Montana is heavily mineralized with proven and untapped deposits of gold, silver, copper, lead, zinc, molybdenum, tungsten, uranium, asbestos, graphite and iron ore. Half the region falls within the Overthrust Belt, an active area for oil and gas exploration. By January 1983, oil and gas interests had almost 90 percent of the Beaverhead National Forest leased or under lease application. One of the deepest wells ever drilled in the state recently was capped in the Big Hole Valley. Time will tell whether mineral and energy developments have the potential to remake the geography of the Southwest.

On the campus of "Western." John Alwin photo.

Dillon

Racing to beat the Northern Pacific that was projecting an east-west transcontinental line across Montana, the Utah & Northern entered from the south in 1880 as Montana's first railroad. Its primary objective was the rich Butte mining district, which was reached in late 1881. Enroute, construction temporarily was blocked by a rancher who refused to grant right-of-way. Several visionary locals formed a partnership, purchased the ranch, gave the railroad the right to pass and developed a town where the line had come to a standstill. With direct access to outside markets they were convinced the Southwest region would blossom commercially and require a regional trade center. For the first year the fledgling town was appropriately called Terminus, but later adopted the name Dillon after Sidney Dillon, president of the Utah & Northern.

The town founders were proven correct as the community quickly eclipsed all others in the region and displaced Bannack as county seat of Beaverhead County in 1889. Within ten years Dillon was one of the dozen largest towns in the state with more than 1,000 residents. It developed as an important center for surrounding ranches and for a time claimed to be Montana's largest wool shipping point. The community also became an educational center in the 1890s when the legislature chose it as the location for the state's Normal School. The political clout of Marcus Daly didn't hurt. The first building was opened on a 20-acre campus in 1897 to serve an enrollment of 75.

Dillon still functions in many of the same roles it has for decades. It remains dominantly an agricultural and educational center. With a population of approximately 4,000 the community is the largest for a radius of 50 miles or more in all directions. Hopping into the pickup truck and heading into Dillon for a livestock sale, to shop, or to take in a movie is routine for thousands in the sprawling trade area of some 15,000 square miles.

The Normal School has evolved into Western Montana College with approximately 900 students. Most are Montanans with about 85 percent coming from the western part of the state. Dr. Evelyn Hively, Vice President for Academic Affairs, points out that "our mission is still primarily training teachers." Education graduates have an excellent record for job placement and are on the teaching staffs in all but two or three Montana counties. Students at Western benefit from small classes and one of the best student-faculty ratios in the state.

Dillon also is headquarters for Beaverhead National Forest which provides about 75 local jobs. The Pfizer talc mill eight miles south of town and the associated Treasure Chest open pit mine 12 miles north in the Ruby Range employ more than 100. The Precambrian rock trucked to the mill arrives in chunks up to three feet across. The rock is hand sorted on a conveyor belt system, ground to various grades of powder and sacked. Dillon talc has a reputation for extremely high purity making it valuable for scores of uses from ceramics and chocolates to paper, plastics and paints.

Ranchers from the Big Hole and Madison and other surrounding valleys, as well as non-locals, have discovered the suitability of Dillon as a retirement community. Its modest size is appealing as are its quiet tree-lined streets, abundant sun and dearth of snow. It is unlikely that Dillon will become another Palm Springs, but then, most residents wouldn't want it that way.

THE YELLOWSTONE ROCKIES

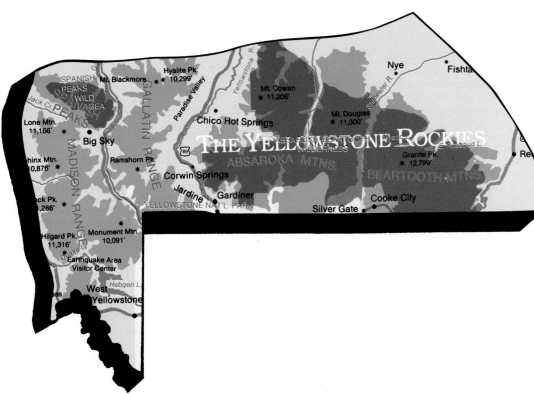

Northwest and Frontier airline flights connecting Billings with Bozeman and Butte provide what must be the most spectacular visual introduction to Western Montana's Yellowstone Rockies. On a clear day it's worth a bit of a scramble at the airport to obtain a window seat on the south side, fore or aft of the wing. These east-west flights pass just to the north of the expansive highland complex, which spreads out as a seemingly endless sea of mountains.

Even from 30,000 feet the scale and ruggedness of this elevated country is awesome — the two-mile-high, bare rock and lake-studded Beartooth Plateau, the peaks of the wild Absaroka Range, the snow-capped Hyalites, the jagged Spanish Peaks, and beyond a mountain world that stretches south past Yellowstone National Park. Between Red Lodge on the east and the western foothills of the Madison Range 120 miles to the west, the Yellowstone's trough-like Paradise Valley south of Livingston stands out as the only major break in this mountainous terrain.

From the air it is obvious that the Yellowstone Rockies is a distinct corner of Western Montana, contrasting with neighboring sections of the state. To the west and north the widely spaced mountains and dry valleys of the Broad Valley Rockies appear rather tame in comparison to the concentration of mountainous terrain in the Yellowstone Rockies. To the east that contrast is even more striking as the steep lower forested slopes of the Beartooth yield to a much more subdued natural landscape of rolling grass and sage-covered hills on the western margin of Great Plains Montana.

Residents of these adjacent sections seem to perceive the region as a distinct and special place. Those in Billings take pride and comfort in the snow-capped peaks on the southwest skyline that local promotional maps and brochures take the liberty of moving to within 15 or 20 miles of town. In communities from Red Lodge to Livingston, Bozeman and Ennis, the mountains provide the scenic backdrop that fills the horizon. Like most tourists, citizens of neighboring areas generally enter the region only for outdoor recreation. It's where they go for some of their favorite Sunday drives and hikes, and best fishing, hunting, and skiing. Three of its communities, Cooke City, Gardiner and West Yellowstone, serve as Montana's gateway cities to Yellowstone National Park.

Western Montana's Yellowstone Rockies remains one of America's most thinly populated, wild and remote areas. Not a single east-west road traverses the region and only two north-south highways run its entire width. Most roads reach only a short distance into the outer fringes as finger-like probes, and even paved highways quickly deteriorate to jeep-grade dirt trails.

Above: Granite Peak in the Absaroka-Beartooth Wilderness and the highest point in the state at 12,799'. Rick Graetz photo.

Right: The Spanish Lakes in the Spanish Peaks Wilderness. Pat O'Hara photo.

Looking to the plains from the Beartooth Mountains along East Rosebud Creek. George Wuerthner photo.

Western Montana's Wilderness Areas

When the first Europeans arrived centuries ago America was wilderness from coast to coast. There were no roads, signs of man's impact were practically nonexistent, and finding solitude certainly was not a problem. From that time forth, large, wild and unsettled areas have been places to be conquered and subdued. Progress has been synonymous with humanizing the land and putting it to economic use. By this century the process of converting natural landscapes to cultural landscapes was almost complete, prompting visionary conservationists to grow increasingly concerned that the few remaining vestiges of America's wild lands heritage soon would succumb to development.

As early as the 1920s the U.S. Forest Service began managing sections of forest land as "primitive" and the next decade adopted both "wilderness" and "wild" designations for some areas. These were strictly administratively based.

It was not until the 1964 passage of the Wilderness Act that this country had the legal mandate and framework for designation of federal wilderness areas. The legislation's primary objective was "to assure that an increasing population, accompanied by expanding settlement and growing mechanization, does not occupy and modify all areas within the United States . . ."

The Act defines wilderness as "an area where the earth and its community of life are untrammeled by man, where man himself is a visitor who does not remain." Federal lands included in the National Wilderness Preservation System must meet specific requirements outlined in the Wilderness Act. First, the land must appear to have been affected primarily by the forces of nature, with the imprint of man substantially unnoticeable. Further, areas must offer outstanding opportunities for solitude or a primitive and unconfined type of outdoor recreation. Individual tracts should total at least 5,000 acres or be at least sufficient in size to make

preservation practical. Finally, areas also may contain ecological, geological, or other features of scientific, educational, scenic or historical value.

If you've walked the streets of midtown Manhattan or strolled along Chicago's State Street with their noise, congestion, foul air and almost totally manmade landscapes of horizontal and vertical concrete and steel, then you've experienced one extreme of this country's environmental continuum. Wilderness areas are at the opposite end of this spectrum. The wilderness experience, as it is called, allows visitors to escape the hustle and bustle of daily life and enjoy spontaneity and solitude within a primordial setting. For some this is the ultimate in outdoor recreation and necessary for spiritual well-being. Others who have never visited a wilderness area and probably never will, gain comfort just knowing that they exist.

Depending on one's perspective, Western Montana has been blessed or cursed with extensive areas that have been by-passed in the settlement process. Most correspond to rugged and high mountainous country. As of 1982, Western Montana still has unprotected wilderness and an active corps of conservationists striving additional designations.

The Forest Service calculates that Montana wilderness areas provided 844,800 visitor-days in 1982. The visitor-day is the standard unit for reporting recreation use on national forest lands; it is an aggregate stay of one person for 12 hours, two persons for six hours, etc. Contrary to popular myth, most visitors are not wealthy out-of-staters. Approximately 80 percent are Montanans, the majority of modest means. All residents of Western Montana are within an hour or two of a wilderness trail head and a growing number have been taking advantage of their proximity. Montana's wilderness areas now rank behind California and Colorado and are tied with Washington for amount of visitor use. That is no small accomplishment considering the state's relatively small population and the fact that most visitors are in-staters. Higher fuel costs may boost visitation by ruling out long-distance vacations and forcing more residents to seek closer-to-home alternatives.

The Wilderness Act stipulates that areas be administered so as to "leave them unimpaired for future use and enjoyment as wilderness . . ." Once designated, they must be managed or the values for which they were originally selected will be lost.

Wilderness management is a new field that has had to rely on the findings of an equally new field of research. Drs. Robert Lucas and George Stankey, both geographers and research social scientists at the Forest Service Intermountain Station's Wilderness Management unit in Missoula, are pioneers in wilderness research. They have studied wilderness users for almost 20 years, and have interviewed thousands. Much of their work has centered around how visitors use and perceive wilderness and how that use impacts the environment.

Studies by Lucas, Stankey and others have shown that most visitors to Montana's wilderness areas are families and small groups who make short visits, commonly one-day outings. Extended stays of a week or longer are rare. Evidently, the wilderness experience is lessened when users encounter others on the trail or at their campsites. Large groups are considered especially offensive. Less than 20 percent of visitors venture much beyond trails and in virtually all areas use is heavily concentrated on a few popular trails. In the Mission Mountains, more than 90 percent of groups enter via two of the areas's 19 trails and in the Bob Marshall, the most-used 25 percent of trail mileage carries 95 percent of all use.

Lucas points out that the "draw-a-line-and-leave-it-alone philosophy of wilderness management is a myth." As well as accommodating hikers, wilderness areas legally may be used for hunting, fishing, grazing by domestic livestock, and even seemingly contradictory mining. All these activities must be managed to assure that natural ecological processes are not impacted.

In some more densely populated sections of the nation, wilderness areas have become so popular that they are being overrun by users. California's John Muir Wilderness, for example, experienced nearly 1.4 million visitor-days in 1975. Administrators of some heavily used areas have been forced to initiate permit systems to control visitation. Montana's sparse population in relation to its 3 million-plus acres of wilderness with more than 3,000 miles of trails have meant that rationing here has not yet been necessary. Soil erosion on heavily traveled trails and loss of vegetation at some popular campsites are warning signs of overuse, but few would argue for a permit system as yet. Stankey has suggested that to some, rationing "might seem akin to charging people to go to church."

In the shadow of the mountains. A hayfield in the Yellowstone River Valley south of Livingston. Tom Dietrich photo.

Two existing and one impending wilderness areas protect much of the heart of this wild domain. The giant among these is the 904,500-acre Absaroka Beartooth Wilderness that sprawls over most of the Absaroka and Beartooth ranges. It is Montana's second largest (over 1,400 square miles) and most popular wilderness area in terms of visitation.

Although a single wilderness, the Absaroka Beartooth is really two different worlds. The Beartooth portion, east of the Boulder River, is dominated by a series of extensive plateaus and deep canyons. Hellroaring, Froze-to-Death, Beartooth, Silver Run and others are nearly level, treeless areas generally around 10,000 feet in elevation. These spectacular and rugged wind-swept plateaus carry vegetation similar to Arctic tundra.

Recreation and scenic values are outstanding in this, the Roof of Montana. The entire territory was heavily glaciated during the last Ice Age, and the evidence is everywhere. Numerous lakes now fill depressions scooped by glaciers; sheer rock walls, waterfalls, and extensive areas scraped down to bare rock are other legacies of the not-too-distant era of ice. The scale of the physical landscape is awe inspiring. It is understandable why some feel the area is unrivaled for its natural, high-country beauty.

In places mountain peaks rise to several thousand feet above plateau surfaces. More than 20 exceed 12,000 feet, including Granite Peak, Montana's highest at 12,799 feet. It and its sister peaks are especially popular with Montana mountain climbers who are attracted by the prevalence of granite (good for climbing) and the glacially imparted ruggedness of the state's highest peaks. The easiest ascent of Granite Peak is considered class four climbing according to professional climber Jack Tackle. That means that you don't have to be an expert with all kinds of fancy gear, but you should have mountaineering experience before attempting the climb.

Climbing in the Beartooths and other Montana ranges is made more challenging by the lack of a guide book. Mountain climbers are an independent lot and are not interested in counterparts to the "how to" and "where to" books on Montana hiking, skiing, fishing, floating, etc. A guide would destroy some of the element of discovery and most likely would lead to increased use and impact. There is an unwritten agreement among the climbing community that no one will write a mountain climber's guide to Montana, according to Tackle. They don't contribute to magazine articles for the same reasons.

61

The Absaroka Beartooth's uniqueness combined with its proximity to Montana's largest urban center help explain why it receives more use than any other Montana wilderness. In 1982 its 392,700 visitor-days were more than twice that of the Bob Marshall and almost equal to all other Montana wilderness areas combined. The 108,000 citizens of metropolitan Billings are within two hours of wilderness trail heads and each year more Magic City residents take advantage of it. Easy access from a dendritic network of roads that terminate just north of the Beartooth portion makes these the most popular entry points. At times in the summer, the number and prevalence of "3 county" license plates on vehicles at Forest Service campgrounds in the upper East and West Rosebud and Stillwater drainages make them seem like Billings city parks.

West of the Boulder River, topography in the Absaroka Range is more gentle than in the Beartooth, but still it is by no means tame. Mountain tops reach well above tree line, and are bare and rocky, but these areas are not nearly as extensive as in the Beartooth. Mt. Cowan, the highest, reaches 11,206 feet, whereas the Beartooth has several extensive plateaus that approach that height. Overall, the Absaroka has broader valleys, more rounded slopes and abundant vegetation, including a luxuriant forest cover on lower and intermediate slopes. Wildlife is also more plentiful in this less harsh and more varied environment. Although different, the Absaroka are not second to the Beartooth or any other Montana range in terms of wilderness value. In fact the northern section was judged by the Forest Service to have the highest possible wilderness quality index rating of any area in the U.S.

Varieties of recreational use of the Absaroka Beartooth and surrounding public lands is typical of that in other areas of the Yellowstone Rockies. Hiking, backpacking and horseback riding, skiing, and fishing and hunting are all popular activities. Nearby Montanans are fortunate to be able to partake of these activities with a minimum of cost and effort. Accommodating visitors from more distant areas now supports a large dude ranching, guiding and outfitting industry within the Yellowstone Rockies.

Dude ranching got an early start in the region with Gallatin Canyon pioneer Pete Karst, who is believed to have started Montana's first dude ranch. He arrived in the canyon in the 1890s and by 1901 was driving his horse-drawn Karst Stage hauling mail, passengers and freight between Bozeman, Salesville (now Gallatin Gateway) and the Cooper tie camp five or six miles up Taylor Fork in the canyon. He evidently accepted his first dudes in 1901, even though his homestead at the mouth of Moose Creek didn't have much by way of accommodations. That year he took in a dozen Easterners who shared a bunkhouse. His Karst Kamp got into full swing in 1907 when closure of the tie camp directed him into full-time dude ranching. He had already added guest cabins and set about drumming up business in places like Minneapolis and Chicago, advertising a week's stay for $12 per guest. His resort grew more popular and became a canyon landmark. Karst has been rebuilt more than once but still occupies the same site.

Dude ranches now are sprinkled around the edges of the Yellowstone Rockies and within the Paradise Valley and Gallatin Canyon. A traditional dude ranch is a family operation that might accommodate 40 to 80 guests at one time. Most have been in the same family for decades, some for as long as three or four generations. Guests, or dudes, as they are called, stay in rustic — usually log — structures and eat family style in a central lodge. Riding is the dominant activity, but dudes might also enjoy herding and branding cattle, fishing, hiking, swimming, and are often the most enthusiastic spectators at nearby rodeos. Emphasis is on healthy, family, outdoor recreation — western style. Members of the Dude Ranchers Association are not allowed to have a licensed bar or to serve alcohol.

Clientele at ranches are usually carefully screened to make sure they will fit into what will almost certainly become a family, of sorts. Screening and above average income levels are a hold-over from earlier times when dude ranches were strictly for a privileged elite. You don't have to be wealthy today to be a dude, but it is important that one fits in. Lifetime friendships are often cemented at ranches, with the same groups of dudes coming back the same week each summer. Up to 85 percent of dudes might be returnees, some for as long as 20 years. So strong is the sense of family and camaraderie that farewells are commonly teary-eyed affairs for all.

Owners view themselves as hosts who have invited friends into their homes. Their style and personality permeate the ranch to the point that when a ranch changes hands a new owner has to start anew to build up his own family of dudes.

After almost 40 years Howard and Martha Kelsey have acquired a loyal clientele at their 9 Quarter Circle Ranch on Taylor Fork in the Gallatin Canyon. The setting alone would seem enough to bring in droves of guests. The ranch's log buildings are nestled in an idyllic, high-mountain valley within the shadow of the Madison Range's majestic 10,000-11,000 foot Taylor Peaks. In an average summer the 9 Quarter Circle is booked full at its 85-guest per week capacity and hosts a total of about 650 during the vacation season. Most are families of from four to six. Arnold Wihtol of Menlo Park, California said he has been coming up for 17 years for "the fishing, the friends and the country, but not necessarily in that order."

A morning bell rings at seven o'clock to start the day for dudes. Breakfast is served and guests are then free to choose from a wide range of activities. For many, a large part of each day is spent in the saddle. Guests are assigned horses for the entire visit. At least four to five trail rides depart from the corral every day. These include morning and afternoon rides and overnight pack trips into the surrounding backcountry. Trail rides are classed by degree of difficulty and range from the Turtle Trot for beginners on up to the thrill seeker's Kelsey Killer. The 9 Quarter Circle runs a string of 140 to 150 head, mostly Appaloosa, which are known for their stamina and good disposition. The ranch breeds, foals, breaks and trains its own horses.

Trout fishing in the nearby Gallatin, family hikes, and other outdoor activities fill the all too short days. Private cabins assigned to each family are used little except for sleeping. The rustic dining room/lodge complex is the focus for most indoor goings on. Guests meet there three times a day for home-cooked, family-style dining. Children are seated at tables with others of their own age and adult seating is shifted periodically for social variety. Three outdoor meals a week include a beef barbecue, steak fry and a late Friday afternoon trail-side trout fry.

Labor Day and the start of school means an end to the dude families until next season and the beginning of guide-outfitting operations. Through the end of September the 9 Quarter Circle holds weekly fly fishing schools under the direction of a professional instructor. During big-game season the ranch becomes base camp for small numbers of hunters who pay for seven-day excursions into the nearby high country.

Guiding and outfitting are big business in the Yellowstone Rockies. Forest Service records show that several hundred licensed guides and about half as many outfitters operate within the region. For some it is strictly a part-time undertaking that might involve taking only a few people fishing each summer. Outfitting ranges from these out-of-the-back-of-a-pickup

businesses to large, full-time operations that might provide services for 100 people annually.

Larry Gaustad operates out of his home north of Gardiner and is one of the large-scale outfitters in the region. Almost 100 percent of Larry's business is out-of-staters, fairly typical among outfitters. Most of his hunters come from Texas with others hailing from New Jersey, New York, Florida, North Dakota, and California. He admits that most of his clients are economically up-scale and very knowledgeable about big-game hunting. Some regulars spend $10,000 to $100,000 each year going after big game worldwide. Their interest in the Yellowstone Rockies is testimony to its world-class reputation. Most come for elk, not for the meat, but for the trophy bulls. In 1982 rates varied from $2,500 to $3,500 per person depending on the type of hunt and length (seven-day or ten-day). Even at these prices bagging an elk isn't guaranteed. Success rates vary annually from 30 to 75 percent. In the 1982 season Gaustad's hunters took home approximately 100 elk.

Outfitting is Gaustad's primary means of livelihood and occupies most of his time from May to February. The annual cycle begins with the spring bear hunt. During summer months he and his guides cater to fishermen and take family pack trips into the Absaroka-Beartooth Wilderness and Yellowstone National Park. Elk hunting starts with the early bugling season in September, expands during the regular October-November general season, and winds up with the special hunt (by draw) around Yellowstone Park from December to February.

Gaustad runs one of the largest tent camps in the Absaroka Beartooth Wilderness. Prior to the start of the season he packs in all necessary equipment on mules and readies everything for the elk hunters. His campsite in the Slough Creek drainage is designated by the Forest Service and is off-limits to other outfitters. Camp includes as many as seven 16x20-foot wall tents. Hunters sleep in the largest tents on cots with thick foam pads and have an airtight wood stove. A similar-size tent serves as kitchen, staffed by a full-time cook, and another is used as a mess tent where all gather around a big table for meals. A smaller secondary, or spike, camp of two or three tents is set up farther into the wilderness beyond a day's ride of the main base.

Like other Yellowstone Rockies outfitters, Gaustad also leases hunting rights on a large ranch. More ranchers are becoming part-time outfitters as a way of augmenting fall cash flow, but those who don't often lease to an outfitter. Gaustad's ranch lease is in the Paradise Valley where hunting privileges range from about $1,000 to $50,000 per year depending on size and suitability. He is convinced that the 15,000 acres he leases adjacent to Yellowstone National Park on the

Top: Guests at the 9 Quarter Circle ranch in the Gallatin Canyon enjoy all sports western including "home-made" horse racing and rodeo. Ranch guest cabins, middle photo. John Alwin photos.
Bottom: The Stillwater River is part of the network of corridors leading to the heart of the wild Yellowstone Rockies from its northern fringe. Gary Apps photo.

western flank of the Absaroka Range has "some of the best elk hunting left in the U.S." His "ranch hunt," as he calls it, is his most popular and most expensive.

Gaustad and other Gardiner operators like Bill Hoppe and Warren Johnson, or Dwayne Neal of Pray, may be booked solid for the season by the first part of the year. Gaustad has been in business 11 years and doesn't even have to advertise. Almost 90 percent of his business is repeat. To be successful, he said, "Show the hunters a good time, run a good camp with good food, and produce the elk."

Even more visitors are lured to the region for fishing than hunting, and catering to this army of fly fishermen is another well developed sector of the regional economy. The legendary waterways of the Yellowstone Rockies from Blue Ribbon waters like the Yellowstone and Madison on down to the Paradise Valley's world famous, but diminutive Armstrong and Nelson spring creeks attract eager anglers from throughout the country and abroad.

In the early 1980s fishermen could hire an outfitter for about $150 per day for a float fishing trip for two. Outfitters and customers commonly meet early in the morning at fly shops, which include national institutions like Dan Bailey's in Livingston and Bud Lilly's in West Yellowstone. Wild Wings Orvis and the River's Edge, both in nearby Bozeman, and others in Livingston, Ennis and West Yellowstone, offer guide services.

At least one of the region's dude ranches has shifted emphasis from horses to fish. The Stillwater Valley Ranch near Nye is now home to the Montana School of Fly Fishing. Here, while wives and younger children partake of a more standard dude week, dad and the older kids can enroll in one of ten weekly programs. These include several days of school at the ranch and then several more days on fishing expeditions. One guest from Arizona has been coming up for years, determined to catch a trophy-size golden trout, a scarce and wary resident of some high-mountain lakes.

Anyone who questions the appropriateness of the recent move of the headquarters for the International Federation of Fly Fishers to West Yellowstone within the Yellowstone Rockies region probably hasn't fished its waters. The "Wall of Fame" at Bailey's in Livingston, which shows the silhouettes of the giants caught with flies, is proof of the region's sport fishing potential.

On a Montana scale of recreational developments, the Yellowstone Rockies' Big Sky is big time. It easily is the state's largest four-season resort and second-home complex, attracting the full spectrum of outdoor recreationists from fishermen to skiers and from hunters to horseshoe pitchers.

Network newsman and national celebrity Chet Huntley, of Huntley-Brinkley fame, is credited with originating the idea for Big Sky. His initial plans,

however, evidently called for a development quite different than what has evolved. Patty Goodrich recalls sitting in the living room at their 320 Dude Ranch in the Gallatin Canyon with her husband Jimmy and the late Chet Huntley in June 1968 when Chet first shared his idea for a dude ranch-working ranch operation.

Huntley was a native Montanan, born at Cardwell just to the west of the canyon and raised on the Eastern Montana homestead frontier. Like many other natives who leave for various reasons he found return visits to Montana especially regenerative, and wanted to share the state and its recuperative powers with the numerous friends he had made throughout the world.

According to Patty, Huntley originally thought in terms of a working ranch that would also include extra accommodations for guests. By that winter the Goodrich's wrote to tell Chet that three parcels in the area could be purchased that would be suffcient to support a 1,000-cow operation. Plans for this somewhat more traditional venture were dropped and before long Chet Huntley had lent his name to a much more ambitious project in the same area. This undertaking was funded by Chrysler Corporation, Northwest Orient Airlines, Burlington Northern Railway, Continental Oil (Conoco), and the Montana Power Company. Even though his name has always been synonymous with Big Sky Huntley's financial interest amounted to about two percent.

These corporate backers weren't interested in a quaint dude ranch. Their plans were much more grandiose. They envisioned a large scale, four-seasons recreational and second-home mecca of national importance. Early plans for Big Sky included an 11,000-acre resort with 2,700 condos, 1,300 homesites, a ski hill with more than 20 miles of lifts and gondolas on Lone Mountain, hotels, convention facilities, a golf course and tennis courts — a multimillion-dollar complex unlike anything Montana had ever seen.

The new Big Sky Corporation didn't have much difficulty purchasing most of the property they needed, a total of 8,721 acres. They ran into a bit more difficulty acquiring the final and critical 1,820 acres at the base of Lone Mountain, which now includes Mountain Village. This was Forest Service land and it had to be acquired through a land swap with Burlington Northern Railway.

From its initial public announcement, Big Sky has been controversial. The necessity of a large-scale swap of National Forest land for private holdings riled the opposition even more. Much of Montana's vocal environmentalist community was adamantly against the scheme. They were concerned about its possible adverse impacts on wildlife, stream and air qualities, and the very appropriateness of such a huge complex for the well-to-do in the middle of the Montana

Top: Elk from the northern portion of Yellowstone Park, where they are not hunted, migrate to winter range in the Gallatin Valley. Ken Reynolds photo.

The two bulls in the middle photo were shot near Gardiner. Phil Farnes photo.

Bottom: The Paradise Valley, shown here near Emmigrant. Rick Graetz photo.

Lettuce Farming—Montana Style

Isabel came west from Wisconsin to the Gallatin Canyon with her mother in 1913. As the stepdaughter of Pete Karst, canyon pioneer and owner-operator of the resort ranch of the same name, Isabel developed a closeness and love of the canyon that has held her there ever since. "I have an idea I've been here longer than anyone," she is proud to point out. During her 70-plus years in the canyon she has seen it evolve from a pioneer country to a popular vacation and summer-home area.

The Karst Ranch was Isabel's home until 1937. As a young girl she worked with the dudes who frequented her dad's resort. In 1923 she married Ed Durnam, a young man who drove the stage between Gallatin Gateway and the canyon in the Teens. They took up residence at the ranch and she recalls they did "just about anything there was to do." Ed had been a golf pro and put his talents to work laying out a nine-hole golf course on the west side of the river that proved short-lived. In 1937 they moved about a mile up the canyon with their two children and set about establishing a rather unconventional farming enterprise.

Ed and Isabel had heard that others had successfully grown head lettuce commercially around West Yellowstone farther up the valley and decided it was worth at least a try in their section of the canyon. Lettuce production in California's hot and low valleys like the Salinas with elevations of only a few hundred feet above sea level, yes, but in this cool, 5,800-foot-high mountain valley? Looking back to that first year Isabel now admits "we didn't know what we were getting into." Their gamble paid off, however, and for the next 25 years the Durnams operated and depended on one of the most unique farms in Montana for their livelihood.

Their first year five acres of sage adjacent to the Gallatin River were cleared and planted in neat rows of lettuce. The field had to be as orderly as a garden and properly sloped and trenched to permit the necessary irrigation. Water was directed out of the river and into a canal about a half mile above the field by a masonry diversion dam that jutted 10 to 15 feet out into the swift flowing stream. By the end of the first season it was apparent that not only would lettuce grow, it would thrive. Evidently the combination of high altitude, cool nights, and fine sandy loam soil was just right for production of excellent quality, crisp

In the '40s Durnam's lettuce was requested by name from as far away as Minnesota. Photos, courtesy of Isabel Durnam.

and sweet lettuce with a delicate texture. Over the years consumers in Montana and neighboring states, and others as far away as Minnesota, Illinois, Oklahoma and Texas were requesting Montana lettuce by name.

The lettuce field was eventually expanded to more than 30 acres and an annual routine soon developed. Plantings were staggered from April through June. It was possible to use machines for seeding, but thinning and weeding required manual labor, and lots of it. The busiest time was always harvest season, which normally started in July and grew progressively more frantic toward the late September, early October finale. Most locals weren't very interested in this type of backbreaking work so the Durnams depended on migrant workers. At the peak of the harvest they employed up to 20, all of whom were housed and fed.

Lettuce had to be cut at night when temperatures were cool — not usually a problem in the Gallatin Canyon. Migrants worked into the wee hours wearing miner's hats or flashlights held on their heads with large rubber bands. Once cut, lettuce was crated and packed in ice. Each crate held from three to five dozen heads, packed in three tiers with layers of crushed ice.

Each winter the Durnams put up their own ice and built their crates. As Isabel remembers, "we had to be industrious." In the beginning they cut the ice out of the Gallatin, but had trouble with a fluctuating river level and soon developed their own ice pond with a packing and ice shed behind their home. Insulated with sawdust, the ice kept until harvest time.

A good harvest filled approximately 5,000 crates, most of which were sold to a wholesaler in Billings. No one kept track of how many night trips their 1940 Diamond-T truck made to Billings with its full load of 120 crates, but when sold five or six years ago to a Gallatin Valley farmer it was still running strong. If the crop was more than the wholesaler could take, the Durnams trucked the lettuce to Bozeman where it was loaded into railroad box cars with ice and sent directly to more distant markets.

An industry-wide change in packaging and improved long distance trucking combined to force the Durnams out of the lettuce business in 1960. The "dry pack" method using cooling plants to draw heat out of entire truck loads of lettuce replaced the traditional ice-packed shipments. Ed and Isabel were not in a position to invest the several hundred thousand dollars necessary to construct their own cooling plant and found it increasingly difficult to compete with others using the improved method. Speedier trucking also meant that lettuce grown hundreds of miles farther from the market arrived just as fresh as Gallatin County lettuce and at competitive prices.

Even before the last lettuce crop the family had started raising cattle. There was so much waste from trimming the lettuce that they had a ready supply of seasonal feed. Ed had homesteaded about a mile up Moose Creek and with that land, coupled with additional railroad and Forest Service leases, they were able to shift to a cow-calf operation. Eventually the lettuce patch was planted in hay.

Thinking back (not so long ago) to the days before canyon residents had the simple luxury of electricity, Isabel is almost apologetic for the satellite dish that provides her with 60-channels of television reception. After working so hard for so many years, Grandma, as her tenants call her, is not one to sit back and do nothing. She rents her original 1937 log home and some of the rustic cabins that housed the migrant workers to young couples employed at Big Sky or other canyon establishments.

Cooke City, which lives largely off the Yellowstone tourist trade, is a recreational retreat in its own right, especially in winter. Republic Mountain is in the background of both photos. Tom Kaiserski photos.

Cooke City

Cooke City is a one-of-a-kind community. Here is a Montana town you can't drive to except by way of neighboring Wyoming. Cooke is served by a single east-west highway. Access from Red Lodge is over Highway 212, but 10,940-foot Beartooth Pass and 8,000-foot Colter Pass (called Cooke Pass by locals) keep that approach closed seven months each year. The community's year-round life line is the stretch of highway through Yellowstone National Park that connects it to Gardiner and the county seat of Livingston, 110 miles away.

Despite its remoteness this is a four-season tourist mecca. Most of the 100 permanent residents depend on the tourist trade for their livelihood. Located at 7,600 feet in alpine-encircled Soda Butte Valley high in the Absaroka Range and along one of the portals to Yellowstone Park, it's a natural retreat and mountain playground.

Cooke is one of Montana's most popular snowmobiling centers. Predictable snow depths of from six to eight feet, an excess of 50 miles of state-groomed trails, and seemingly limitless routes over virgin snow for the more adventuresome — it's pure paradise for snow machine enthusiasts.

The Cooke area has grown increasingly popular among cross-country skiers seeking remote and scenic country with consistently superior snow conditions. Even the U.S. Olympic Nordic Team has been drawn to the area for training. With its winter accommodations and eateries, Cooke is an excellent base camp for skiers seeking the unrivaled pristine solitude of nearby Absaroka-Beartooth Wilderness, North Absaroka Wilderness across the state line in Wyoming, and remote backcountry sections of Yellowstone Park — all three off limits to snow machines. Local retailers are happy to see more winter recreationists but lament that cross-country skiers are a more self-sufficient lot who don't generate nearly the same per capita trade as their snowmobiling counterparts.

Summer is when things really start hopping in Cooke and the hamlet's population expands 300 to 400 percent. More than 300 seasonal residents and summer home owners converge on the region from as far away as Florida, Pennsylvania, Illinois and California. Most don't escape to rustic little cabins left behind by miners. More common are luxury homes in the six-figure price range.

They share their area with other tourists lured by exceptional opportunities for hiking, backpacking, fishing and sightseeing. The mountains provide the gamut of hikes from short, simple day-outings to rigorous week-plus expeditions into wild and remote country. High mountain fishing in gem-like lakes provides anglers an opportunity quite literally to fish among the clouds. According to Bill Sommers, owner-operator of Sommers Motel and Top of the World Guide Service, Grasshopper Glacier north of Cooke is an especially popular attraction. A backcountry road takes visitors to within a short hike of this peculiar glacier that contains millions of grasshoppers frozen and embedded in its ice. The insects are so well preserved that birds and fish feed eagerly upon them as they are released by melting ice.

Still other visitors are captivated by the ubiquitous relics of past mining activity. This was the center of the historic New World Mining District. Four trappers fleeing Indians who had robbed them of their horses retreated into the area in 1869 and are credited with bringing word of the region's promising mineral potential to the outside world.

From the beginning, processing was essential since the district's remote location made cartage of anything but concentrated ores uneconomical. The earliest smelter began treating lead ore in 1875. An account of its production is unknown since some of Chief Joseph's Nez Perce warriors swept through on their 1877 retreat, pillaging the mill, and apparently using its lead for shot. Over the years mines like the Republic, Albert A., Homestake and Daisy produced gold, silver, lead and copper. Production peaked in the late 1800s, but always was limited by inadequate transport. Operations continued into the 20th century on a reduced scale, but a promised rail link northward through the Stillwater River Valley to Columbus never developed. The last two mines ceased operation in the 1950s.

Modern mining buffs find the richest pickings north of town in the Henderson Mountains, Daisy Pass, and Lulu Pass area. The region is spattered with abandoned mining shafts, weathered ruins of deserted buildings, and even the dilapidated remains of a tramline in the Fisher Creek drainage.

Gene Wade anticipates a revival of mining in the district. He and a group of associates have been coring and testing the extent and values of a gold-copper-silver ore body in the old McLaren pit in the Daisy Pass area. Testing to date has been encouraging, and those findings coupled with other known ore occurrences, have convinced Wade "there will be mining again in the Cooke City area and it could be a big operation." He points out that physical distance and topography should somewhat buffer the site of Cooke and summer homes from the less desirable aspects of mining activities.

Cooke is no longer an outfitting center for prospectors, and residents are not held in the area by the hope of quick treasures from the highly mineralized mountains. Mining may experience a resurgence in the New World District, but for now it is an infatuation with the place that holds residents. As one local put it: "The Beartooths turn me on." Gene Wade, like his neighbors, enjoys the pervasiveness of nature. "Where else can you live where any day of the year you can hop in your car and within a few minutes be viewing elk, moose, buffalo and all kinds of big game animals," he says. Sometimes you don't even have to leave your home. The annual "invasion" of Cooke by both black and grizzly bears in search of easy food (garbage) elicits mixed emotions among residents, but is frowned upon by wildlife managers.

Remoteness and sparsity of population is considered a plus by residents. Locals learn to live with things like winter's three-day-a-week mail delivery, the closest law enforcement officer stationed 56 miles away at Gardiner, and attending a one-room school that had only two students in the 1982-83 school year. Few consider themselves isolated, even in winter. The National Park Service discontinues plowing Beartooth Pass on October 15 and usually doesn't have it open until late May or early June, but the highway from Cooke to Gardiner is plowed on a regular basis. This stretch is kept in better winter driving condition than many main streets in downtown Western Montana communities!

Bus driver Warren Patten probably knows the Cooke-Gardiner highway as well as anyone. For years his job has been making the five-day-a-week run that carries junior high and high school students across the northern reach of Yellowstone National Park to school in Gardiner. In the last six years he has been stuck only once or twice. Warren is sure his is one of the most interesting school bus runs in the nation. He and his passengers regularly see elk, bighorn sheep, buffalo, deer and, on occasion, have spotted mountain lions and grizzly bears.

There is talk of keeping the highway open year-round between Cooke and Cody, Wyoming. Now, plows stop about ten miles southeast of town on the other side of Colter Pass. A year-round highway undeniably would boost winter tourist trade, but it also would mean an end to Cooke's novel end-of-the-road location each winter and the tranquility that distinction has helped assure.

The Big Sky recreational development complete with 600 condominiums, a ski area having 48 miles of runs and a generous golf course is Montana's only truly large-scale resort. John Alwin photos.

wilderness. Others pointed to the project's energy consumption in construction, maintenance and heating and expended by people traveling to and from the resort — all at the height of the national energy crisis of the 1970s. Proponents argued that it was just what Montana needed, a boost to the all-important tourist industry and a signal to the nation that the state was willing to develop and share its recreational lands.

Some of the strongest opposition came from long-time Gallatin Canyon residents who cringed at the thought of a huge tourist complex, filled with strangers, disturbing the tranquility of their peaceful and pristine valley. Isabel Durnam, a 70-year resident, recalls, "We weren't too happy about it — we figured we didn't need anything like that here." Her late husband, Ed, had been a fire guard on Lone Mountain in 1918. Each day he rode his horse to the summit and watched for fires. At night he rode back down to camps in the protection of the trees. Like some other decades-long canyon residents, Isabel prefers to remember the mountain as it was before its face was scarred by ski runs.

Big Sky is a reality and a dominant economic and political factor in Gallatin Canyon. Big Sky landowners are the majority and other canyon residents, including Isabel Durnam, now are listed in the phone book under the heading of Big Sky.

The energy crunch of the 1970s coupled with the recession and high interest rates of the early 1980s meant growth at the resort during its first decade did not meet projections. As of 1983 there were approximately 600 condominiums between the two major residential areas of Meadow Village and Mountain Village and a total of 75 family homes on the 400 single-family homesites. John McCulley, Managing Director of the Big Sky Owners Association, estimates that, excluding employees, there are only about 100 permanent residents.

Even though not as large as initially planned, Big Sky probably would please Chet Huntley, who was interested in making it possible for others to enjoy Montana. In all, residents from 42 states and five foreign countries own property at Big Sky. The top five states and their respective percentage of property owners are 1) Montana (36%); 2) Minnesota (13%); 3) California (8%); 4) Illinois (6%); and 5) North Dakota (5%).

Big Sky has an 18-hole, Arnold Palmer designed golf course, tennis courts, pools, and other recreational amenities, but is best known for its winter skiing. It, along with Big Mountain outside of Whitefish, are Montana's only two destination ski resorts. Snowfalls of more than 400 inches per year, 48 miles of runs on 32 slopes, up to 2,500 feet of vertical drop, two gondolas plus other high-capacity lifts, and a season that stretches from mid-November to May explains why this is one of Montana's most popular ski areas. During the winter of 1981-82, the 144,500 skiers who used Big Sky made it the state's third most popular ski area. Out-of-staters conditioned to the long lift lines at Vail and Sun Valley find Big Sky a pleasant change.

Ski charter flights into nearby Gallatin Field outside Bozeman bring groups like the Atlanta Ski Club and each year Big Sky's promotional team is out extolling the virtues of "Skiing the Sky" at ski shows nationwide. Even so, the resort's most optimistic promoters

Left top: The Lone Mountain Guest Ranch caters to the nordic skier. Rick Graetz photo. Heli-skiing is available through Omniflight out of Big Sky, left bottom. Mitch Thompson photo.
Above: Beartooth Pass holds plenty of thrills from the road. Charles Kay photo.

admit it will be a long time before Big Sky has to cope with the more than 1.2 million skiers per winter that now flock to Vail.

Skinny ski enthusiasts rank Lone Mountain Guest Ranch at Big Sky among the top ten nordic ski centers in the country. It boasts 43 miles of groomed and tracked trails, authentic rustic family accommodations in 60-year-old log cabins, and family-style meals prepared by a gourmet cook. In summer season owners Bob and Viv Schaap operate the 45-guest capacity ranch in the style of a traditional dude ranch with an obvious emphasis on the ecological.

Beginning with the winter of 1982-83 skiers at both Big Sky and Lone Mountain Ranch could take advantage of helicopter skiing provided by Omniflight. A helicopter ride to the summit of Lone Mountain adds another 1,266 vertical feet and provides skiers with a total drop of almost 3,800 feet. That's a run of some four miles and a 30- to 45-minute trip between the peak and the lodge. Pilot Mitch Thompson says that right after a heavy snowfall everyone wants to be first. "The whole idea is to ski the virgin powder," Thompson says. The most common question he gets is, "Do you still have untouched snow up there?"

Before a day of heli-skiing, Thompson and his guides fly and ski the mountain eliminating avalanche problems, blasting when necessary. All skiers are instructed in safety and rescue procedures before their descent and must remain within sight and sound of each other and their guide while skiing. Thompson says that heli-skiing isn't just for the experts, but cautions all to be in good physical shape since deep, virgin powder is much more demanding than nicely packed slopes.

Environmental issues have high public awareness within the Yellowstone Rockies. No sooner is one controversy seemingly resolved, than another one or two arise to take its place. As of early 1983 numerous environmental issues dominated the minds of residents and those with a special concern for the region. In the Big Sky area these included the routing of a high voltage transmission line from Ennis to Big Sky over the crest of the Madison Range. Environmentalists resisted the bisecting of this de facto wilderness and expressed concern that a power corridor would invite a

Red Lodge

With its 1,896 residents, Red Lodge easily is the urban giant in the Yellowstone Rockies, almost three times the size of second-ranking West Yellowstone. Like many of the region's other hamlets and towns, this, too, is primarily a tourist center. It also serves as a regional trade center for farmers and ranchers, but catering to visitors is the biggest industry in town. Beginning around Memorial Day each year, the scenic Beartooth Pass is opened and Red Lodge becomes the eastern gateway to this engineering marvel and popular approach to Yellowstone National Park. During summers, area streams and forests attract a steady flow of outdoor recreationists. Each big-game season Red Lodge serves as a jumping-off point for backcountry-bound hunters. Nearby Red Lodge Mountain attracts approximately 100,000 skiers per winter from a three-state area and enjoys a reputation for excellent spring skiing. The Red Lodge area is especially popular among Billings residents and might even be considered its recreational satellite.

Red Lodge has undergone a metamorphosis. Its origin and early years had little to do with serving tourists. From its beginnings in the 1880s until the 1940s, this was primarily a coal-mining center.

Major development of the Red Lodge Field began in 1889 with the arrival of a branch line of the Northern Pacific Railroad, which provided all-important access to outside markets. Before long, bituminous-grade coal from local mines fueled the Northern Pacific's steam locomotives and found other uses within an area that stretched from Washington to North Dakota. By 1910 the field was the state's largest producer and Red Lodge's population had ballooned to 4,860. Residents in other nearby coal towns like Washoe, Bearcreek and Fromberg added to the regional population. Both production and population peaked in the late Teens.

Red Lodge of the early 20th century had a large foreign-born population. The backbreaking, dirty and dangerous life of an underground coal miner didn't appeal to many American workers, but hundreds of Finns, Slavs, Poles, Italians, Scots, Germans, Irish and other Europeans were drawn to the region by just the prospect of those jobs.

Above: Near Red Lodge. Tom Dietrich.

Below: This is the old Smith coal mine in the vicinity of the 1943 mining disaster that claimed 74

and is the state's worst coal mine disaster. John Alwin photo.

Eli Ponich left his native Austro-Hungary in 1910 at age 18. He still vividly recalls the March 13 when his boat landed at the port of New York. From there he traveled west to California where he worked on the railroad for five years before moving on to a steel job in Colorado. In 1917 he made a final move north to Red Lodge and a career in the mines.

Eli arrived at the peak of the coal-mining boom. "When I came to Red Lodge it was a miner's town," he recalls. Men were paid every two weeks and there were plenty of places to spend their hard earned dollars. "It was just like Las Vegas," Eli remembers, with 13 saloons, gambling, women, the works. He continued working even though mines began closing one by one in response to a shift to oil and natural gas as energy sources and competition from cheaper strip-mined coal at Colstrip starting in 1924.

The Smith Mine disaster of February 27, 1943, caused by an explosion of natural gas, was a further setback to Red Lodge mining. It took more than 70 lives and still ranks as the worst coal-mine disaster in Montana. Luckily for Eli, then employed at the Smith, the explosion occurred during the morning and he had left his afternoon shift at 11:00 p.m. the previous night. He knew every one of the men who lost their lives in the explosion. He continued working until 1952, when the last major operation shut down and he retired after 35 years in the mines, having "never as much as scratched a finger."

Most of the original miners from the early part of this century are gone, but their descendants and an interesting ethnic mix remain. In the interest of recognizing and honoring the various ethnic groups who were so vital to the community's development, Red Lodge's Festival of Nations was begun in 1950, long before ethnic was "in." This colorful celebration begins on the first Saturday of every August and runs for nine days and nights. One day is designated All Nations Day, another Montana Day, and each one of the remaining seven days honors a specific group (Scandinavian, Yugoslav, Italian, German, Scot, Finnish, and English/Irish). The town goes all out for the festivities and is joined by thousands of visitors. Each day there is a parade, and booths and arts and crafts displays are set up along the main street. Each evening, folk dancing and music honor a nationality at the Civic Center.

parallel road. Pro-development forces in both Big Sky and Ennis applauded the prospect of an east-west highway.

Lumbering has been important in the regional economy since the days of the tie camp on Taylor Fork before the turn of the century. In the 1980s a growing number of people are questioning the appropriateness of extensive commercial lumbering activities in the Yellowstone Rockies. Much of the forest land is of marginal timber value compared to better suited areas farther west in Montana or in the Pacific Northwest. It may be debatable whether such activity can be justified on strictly economic grounds. The Gallatin National Forest's own planning team has concluded that only 15 percent of the Gallatin's value is timber and range while attributes like wildlife and recreation total 85 percent.

A decade-old plan to develop the resort complex of Ski Yellowstone on Mount Hebgen 12 miles from West Yellowstone remained controversial in early 1983. The plan has called for a major ski facility on the east face of the 9,721-foot summit and a mountain top restaurant along with an 8,300-foot-long gondola connecting it to a lower Mountain Village. Proponents say it would provide the final critical link in a ski corridor that would then stretch on the north from Bridger Bowl outside Bozeman, south to Big Sky, Ski Yellowstone, Grand Targhee in Idaho and Wyoming's Jackson Hole. One environmentalist described it as "merely one more arm of a land development monster which threatens to make Montana a miserable mess."

Farther to the east, along the north face of the Beartooth, possible renewal of mining of the Stillwater Complex is a hot environmental issue. The Stillwater Complex is a unique geological belt about 25 miles long and one to six miles wide. Chromite, a steel alloy, was mined from the Stillwater at intervals from several mines (Benbow, Mouat, and Gish) between 1941 and 1961. The ore is low grade, but war conditions, which cut off traditional sources of higher grade overseas ore, and a national stockpile program for strategic minerals were sufficient impetus to justify mining.

The Stillwater Complex is a veritable treasure chest of minerals. It is estimated that the complex still contains 70 percent of our country's domestic reserves of chromite ore. The mineral-rich formation also constitutes one of the nation's largest nickel resources, although it also is considered too low grade to be mined at this time.

Current interest centers on platinum and palladium deposits. The Anaconda Company (Arco), Johns-Manville, and Chevron have mining claims in the area and production could commence in the 1980s if platinum prices rebound. Two planned mines would create more than 750 mining jobs and increase population several

Above: The Yellowstone Rockies claim three of the entrances to the oldest and perhaps the most famous of the country's national parks, Yellowstone. Shown here is the 1929 dedication ceremony of Gallatin Gateway, billed as gateway to Yellowstone Park even though it is some 70 miles distant from the park itself.
Courtesy Isabel Durnam.

Left: Small communities in the fringe of the mountains have a special character bred of isolation and hard winters as reflected in the friendly wood tones of well used P.O. boxes at Roscoe. John Alwin photo.

Left top: The Broadwater River in the north Beartooth country. George Wuerthner photo.

Left bottom: Gardiner guards the northwest entry to the park. John Alwin photo.

Above: The controversy rages over management of the threatened grizzly bear. Michael Quinton photo.

times that number in Sweet Grass County (population 3,216). The impact of such mining and associated milling activities in this thinly populated and most scenic of Montana areas adjacent to the Absaroka-Beartooth Wilderness must be weighed against the economic benefits, including badly needed local employment. The debate has pitted neighbor against neighbor.

Conservationists and biologists consider Montana's Yellowstone Rockies the northermost portion of a much larger Yellowstone Ecosystem. This five-million-acre territory includes Yellowstone National Park and the surrounding wild lands in Montana, Wyoming, and Idaho. As an ecosystem, or an intertwined ecological community together with its physical environment, changes in one area have implications for others. The Montana portion is an integral part of this ecosystem and essential to the integrity of Yellowstone National Park. This already world-famous park recently gained

even more international recognition with its selection as a world biosphere reserve by the United Nations and designation as a world heritage site.

The largely unroaded backcountry of the Yellowstone Rockies helps explain why it is one of only two strongholds for the grizzly bear in the lower 48 states. Grizzlies within the ecosystem are an emotional issue, especially since their 1975 designation as a threatened species under the federal Endangered Species Act.

Bear researchers have warned of declining grizzly numbers in the region since the 1960s, and in late 1982 in a National Park Service memo it was estimated that grizzly population may have dropped below 200 in the greater Yellowstone area. Even more alarming than the total number is the possibility that the population might include only 30 breeding females. Such a diminished population cannot continue to sustain losses of recent years. Estimates of number of grizzlies killed within the region over the last five years range between 100 and 200.

Most researchers acknowledge loss of habitat as the number-one threat to the big bear. Within the Yellowstone Rockies, as in much of its range, encroachment by man in the form of summer homes, subdivisions, recreational development, mining, timber harvesting and associated roading nibble away its habitat. Each individual "bite" in itself may not be major, but the cummulative effect has been to crowd the bear out of former habitat. Greater use of backcountry by recreationists increases the likelihood of direct man-bear contacts which usually prove more fatal to bears than humans.

Experts don't agree on the impact of illegal hunting, but it would be naive to assume that deals haven't been struck at night spots in West Yellowstone, Gardiner and Cody. Some unscrupulous hunters are willing to

pay dearly for a grizzly: the more endangered the quarry, the more prized it seems to be. Poaching can be lucrative. On the black market, a dead grizzly may fetch several thousand dollars. The hide is sold for up to $1,500 and each claw for up to $200. Even the gall bladder finds a market in Asia where it is thought to be an aphrodisiac. Sheep ranchers have shot many grizzlies that have wandered onto their high mountain grazing allotments. The Centennial Range just west of Yellowstone National Park has had especially high losses of grizzlies at the hands of sheepmen.

Unless things change, and quickly, Montana's state animal and this ultimate symbol of wild nature uncontrolled by man may be exterminated from the Yellowstone Ecosystem in short order. Survival of the bear will depend on protection of existing habitat. Critical habitat for the bear must be designated and protected, as stipulated by the Endangered Species Act. Management of these areas could then rule out impacts — whether minerals, lumbering, resorts, or hikers — that would adversely affect the bear. This may entail closer management of recreationists in some backcountry areas and perhaps phasing out grazing allotments on public lands in and adjacent to grizzly areas. The loss of grizzly bears shot mistakenly for black bear may end only when all bear hunting is eliminated in grizzly country. Grizzly cannot be taken legally in the Yellowstone Rockies, but there are those who are pushing for a grizzly season in the area, while at the same time others are suggesting raising its designation to an endangered species.

Stricter enforcement of existing laws against killing a threatened species may help deter poachers. Sentences handed down for illegal kills in Montana have been consistently minimal, especially in comparison to the black market value of a carcass. The penalties for violating the federal Endangered Species Act can be as much as a year in prison and a $20,000 fine, but to date prison terms, if any, have been suspended and the hunter given a small fine and forfeiture of his hunting privileges for a brief period. In the hope of helping to reduce the grizzlies' mortality rate, the National Audubon Society recently upped its reward for information leading to the arrest of grizzly bear poachers from $2,000 to $10,000.

Public education programs also may help keep the grizzly a part of the Yellowstone Ecosystem. In early 1983 state and federal officials announced they were preparing a new program to help protect the grizzly in the Yellowstone region. Unified efforts in support of the grizzly are welcomed. Critics have claimed that lack of coordination between various government agencies, including between neighboring National Forests and even among ranger districts within the same forest, have hampered management efforts to perpetuate the grizzly.

71

THE EASTERN FRINGE

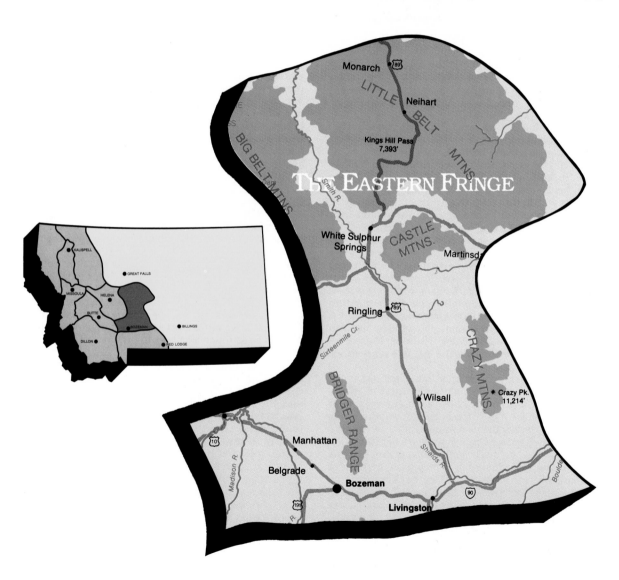

West of Browning and Choteau and other northerly towns, the ramparts of the Northern Rockies thrust skyward leaving little doubt where the Great Plains end and the mountains begin. In the Eastern Fringe the contact is less precise. Its physical landscape is a mix of high and low, steep and flat, an area over which each only grudgingly yields to the other. Within this transition zone is one of Montana's most varied natural landscapes and the physical base for a most diverse and stable regional economy.

The Yellowstone Rockies is mainly a high mountain wilderness and recreation area, and the Southwest a historic region still dominantly cattle country. Within the Eastern Fringe the unifying element or regional character is one of internal diversity. Its heterogeneity encompasses elements of physical geography, historical development and contemporary economic activity.

As in other sections of the Broad Valley Rockies the Eastern Fringe is a land of characteristically wide, level valleys between widely separated mountain ranges. The region's spacious valleys include the lineal Smith, Shields, and Yellowstone, and the even more roomy, saucer-shaped Gallatin Valley. Their naturally sage and grassy floored lowlands rise to the foothills of a surprisingly varied array of detached ranges.

On the north the extensive and heavily forested Little Belt Mountains spread over almost a fourth of the region with their rounded 8,000-foot peaks. On a clear day those daring enough to climb to the top of the fire watch tower at King's Hill Pass will be rewarded by a view of the entire width of Montana, from the Sweetgrass Hills hugging the Canadian border south into the mountain world of Yellowstone. From that vantage point the other Eastern Fringe highlands can be picked out to the south and west. The diminutive Castle Mountains contrast with the dramatic and glacially honed Crazy Mountains with its crown of peaks higher than 10,000 feet including 11,214 foot Crazy Peak. On the west, the tall, narrow north-south trending Big Belts constitute an obvious barrier to transportation and are crossed by but one paved road. Farther south the ridge-like Bridger Range is almost continuous with the Big Belts. On the horizon the wild ranges of the Yellowstone Rockies clearly mark the southern limit of the Eastern Fringe.

When the first white men entered this area they found a wildlife-rich region. Passing through the Gallatin Valley on the return from the Pacific in the summer of 1806, Captain William Clark commented on the abundance of animals including elk, deer, antelope and "multitudes of beaver." Clark also reported signs of buffalo almost everywhere, including their deeply worn "roads" or trails.

Above left: The Smith River with headwaters in the Castle Mountains empties into the Missouri. George Wuerthner photo.

Left: The Shields River originates in the Crazy Mountains and flows to the Yellowstone. Rick Graetz photo.

Above: The Bridger Mountains, much beloved by Bozeman residents. Tom Kaiserski photo.

Left: Upper Twin Lake, Crazy Mountains. Charles Kay photo.
Above: The ghost town of Castle. Rick Graetz photo.

So game-rich was the Gallatin Valley that no tribe, not even the powerful Blackfeet, dared claim it for their own, at least not for long. The region was a crossroads area for several tribes and served primarily as a common hunting ground. Archaeologists have documented many pishkuns, or buffalo jumps, within the region. One of the most impressive was used for thousands of years and now is protected as Madison Buffalo Jump State Monument southeast of Three Forks in the western part of the region.

No sooner had Captain Clark left our Eastern Fringe area than the earliest white fur trappers of record began setting their traps along its beaver-full rivers. One attractive area for these mountain men was the Three Forks of the Missouri, which had not been trapped by white man before, but already was trapping grounds for Indians who carried pelts northward to present-day Alberta where they were traded for European goods at Hudson's Bay Company and Northwest Company posts. The Blackfeet especially resented this trespassing onto their prized trapping grounds and did their best to make life miserable for any white trappers who dared enter the region.

Fur trappers and traders of rival corporations and independent mountain men continued to scour the Eastern Fringe and most of Western Montana for decades. During this colorful era the Fringe was worked by now legendary mountain men including John Colter, Jim Bridger, Peter Skene Ogden and Osborne Russell. The fur trade era was an ephemeral one. Trappers and traders explored the region and blazed trails which would carry settlers, but few remained behind. Permanent white settlement within the Eastern Fringe had to await the discovery of gold in southwest Montana valleys and the resultant regional market for agricultural products.

The Gallatin Valley had the best reputation as a prospective farming area. Even the fur traders noted the agrarian qualities of the generous valley. When veteran trapper Osborne Russell passed through in May of 1838 he commented on its large size and its smooth and fertile nature. Natural fertility was especially good in the wetter, eastern end of the valley where native grasses had contributed to soils rich in nutrients and organic material.

The pace of agricultural development in the Gallatin Valley paralleled the filling of western gulches by gold seekers. Bannack, Virginia City, Nevada City, Helena and other Western Montana mining camps and towns were supplied with some goods hauled up from Salt Lake City, but it made better economic sense to produce grain, potatoes, vegetables, and livestock regionally in areas with outstanding agricultural potential like the Gallatin Valley. Perceptive settlers

Colter's Run—Fact or Fairy Tale

Mountain man John Colter's naked run for his life in advance of hundreds of pursuing Blackfeet at the Three Forks of the Missouri is one of Montana's most famous legends. State historians have accepted it as fact and each year hundreds of runners commemorate Colter's escape with a challenging cross-country and through-river fun run. Colter may have made a miraculous escape that summer day back in 1808, but long accepted inconsistencies and implausibilities in various accounts coupled with a yet unreported reference in the Hudson's Bay Company Archives require that the legend be, at the least, re-examined.

The basic story is that Colter and a companion trapper, John Potts, traveled to the Three Forks from Manuel's Fort at the junction of the Big Horn and Yellowstone rivers in pursuit of beaver. As a former member of the Lewis and Clark Expedition, Colter knew firsthand that the Three Forks country was the richest in furs of any section in the Northwest. A party of several hundred Blackfeet discovered them, killed Potts, stripped Colter naked and allowed him to run for his life. Pursued by hundreds of warriors and running barefoot across a cactus and sage covered plain, Colter escaped and managed to get back to Manuel's Fort more than 200 miles away.

Important details of this story vary from author to author and all accounts contain extravagant claims that raise doubts about the likelihood of the incident. Was Potts killed by a hundred bullets or by innumerable arrows? How much of a lead did Colter have, 80 to 100 yards or 300 to 400 yards? If the Indians threw off blankets, leggings, and other encumbrances before they started the chase, how is it that the one Indian who caught him still carried a blanket in his left hand? Did Colter kill that brave with a tip of the Indian's own spear that had already broken off or that Colter had snapped off with his bare hands? Having reached the Madison River how could 5-foot-10-inch Colter have accomplished the unlikely task of sequestering himself in a beaver lodge by entering via the animal's tiny underwater opening? Or in another version of the story, how could he have survived naked, in the chilly Madison River,

A popular Bozeman-area foot race, the Colter Run, embraces the Colter legend, true or false. John Alwin photos.

immersed from the neck down for a day hiding beneath a log jam? When he arrived at Manuel's Fort was it after a 7-day or an 11-day journey and did he have an Indian blanket and spear, or was he empty handed?

Specifics aside, it seems unlikely that a man in his mid to late thirties running barefoot over sage and prickly pear cactus could outpace hundreds of pursuing braves. As a mountain man Colter may well have been in good physical condition, but not necessarily an outstanding distance runner. Even with his adrenalin on full tap it seems improbable that Colter could have outdistanced what must have included scores of wiry young warriors in their teens and early twenties equally fired up by the excitement of the chase and wearing some type of footwear.

On October 2, 1808, the Hudson's Bay Company post commander at the trading establishment of Edmonton House (precursor of Edmonton, Alberta) recorded that several Blood (Blackfeet) Indians arrived with the booty and story of attacks on two different groups of white trappers "on a southern branch of the Mississoury." According to their account they killed one of the trappers (Potts?) and stripped the rest who were then "permitted to escape." If this is a factual

account, one of the parties attacked may have been the Colter-Potts pair. This would have meant that Colter was stripped naked, but instead of winning a miraculous marathon, simply may have been set free. This method of humiliation evidently was used by the Blackfeet more than once.

The fur trade era is one of the most romanticized branches of western history. This is undoubtedly at least partly linked to the mountain men who had developed storytelling to the highest level. A yarn wasn't worth telling if it didn't have at least several references to super-human strength, speed or cunning. Getting the best of the Indians, the more the better, was central to many fur trade fairy tales. Retellings of yarns only added to their astounding proportions. Imagine how quickly the Colter run legend would have been discounted and discredited had it involved anyone other than a mountain man.

One possible explanation for the Colter yarn may be as follows. Like any good tale it helps to be at least partly based on fact, as this one evidently is. Colter and Potts did travel to the Three Forks the late summer of 1808, Potts was killed and Colter apparently was stripped naked. From this

point on actual facts may have differed from popular accounts. If Colter had been stripped and humiliated by the Indians and allowed to escape, what better way would there have been for a rugged he-man to save face and come out of an embarrassing situation as a hero than to fabricate a superhuman escape. Perhaps in its initial telling the story lacked many of the embellishments that may have been added in subsequent retellings. Even the two accounts obtained directly from Colter, one in 1809 in Montana and the other in St. Louis the next year differ in important details in their published versions.

Even Colter's family perpetuated legends about their relative. One claimed that he had retired from Indian country with 101 Indian scalps and another that he always propped his victims up in a distinctive sitting position as a warning to other Indians. In fact, Colter may never have taken the life of even one Indian, unless, of course, the race at the Three Forks actually took place and he killed the swiftest warrior in self-defense. Perhaps the historic run did take place largely as reported, but it is also possible that a gifted storyteller, assisted by authors caught up in the romance of the era built this fur trade whopper.

realized they were more likely to strike it rich in farming and ranching ventures geared to supplying the lucrative mining-camp markets. Even the editor of the Virginia City newspaper encouraged miners to become farmers when on August 27, 1864 he wrote, "Let a portion of our citizens turn their attention to farming and stock raising, they will make money, and the people will receive provision much lower . . . directing the attention of some among the many enterprising men in this newly developing country into an excellent channel for its remunerative exercise. . . ." By the next month the same *Montana Post* could report that the Gallatin Valley rapidly was being filled by farmers.

Historians tell us that the first wheat was planted in the valley in 1864. The next year the Gallatin produced 20,000 bushels, and by 1867 valley wheat acreage had expanded to 8,351 acres and production to 300,000 bushels. In the late 1860s the Gallatin Valley had three flour mills and was the territory's granary, a title it could claim until the agricultural settlement of the Eastern Montana plains.

Farther to the east in the Smith, Shields and Yellowstone valleys stockmen and farmers moved in. From the beginning agricultural emphasis in this section of the Eastern Fringe has been on livestock ranching, with valley bottoms used predominantly for hay production. The 1867 establishment of a military post northwest of White Sulphur Springs helped secure the area, generate greater local demand for foodstuffs, and encouraged additional settlement in that area. Fort Ellis, opened the same year a few miles east of Bozeman, had a similar impact on the Gallatin Valley.

The Eastern Fringe of the late 19th century was not solely a supplier of food products for mining communities farther west. The region had its own mining towns to supply by the 1880s. Most were in the northern section within the Little Belt and Castle mountains. Here smaller igneous intrusions, called stocks, had forced their way into overlying rock and generated upward migrating, super-heated waters which deposited minerals as vein fillings.

Stocks are most common in the Little Belts and not surprisingly, so were mining boom towns. These were silver producers, and some also yielded lead. Ghost town enthusiasts know where to find the sites of former mining towns like Barker, Hughes (Hughesville) and Galena, but any state highway map shows the location of Neihart, the largest of these former silver mining centers. Today Neihart has a year-round population of around 100. At one time this former silver mining town eclipsed even Great Falls as Cascade County's largest community. Founded in 1881, Neihart developed atop what proved to be one of the richest

Above: The Castle, a White Sulphur Springs landmark, and now an art gallery and community museum. John Alwin photo.

Above right: In the Little Belts. William Koenig photo.

Right: The Crazy Mountains from the Belts. Rick Graetz photo.

silver-lead ores in the Little Belts. This was especially important in the early years since only high grade ore could justify the expense of long-distance transport. After being hauled by wagon to Fort Benton on the Missouri, the ore was shipped downriver to St. Louis or New Orleans and then across the Atlantic to a smelter at Swansea, Wales! The opening of a silver smelter in Great Falls in 1888 and an even more local operation eased the transport burden somewhat, but inadequate transportation hampered growth and the community languished between 1887 and 1890 after easily worked high grade ores were depleted. Anticipated arrival of a branch line of the Montana Central spurred development in 1890 and finally, on November 15, 1891, rails reached Neihart. The occasion was celebrated with the driving of a "Silver Spike" cast of silver from Queen of the Hills ore — the first area mine. Neihart flourished for two years until the 1893 Congressional repeal of the Sherman Silver Purchase Act and the ensuing crisis which knocked the floor out of silver prices.

To the south beyond the Mussellshell River Valley Castle easily was the largest mining community in the Castle Mountains. Silver had been discovered there in the early 1880s and the town founded in 1887. At its peak in 1890-91 there may have been 2,000 people in the vicinity. The town boasted numerous stores, including a bakery and millinery, bank, hotels, newspaper, daily stage service in virtually all directions, and of course, innumerable saloons and brothels. The appropriately named "Princess" (of the Castles) and "Yellowstone" were the most productive local mines. At the time one of its three smelters was the state's largest lead producer, despite the fact that the 100-pound bars it produced had to be hauled to the railroad at Livingston via oxen-drawn wagons. The handicap of inadequate transport and the 1893 collapse of the world silver market proved fatal to the community. The last mine closed the next year. The nearby town of Martinsdale was, in part, built with the bones of Castle as building after building was moved to the embryonic community. Castle, which once boasted a water company that could have met the needs of 50,000 residents, is now one of Montana's many ghost towns.

Smelting operations in the Castle area tied into another mining district on the southern edge of the Eastern Fringe. The same wagons that carried processed ore from Castle to Livingston returned with coke that had been produced from coal in the Bozeman-Livingston Coal Field south of Bozeman Pass. Colonel James Chestnut began Montana's first major coal mining operation there in 1867. His first contract was to supply coal to the new, nearby garrison at Fort Ellis and soon provided fuel for home heating in Bozeman. Other mining camps sprung up in the field.

When the boom was on. The town of Castle, 1888. Montana Historical Society photo.

The Bozeman coal was bituminous grade and of a good coking quality, ideal for the smelters of not-too-distant Castle.

Coal mining in the district expanded exponentially with the building of a railroad across Bozeman Pass in 1882. The railroad generated its own demand for coal and even more importantly, provided the all-important transport link that allowed for a wholesale expansion of smelting ores in Montana, which created even more demand for coal. The Northern Pacific leased Chestnut's mine, but that alone proved insufficient. In response to demands, other mines were opened and towns took root south of Bozeman Pass and along Trail Creek, which was eventually served by a spur line known as the Turkey Trail Railroad. Cokedale, south of the pass, claimed 500 residents in its heyday and had a continuous line of 130 coke ovens nearly a half-mile long. Other area coal mining towns included Chestnut, Timberline, and Hoffman, and the curious, short-lived company town of Storrs. This was a carefully planned, model mining town built in 1901-02 by the Anaconda Copper Mining Company along Trail Creek to supply coke to its smelters. As many as 800 may have lived there, some in the straight rows of tiny, company-town homes on the hillside above the 50 coke ovens. The town shut down almost immediately when a Utah supplier reduced the price of its coal and the Anaconda Company returned to this former supplier. The houses were sold, many being moved to nearby Bozeman and Livingston. Other area coal towns quickly followed suit as state production shifted to more easily worked fields like those at Red Lodge and in the Bull Mountains.

Just as the arrival of the railroad spurred coal mining, so too, did it eliminate much of the isolation that had held back agricultural development within the Eastern Fringe and other parts of the territory. In the decade of the 1880s Montana experienced a transportation revolution that saw freight wagons pulled by teams of oxen or horses begin to be replaced by steam locomotives. This much swifter and more economical mode of transport opened seemingly unlimited new and distant markets for Montana products.

Improved transport unlocked the agricultural bounty of the Gallatin Valley. Irrigated farming greatly expanded and earned the Gallatin the title of "Egypt of America." The valley was billed as a veritable agricultural cornucopia. At times regional hype may

have gone a little far, as was the case in a December 1890 article in a Bozeman newspaper that claimed the average yield of cereal grains in the valley "is much larger than that of any state or territory in the Union, or even the civilized world." The same month an ad in the *Butte Daily Miner* referred to the Gallatin Valley as having "no equal for productivity in the world" and as "a dimple in the fair cheek of nature."

Even without the hyperbole the agronomic attributes of the valley were undeniable and it would have been difficult to keep settlers out. Expansion of acreage and greater mechanization boosted production, especially of grain and hay crops, and livestock became an even more entrenched component. The first steam tractors were used in the 1890s and after the turn of the century gasoline tractors, trucks, and other innovations continued to transform agrarian life. Around 1910 cultivation of peas began and by 1913 the harvest from 17,000 acres was processed locally. Bozeman's annual summer Sweet Pea Carnival, recently reactivated, was famous throughout the Northwest.

The Gallatin Valley is no longer the state's granary, but it is still one of Montana's premier agricultural areas. Regionally, livestock and livestock products generate more income than crops, common throughout most of Western Montana, but those two aspects of agriculture are much more balanced here than in most other agricultural regions in Rocky Mountain Montana. With about half of the cropland irrigated, the valley has more irrigated land than all but a very few of Montana's counties. Hay, especially alfalfa, is grown on 70,000 acres and is the most extensive crop. Barley and wheat, mostly winter wheat, each account for approximately 50,000 acres.

The Gallatin Valley's most distinctive and prosperous agricultural area is the section centered on Amsterdam and Churchill. Neatly kept homes, finely manicured yards, an occasional miniature windmill on a front lawn and names on mailboxes like Van Dyken, Flikkema, Braaksma, and Dykstra are obvious signs that this is a Dutch area, still sometimes referred to as the Holland settlement.

The first Dutchmen arrived in the area in 1893. They came at the invitation of the Manhattan Malting Company which already had built a sizable elevator and malting house at Manhattan, dug miles of irrigation ditches and purchased or leased in excess of 50,000 acres they planned to irrigate. With everything ready to go all they needed were the farmers to purchase the land and produce grain for their mill.

Then, as now, Dutch farmers had a reputation for industriousness and agrarian talents that made them desirable candidates. The company sent a minister of the Reformed Church to the Netherlands with pictures

Top: Sheaves of wheat, Gallatin County, date unknown. Montana Historical Society photo.
Bottom: Sheep grazing in the Bridgers. Phil Farnes photo.

Above: The encroachment of subdivisions on agricultural land in the Gallatin Valley concerns ranchers and farmers. John Alwin photo.

Right: The Gallatin Canyon, south of Bozeman, taken from just north of the canyon. John Alwin photo.

and samples of Montana-grown products to lure settlers to this newly planned Dutch colony. They placed ads in Dutch language newspapers throughout the United States extolling the virtues of the fertile valley and inviting new settlers. The earliest efforts were successful and the initial trickle of Dutchmen expanded to a steady stream after the turn of the century. They came directly from the Netherlands and from other Dutch areas in the United States, including southwestern Michigan to which many in this area still have family ties.

Prohibition in 1916 dried up the market for malting barley. Luckily for the Manhattan farmers the hostilities in Europe caused by World War I created heightened world demand for wheat and allowed emphasis to shift without major disruptions. Recent decades have seen a continued evolution of agriculture. Today the Holland settlement ranks as the state's premier dairy region accounting for approximately one-fourth of all milk cows in the state. It is also Montana's second largest potato producer, although growers claim they are number-one in terms of quality.

Dairying in the Gallatin Valley has an obvious ethnic flavor. Almost 90 percent of the 66 family dairy farms are owned by people of Dutch descent, many related to one another. The heaviest concentration is in the Churchill-Amsterdam area. Hilco and Nell Van Dyken's Greenline Dairy northeast of Amsterdam is a bit bigger than average. Hilco, his two sons and a hired man milk 140-150 head. Increasing herd size has been one of the recent trends.

Hilco has been on the farm for 39 years and admits he knows all too well the daily routine of a dairy farmer. Seven days a week, 52 weeks a year the day begins at 4:50 a.m. and by 5:30 the first milking of the day is underway. Other chores, including "changing water" (moving sprinklers) during the irrigation season, easily fill the hours between the end of the first milking at 8:00 a.m. and the start of the second milking at 3:45 in the afternoon. The Greenline and other valley dairy farms run almost exclusively Holstein herds because of the low butter-fat content in their milk and good production, 200 to 230 gallons per year per animal. Hilco sends all his milk to Darigold in Bozeman, but others also ship milk to plants in Butte, Great Falls and Billings. Gallatin Valley milk is marketed throughout Montana under various labels.

From the onset potato growing in the Gallatin has, like dairying, been closely associated with farmers of Dutch descent. Only a few of the 17 growers in the valley are not Hollanders.

John Weidenaar and Sam Dyk are credited with starting commercial potato farming in the Churchill-Amsterdam area. From 1937 until the early 1950s emphasis was on production for the fresh market. Now most go to growers in other states for use as certified seed potatoes. Approximately 70 percent of the potatoes are shipped to eastern Washington and lesser amounts to Idaho, Oregon and Colorado. Soils in the vicinity are well suited for potato growing and the county is relatively disease free, critical for seed potato production. Winters are cold enough to rule out virus-carrying insects like the green peach aphids which, for example, keep eastern Washington farmers from growing their own seed stock. Even though free of some of the disease problems that plague other areas, growers must still exercise caution. Potatoes are usually only grown one out of every six years on the same plot of ground. A standard rotation scheme is three years of alfalfa hay, one year of potatoes and two years of wheat or barley. This minimizes disease problems and conveniently produces large amounts of feed which complement the area's sizable dairy herd. While stored from fall harvest to shipment the following spring in the distinctive garage-like potato warehouses, spuds must be maintained under correct humidity and air circulation conditions.

Some growers like John Weidenaar, Jr., still separate out the larger potatoes and sell them in the fresh market. John says most of these go to Texas, where "people still appreciate top quality potatoes and are willing and able to pay for them."

Productive agricultural areas like those centered on Churchill and Amsterdam seem destined to become even more important to the Gallatin Valley's agrarian economy as subdivisions take other farm land out of production. Disappearing farm lands are most common within the Bozeman centered region where thousands of acres of one-time farmers' fields have been broken haphazardly into a vast oversupply of suburban lots and ranchettes.

The Bozeman city planning staff estimates that 7,000 acres have been subdivided within the 4½-mile-wide jurisdictional belt surrounding the city. An additional several thousand acres beyond the belt and within commuting distance of town also have been subdivided. In an admittedly optimistic projection, the planning office estimates that the 14,000 new regional residents by the year 2000 will need only 1,700 of those 12,000 subdivided acres. Most of the land sits idle, awaiting homes that may not come for generations.

A

B

C

The Eastern Fringe region has a distinctly Eastern Montana feeling to it at times. Witness (A) the popularity of rodeo. (B) The Gallatin Valley threshing bee. (C) the main street of Livingston. (D) prize draft horses at the Bozeman Winter Fair. Photo A. Phil Farnes; photos B, C, D. John Alwin.

D

The impact of subdivisions on agriculture has been amplified by the tendency to break land into large lots. Around Bozeman this averages almost 1½ acres, with many ranging from several acres up to ranchettes of more than 10 acres. Big lots help create the semi-rural and uncrowded setting sought by those who purchase them, but also mean greater loss of farm land. Local planners are encouraging new home development within Bozeman city limits, in fringe areas already served by utilities, or within designated growth nodes. Outlying growth nodes ideally would be developed with more cluster-type grouping of residences in areas not considered prime agricultural land.

Their almost instinctive desire to keep land in production clashes with the economic realities of farming and puts some agriculturalists in an awkward position. This is especially true for farmers in the wake of the advancing suburban sprawl who are contemplating retirement.

George Dusenberry was born and raised on the family farm south of Bozeman and has operated it with his wife, Frances, since 1947. In the 1970s as George approached retirement age he, like many other Gallatin Valley farmers, reluctantly sold a portion of the farm to subdividers. "I would have to live 100 years to farm that out of it," Dusenberry said of the price he received for his sale. He has watched home after home sprout from his former hayfield, but gains some solace from knowing that the quarter section sold was gravelly and marginal cropland. Looking around the valley it concerns him to see good farm land going out of production. Still, like most of his farming neighbors, George feels very strongly about personal rights. He isn't interested in land use planners telling him what he can and can't do with his land. "When it's your own land it's the man's own option to do what he wants."

Tourism and recreation are big business within the Eastern Fringe. A major draw is nearby Yellowstone National Park. Bisected by Interstate 90 and located just north of the park the region counts on a heavy tourist trade each summer. Local KOAs, public campgrounds and motels are usually full during summer season. Bozeman and Livingston serve as northern hosts for tourists heading in and out of Yellowstone National Park and traveling between there and Glacier National Park. Serious competition between these two towns for the lucrative Yellowstone Park trade dates back to at least the 1880s. In 1883 the Northern Pacific built its branch line up the Paradise Valley to just north of Gardiner and the park, and Livingston quickly eclipsed Bozeman as a portal city. It was not until the late '20s that the rival Chicago, Milwaukee, St. Paul and Pacific Railroad built its elegant Gallatin Gateway Inn west of Bozeman.

The Eastern Fringe is a destination, four-season tourist area in its own right. Bridger Bowl in the Bridger Range north of Bozeman is Montana's second most frequented ski area. Bridger is known for its dry powder snow, "cold smoke" to local powder hounds. Even though the skiing is highly regarded and the Ptarmigan run is nationally acclaimed, Bridger is essentially a local ski area. More than 80 percent of skiers are Montanans with more than 60 percent coming from the Bozeman area. Efforts by some to sell Bridger beyond its present out-of-state drawing area of North Dakota, Alberta and Saskatchewan have been resisted by locals who rather like their "private" uncrowded slopes. Showdown, the region's other downhill ski area located eight miles south of Neihart in the Little Belt Mountains, is only an hour's drive from Great Falls, and draws much of its business from the Electric City.

The Crosscut Ranch is developing as the regional center for cross-country ski enthusiasts and even die-hard downhillers from next door Bridger who want to give skinny skis a try. The ranch maintains 20 kilometers of varied groomed trails and provides extras like sleigh rides and an Eastern country-style restaurant. Operations don't end with the last of the spring snow. The resort shifts to family-style dude ranching during summer and is becoming increasingly popular as a retreat for corporations or other groups seeking a quiet and peaceful setting.

One of the most unique testimonies to the recreational appeal of the Eastern Fringe is the fact that the Wally Byam Caravan Club International has selected the region for its annual, international rally on three occasions. In 1973, 1977 and 1982, several thousand aluminum Airstream trailers and their occupants converged on Bozeman and the Montana State University campus. No other city has ever hosted the rally more than twice. This group of mostly retirees is as close as one can get to expert tourists. John Harmon, a Wally Byam member from Kirkland, Washington, mentioned favorable climate, beautiful scenery and high quality fishing at the top of a long list of attractions that lured him back for his second Bozeman rally in 1982.

The Eastern Fringe isn't part of the nation's industrial heartland, but it does have a manufacturing component that produces goods ranging from two-by-fours to cement, mobile homes, knapsacks, and high tech electronic products. Most of the region's food processing operations are closed now and the bountiful agricultural production is processed outside the region. Sawmilling is the most ubiquitous type of manufacturing. Several area towns including White Sulphur Springs, Livingston, Bozeman and Belgrade each have a sawmill, but only in White Sulphur is it the

Bozeman is the only community in the U.S. to be visited three times by Wally Byam's Caravan Club International rally. John Alwin photo.

largest private employer in town. Belgrade's Gallatin Homes is the community's largest private employer with 100 employees. Approximately 10 mobile homes per week, up to 26 feet by 71 feet, roll off the assembly line destined for customers in a six-state area.

The 500 people who work for Burlington Northern Railway in Livingston make it the town's number-one employer. Not too many years ago that number was closer to 1,000 and Livingston was undeniably a railroad town. Despite its reduced operation, Livingston is still the Burlington Northern's largest locomotive repair facility in the state. Right-of-way equipment from cranes to bulldozers are also sent here for repairs.

In 1983 Burlington Northern was conducting a comprehensive corridor study to determine which of its east-west lines would be designated major routeways, especially for heavy west-bound unit trains of grain and coal. The company has been upgrading the Laurel to Shelby line to accommodate these heavyweights and there is local concern that a permanent routing of trains there instead of through Livingston will mean more lost jobs. The problem is that the grades at Bozeman Pass and MacDonald Pass west of Helena are twice as steep as the one at Marias Pass south of Glacier National Park. At both Bozeman and MacDonald passes, unit trains, even after being broken in half, still can't crest the summits without helper engines.

Many of the same qualities and attractions that lure large numbers of tourists to the Eastern Fringe are beginning to attract a new breed of manufacturing —high tech. Most high technology firms are examples of "foot loose" or amenity based industries. Unlike some other manufacturers that have to locate close to raw material sources or near major market areas, high-tech manufacturers are relatively free to locate wherever they choose. Both the limited raw material

inputs and products produced have a very high value per weight and can be shipped long distances economically. Such firms tend to locate in high amenity areas where both owners and employees can benefit from a presumed higher quality of life.

The Bozeman area has received most of the region's new high-tech firms and although local proponents don't see the Gallatin developing as another Silicon Valley, they wouldn't be surprised to see it become at least a Silicon Gully. Bozeman offers many attractions to high-tech firms looking for a home. The community's modest size, minimal traffic congestion, clean and attractive environment free of befouling smokestack industry, low crime rate, access to unlimited outdoor recreation, and excellent air and ground transportation make it sound like a bit of utopia. Montana State University is an added plus. It provides an extra cultural dimension to the community, and its engineering programs and staff complement high-tech firms.

Summit Engineering has been the largest local high-tech firm since its startup by members of the Montana State University faculty in the late 1960s. In 1974 Summit was acquired by Dana Corporation and in 1983 was sold to a midwestern company, Allen Bradley. Summit continues to manufacture electronic controls for machine tools which are marketed internationally. Employment at their 55,000-square-foot plant south of the MSU campus peaked at more than 300 in 1981.

Bozeman's limited supply of labor, for one thing, makes it unlikely that the area will attract huge corporate installations employing thousands. Probably few residents would support such massive, boom developments that have the potential to change the very nature of the community. The proposed revision of the Bozeman Area Master Plan projects up to 800 new industrial jobs in the Bozeman area by the year 2000. This includes *all* types of manufacturing.

When most people talk of high tech in the Bozeman area they are referring to corporate offices, research facilities and manufacturing plants of smaller scale, perhaps even home-grown companies. Roger Robichaud's Orionics, Inc., which set up shop just east of Bozeman in 1980, is the type of high tech that may have a promising future in the area. His 15-employee plant manufactures a splicer for optical fibers and another apparatus for testing fibers. The facility could have been located anywhere with scheduled air service and telephones. Bozeman was selected from a list of candidate sites including Spokane, Missoula, and Kalispell. It won out because of its size, clean and attractive environment, and the cultural opportunities of a university town. "We can enjoy the location, the mountains, the relaxed atmosphere — this isn't a pressure-cooker type area," Robichaud said.

Above left: Bozeman, 1875. Montana Historical Society photo.

Above right: Downtown Bozeman today. John Alwin photo.

Bozeman

Bozeman has been discovered. It is one of a select group of Western Montana communities that have experienced explosive population growth over the last 20 years. Between 1960 and 1980 the Bozeman urban area doubled from approximately 15,000 to 30,000 as enrollment at Montana State University climbed to record levels and thousands of Paradise Syndrome victims sought relief in the mountain rimmed valley. Growth is expected to continue and population to climb to 41,000 by the year 2000. Planners and long-time residents have yet to discover where all these new Bozemanites are employed.

Until well into this century Bozeman was smaller than neighboring Livingston. Then it was much more of a farming community and a blue collar town, with hundreds of workers from north side neighborhoods employed with the railroads or in nearby food processing plants. The south side developed later and had a greater number of professional and moneyed residents. The homes of

some of these well-heeled early Bozemanites still can be seen within the South Willson National Historic Neighborhood.

Today the blue collar element is greatly reduced and the community has metamorphosed into a white collar town with an abundance of highly educated and professional people. Serving regional farmers and ranchers is still a big part of Bozeman's role, but the move of several agriculturally related retailers to Belgrade reflects the shift away from agriculture. The annual Montana Winter Fair, Sweet Pea Festival, and College National Rodeo Finals, even the life-size revolving horse in front of McCracken's in downtown Bozeman helps keep residents in touch with the community's agrarian foundation.

Montana State University has grown to dominate many aspects of Bozeman and makes this the state's only true university town. Its student body accounts for over half the city's population and its 2,000-employee payroll provides 44 percent of the total non-farm base for the regional economy, greater than tourism, manufacturing and trade combined. If the

university's students, faculty and staff and the townspeople they support from shoe salesmen to ministers, lawyers and bank tellers were somehow magically lifted from the scene, Bozeman area population would probably shrink overnight to less than 10,000, not much larger than Livingston.

With 11,000 students, MSU is the largest university in a five state area. From its beginning in 1893 as the Agricultural College of the State of Montana, the school primarily has served in-state students. During the 1982-83 school year more than 80 percent of students were Montana residents. Among the state's four-year colleges, Montana State drew the most students from 38 of the state's 56 counties, while second ranking University of Montana dominated in seven counties. International students are one of the fastest growing segments of the student body. Their numbers have tripled in the last three years to about 370. They hail from 55 countries including Upper Volta, Lesotho, Finland, Venezuela, and China. The largest contingent is the 75 Malaysians. Most international students are enrolled in engineering or agriculture programs.

As Montana's land grant college MSU has a threefold mission of instruction, research and service to the state. Students at the Bozeman school can choose from among 123 majors in 42 fields and 16 PhD programs. The school's engineering and business courses have been especially popular among today's job oriented students and help explain the record enrollments while other dominantly liberal arts universities have seen steadily declining numbers.

MSU has evolved into a major research institution with more than $20 million in funded research efforts underway during the 1982-83 school year. Staff and research associates are actively involved in hundreds of projects in areas as diverse as barley and Dutch elm disease, coal liquefaction, mine reclamation, snow and ice, hydrology, early man in Montana, western history, and biofeedback. In 1982 MSU ranked along with MIT, Harvard, Northwestern and the University of Wisconsin in the top half-dozen American universities for number of biotechnology patents granted.

The outreach efforts of the University may be best known by rural residents through their local county agricultural extension agents, all MSU employees. These on-the-spot agents channel the latest information directly to both urban and rural Montanans. They are backed up by approximately 40 specialists and other agricultural researchers on the Bozeman campus and eight off-campus Agricultural Research Centers. These centers are designed to serve the needs of area farmers and ranchers. They allow staff to adapt their research to local climatic and soil conditions. Testing of crop varieties and weed and disease control are major efforts at most centers.

MSU's Museum of the Rockies, located on a five-acre site south of the main cluster of campus buildings, is dedicated to interpreting the physical and cultural diversity of the northern Rockies. A theme of "One place through all time" ties all aspects of this excellent and surprisingly large regional museum together. Permanent exhibits on geology, paleontology, ethnology and history, and monthly gallery shows and traveling exhibits attract 66,000 visitors annually. The museum is gaining international notoriety for its dinosaur finds and soon may be *the* place in the nation to view dinosaur fossils.

A

B

C

D

Bozeman (A), is home of Montana State University (B), where football is big medicine, and site of the College National Rodeo Finals (C), and the Museum of the Rockies (D). Photos A, B, C, John Alwin. Photo

D, courtesy of the Museum of the Rockies.

THE MINING AXIS

The Mining Axis

Geology endowed this Montana corridor, from the Garnet Range on the northwest to the Tobacco Roots in the southeast, with numerous rich ore deposits. During the formation of the Rockies the region experienced more igneous intrusions and associated intense mineralization than any other section of the state. Bonanza gold placers and later rich lode deposits of gold, silver, copper, lead and zinc were the basis for early town formation. Some remain today as the region's major urban centers; others are ghost towns.

As within our Southwest region, cattlemen preceded miners and constituted the region's first permanent white settlers. Former Hudson's Bay Company trader Richard Grant and his sons had used the Beaverhead Valley to the south to fatten cattle they traded to travelers on the Oregon Trail. In the 1850s, son Johnny Grant moved north into the free grazing lands of the Deer Lodge Valley and built his own trading post and ranch headquarters along the Mullan Road, which linked Fort Benton and Walla Walla, Washington. A few years later he moved south and built a new headquarters at present-day Deer Lodge. Undoubtedly with a little assistance from his father, then an established trader in the Bitterroot Valley with a personal estate valued at $10,000, Johnny became one of the founders of Montana's cattle industry.

Grant sold out in the mid-1860s to Conrad Kohrs, a businessman with firsthand knowledge of the potential for profit from beef in Montana's southwest mining camps. Kohrs started with a rather modest operation and built it into one of the largest cattle empires in Montana. In 1870 Kohrs may have initiated the movement of the range livestock industry out of the western valleys and onto the range of Great Plains Montana when, finding the local range full, he drove a herd into the Sun River Valley. Eventually this cattle baron owned 30,000 acres in the Deer Lodge Valley and controlled between one and five million acres of range scattered from western Canada south into Colorado.

The opulence with which Montana's cattle magnates lived in the 1870s and 1880s can be seen today at the Grant-Kohrs Ranch National Historic Site operated by the National Park Service. The original log building completed by Johnny Grant in 1859 and subsequently expanded by Kohrs into a palatial 23-room ranch house and social center for the territory's wealthy and influential, is now open to visitors year-round. In 1982 27,000 toured its elegant Victorian interior and inspected the operating ranch's century old bunkhouse, blacksmith shop and other outbuildings.

Agriculturally, the valleys of the Mining Axis are still almost exclusively devoted to cattle, although numbers are not as great as in the Southwest. Climate and slope limit the amount of cropland and choice of crops. Most farmland is found on valley bottoms along streams for

A

B

D

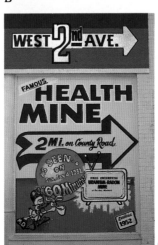

C

(A) Electric Peak, Mt. Warren and Maloney Basin in the Anaconda Pintler Mountains. Ron Glovan photo.

(B) Lost Creek State Park near Warm Springs. Ron Glovan photo.

(C) Abandoned mines of the Boulder Valley draw customers from thousands of miles. They come for what they believe are the health-giving properties of the mines' mineral waters and radon gas. John Alwin photo.

(D) Remains of a stamp mill at Clark, near Philpsburg. Jim Romo photo.

Above: Georgetown Lake.
John Alwin photo.

Right: Safely off Homestake Pass east of Butte, rolling into Whitehall. John Alwin photo.

ease of irrigation, and almost 90 percent is planted in hay. Livestock yards in Butte and Missoula vie for cattle and calves produced in the region. Cattlemen from Drummond might truck their livestock all the way to Butte, or Deer Lodge Valley ranches may opt for Missoula if the price looks better. The large sign at the western community of Drummond proclaims it the "World's Largest Bull Shipper." World's largest, maybe not, but a number of area ranchers, including one of the biggest registered bull raisers in the country, do market bulls.

Indians undoubtedly were the first to discover gold in Western Montana, perhaps thousands of years ago. The initial date of its rediscovery by white men is clouded. Some say Francois Finley, one of the tribe of half-breed French Canadian fur trappers who settled in the Flathead country, should be credited with its rediscovery. The story goes that he discovered gold in the river sand at Gold Creek east of today's Drummond, and in 1850 took less than a teaspoonful to the Hudson's Bay Company's Fort Connah in the Mission Valley. Post commander Angus McDonald evidently did

nothing at that time, but wrote to his superiors at Victoria when Finley brought in more gold within a year or two. McDonald was told to keep the discovery a secret since fur trappers and hordes of settlers didn't mix.

A party including James and Granville Stuart usually is credited with the first discovery of record. It was the spring of 1858 and the site was the same Gold Creek area. Four years elapsed before serious mining began on the site and the short-lived and tiny encampment of American Fork appeared at the junction of the Clark Fork and Gold Creek. It never amounted to much and quickly was eclipsed by major gold discoveries in other western gulches. Within the Mining Axis colors were struck in other drainages and quartz mining operations already begun by 1870 when communities like French Gulch, Butte, Emmettsburg, Philipsburg, Silver Star, Pony and even Pikes Peak struggled for survival. With its more varied economic base Deer Lodge was the metropolis of the 1870 Mining Axis claiming 788 residents.

Even the largest communities did not take on urban dimensions until the '80s when rail service and a boom in quartz mining and refining ushered in a period of growth and assumed permanence. Butte moved rapidly from a silver mining center to a major copper producer and became the largest town in the Axis. It surpassed Helena in the '90s to become the state's biggest city, a position it held for decades.

Other larger communities went their own ways and developed distinctive personalities. The Philipsburg mining district was Montana's premier silver producer. Mines at the mountaintop town of Granite high in the Flint Creek Range several miles east of Philipsburg were the major producers. Development of this rich iode atop the Philipsburg Batholith began in earnest in 1880. Census enumerators counted 1,310 in Silver Queen City in 1890. At an elevation of 7,000 feet, this was easily Montana's highest community of any appreciable size.

On the town's 10th anniversary both the Granite Mountain and Bi-Metallic silver mines were sending their ores to mills lower on the mountainside. The Granite Mountain miners transported theirs via an 8,900-foot-long tramway to a mill at Rumsey, two miles to the south. A community of 500 mill workers and their families developed around the mill site. A similar-size settlement grew around the Bi-Metallic's mill at Kirkville (Clark) just south of Philipsburg. A two-mile-long tramway of 500-pound capacity iron buckets linked the gigantic mill to Granite.

Population and production at Granite peaked just prior to the Silver Panic of 1893. By then the town had

A

B

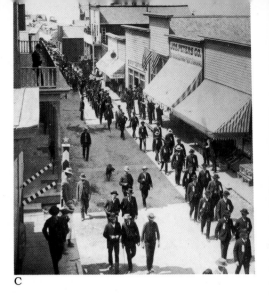

C

D

(A) At the ghost town of Comet. Rick Graetz photo.
(B) Overlooking Philipsburg. John Alwin photo.
(C) Miner's Union Day in Granite, 1890. Montana
Historical Society photo.
(D) The Flint Creek Range from south of Drummond.
Tom Dietrich photo.

an estimated 3,000 residents and boasted a classy three-story hotel, newspaper, four churches, hospital, fraternal lodges, Rod and Gun Club and 18 saloons. Plummeting world silver prices hit Granite with a vengeance in the summer of 1893. Word arrived to close the mines and, according to a reputable eyewitness, the town's population dropped to zero within 24 hours. Production returned periodically afterward, but Granite never again merited town status. Today it is a ghost town. Visitors able to conquer the steep dirt access road east of Philipsburg will find enough remains to sense some of what Granite must have been like in the early 1890s.

Nearby Philipsburg served more as a trade, supply and entertainment center for the surrounding mining district than as a mining town in its own right. Development of the next-door Hope mine led to the town's founding in the late 1860s, but this was not a town of miners. Rather it was home to those who provided goods and services to miners and mill workers in nearby communities like Granite, Hasmark, Princeton, Black Pine, Clark and to the farmers and ranchers who filled the Flint Creek Valley. The economic slump following the Silver Panic was eased somewhat for Philipsburg by its designation as seat of the newly created Granite County.

For decades population has remained remarkably stable. Its total of 1,138 residents in 1980 was within 31 of both the 1970 and 1960 figures. Philipsburg still serves as county seat, trade center for area ranchers and is now a popular stopover for tourists selecting the alternate Pintler Scenic Route along Highway 10A instead of I-90. Higher silver and gold prices have raised hopes that the community may benefit from a resurgence of mining and milling in the district. In

Above: From the ruins of the past...This silver milling operation of the Contact Mining Company was built on the ruins of the famous old Bi-Metallic mill near Philipsburg. John Alwin photo.

Below: Golden Sunlight Mines, operating near Whitehall, is another small, efficient mineral company working old mining country in the wake of higher gold prices of the '80s. Here the company's first gold bar is poured. Photo courtesy of Golden Sunlight Mines, Inc.

Below right: The Anaconda smelter and the town it built, 1887. Montana Historical Society photo.

1981 production restarted at the Black Pine Mine across the Flint Creek Valley and the Contact Mining Company built a 1,200-ton capacity mill on the site of the old Bi-Metallic. They are emphasizing silver, but also can extract gold and copper.

Lean, efficient, small-scale operations like the Black Pine Mine and its small mill near Philipsburg, with a combined employment of approximately 85, may be the future of mining in the Axis as well as the rest of Western Montana. Few analysts expect to see many new huge mines and processing mills.

Placer Amex Inc.'s new Golden Sunlight Mine at the opposite end of the Axis is perhaps an even better example of what may be the beginning of a trend. Night travelers on Interstate 90 can't miss the floodlit complex on a hillside north of the interstate and just northeast of Whitehall. Production at this Canadian-owned, open-pit gold mine began in early 1983. The computer controlled facility includes its own onsite crusher, mill and refinery. During its projected 13-year life it is expected to yield 72,300 ounces of gold annually from ores that contain only .05 ounces of gold per ton. In another shift from tradition, the 120 employees are non-union.

Anaconda, the region's second largest city since the mid-1880s was never a mining town. From 1884 until 1980 it was home to Anaconda Company's gigantic smelter. Marcus Daly, one of the famed Copper Kings' selected the site 26 miles west of Butte because of available water and timber, both scarce in Butte. Daly had hoped to name the town Copperopolis, but settled for Anaconda when it was discovered that another Montana community already claimed that unlikely name.

The carefully planned town took form within a matter of months in 1883 and the next year the Washoe Smelter on the north side of Warm Springs Creek began processing Butte ores. This was a company town under the tutelage of Marcus Daly. He assumed it eventually would replace the temporary capital of Helena and he set about building a city worthy of such a designation. His Montana Hotel, much larger than was needed, was the most elegant in the territory. Carefully landscaped Washoe Park may have been Montana's first formally planned city park. When ballots were counted in 1894 Anaconda lost to Helena by only 1,000 votes from more than 50,000 cast. Administratively, Anaconda had to settle for designation as the new county seat of a then much larger Deer Lodge County three years later.

From its inception the fortunes of Anaconda were tied to those of Butte. To assure ore supplies Anaconda completed its own rail link between the two towns in 1893 and grew as Butte production climbed. A new smelter was completed on the south side of Warm Springs Creek in 1902 and the 585½-foot-tall smoke-stack, then the world's largest, was completed in 1919. Anaconda's population peaked at 12,500 in 1930 and remained fairly steady for several decades.

Above: Silent since 1980, the old Anaconda smelter is testimony to the size of mining operations of a half century ago. John Alwin photo.

Right: Turret of the Montana Territorial Prison, Deer Lodge, now home to the internationally famous Towe Antique Ford collection. John Alwin photo.

The September, 1980 announcement of the June closure of the Anaconda Smelter and loss of 1,000 jobs has impacted local population. Wrecking balls began demolition of the 80-year-old smelter in 1982. It is planned that the smelter will be leveled for maximum tax write-off advantages and the entire hillside will be reclaimed. The heavy mineral contaminated slag piles generated by almost a century of smelting present reclamationists with their greatest challenge. Some residents still hope to save the stack, but were not encouraged by the fate of the Anaconda stack in Great Falls.

Among major communities in the Mining Axis, Deer Lodge is most removed from its mining past. This town of 4,000 is the site of Montana State Prison. Construction of the first territorial penetentiary began in 1870 and the first prisoner was accepted the next year, but the castle-like structure on Main Street was not completed until the 1890s. Originally internees were housed in tents behind a wooden wall. In 1893 prison labor was used to build the massive rock wall and in 1896 inmates completed their own brick cell block within its confines.

The last of the prisoners were moved from the 1890s facility in 1979 and transferred to a new penetentiary seven miles out of town. The Powell County Museum and Arts Foundation has signed a 25-year lease for the old prison and now provides summer tours. The original 1896 Cell Block is gone, destroyed by the same 1959 earthquake that triggered the Madison Slide and created Quake Lake, but visitors can still tour the somber 1912 block.

Few Montana communities are more historically cognizant than Deer Lodge. Residents have realized the tourist potential of their historic attractions on the well traveled corridor between Glacier and Yellowstone national parks. The Grant-Kohrs Ranch National Historic Site and the Old Montana Territorial Prison are two examples. Internationally, Deer Lodge is most noted for another attraction, the Towe Antique Ford Collection, known and respected by car buffs the world over.

The private collection of Edward Towe is housed in sections of the Old Territorial Prison that once were the Industry Building, dormitory and laundry. The 30,000-square-foot facility accommodates 150 vehicles and according to museum director Ernest Hartley, is "the most complete collection of antique Ford cars in the world." It includes every year and model of Ford from 1903 to 1942 and is about to be extended to 1952. Ford aficionados will appreciate its complete sets of pre-Model Ts, Phaetons (1928-37), and Roadsters (1929-37). The 30,000 annual visitors soon may be able to admire a Ford Tri-Motor airplane. Only 199 were built between 1925 and 1932 and perhaps only six to eight are still airworthy. If Towe is successful, one may soon find a new home in Deer Lodge.

Above: Uptown Butte.

Right: From uptown, looking to "the flats." John Alwin photos.

Butte, America

Butte, America, Montana's Mining City, gets more national and international press coverage than any other community in the state. It has "enjoyed" front-page billing in the *Wall Street Journal* and seems to be mentioned more than once a year in the *New York Times*. All this notoriety would be fine except that most of it is unflattering, a fact that at once perturbs and perplexes proud Butte natives. Recently described in the national press as "the ugliest city in America" (in the *Reader's Digest*, no less), "almost pathetic," and "bombed out," it is easy to see why the community is a little defensive.

Like many other communities in the Mining Axis, Butte started as a placer gold mining camp. Word of the 1864 discovery along Silver Bow Creek reached the Virginia City area and sparked an almost instantaneous rush to the new diggings. It has been estimated that several thousand placer miners worked the Silver Bow drainage during the summers of 1865 to 1867. By 1867 Butte, still a camp, peaked at about 500 residents and had a well-deserved reputation as one of the territory's most disreputable places.

The easily worked alluvial deposits were depleted in short order and as the number of white miners fell, the Chinese population rose — a sure sign of the waning years of a gold camp. Initial efforts to work the quartz deposits on Butte Hill were unsuccessful and by 1870 the census tallied only 241 in Butte, of which 98 were Chinese. Four years later Butte was just another dying camp with a population that may have fallen below 60.

Just when Butte City's fate seemed certain and its place among a growing list of deceased territorial mining camps assured, this played-out gold camp was reborn. In 1875 it was found that the rich quartz ores of the Hill could be mined for silver and milled locally at a respectable profit. This discovery ignited a second invasion, one that brought larger numbers of miners and a permanence previously lacking. By 1880 Butte was riding high on a silver boom and claimed title to Montana's second largest town with 3,364 residents.

Silver kicked off Butte's second boom, but it was copper that soon catapulted it to a position of

world-class mining center. The 1882 discovery of rich copper ores in the legendary Anaconda Mine ushered in a phase of mining that would span a century and prove Butte to be the Richest Hill on Earth.

The pace of development quickened in the '80s, and copper production increased from nine million pounds in 1882 to almost 130 million in 1890, while silver production just doubled. Butte tripled its population during the decade as supplier of copper to a world in the grips of an electrical revolution. The timing couldn't have been better for maximum growth. With the 1879 introduction of the electric light bulb and adoption of electric motors, demand for copper wire accelerated. Butte took on the traditional copper producing center in Michigan's Keweenaw Peninsula in a vicious price war for national dominance and emerged victorious.

The '80s also witnessed the opening salvos in the so-called War of the Copper Kings. No school child in Montana gets much beyond the fifth grade without knowing the story of this extraordinary 12-year conflict between Butte's first two copper barons, Marcus Daly and W. A. Clark. The clash of these powerful personalities had implications for much of the state and even reached into the hallowed U.S. Senate chambers.

Mines like the Anaconda, Parrot, Alice, Colusa and Lexington called for miners, and lots of them. The rosters of the mines and smelters largely were filled by foreign-born workers who arrived in Butte in droves starting in the 1880s. Almost 24,000 people lived in Silver Bow County in 1890, nearly all in Butte and its environs. Just under half of the populace, about 10,700, were foreign born.

Prior to the turn of the century the British Isles accounted for more than half the city's foreign born. The largest number, some 2,500, hailed from England. Most were Cornish, from the little 1,300-square-mile county of Cornwall in southwest England. A long history of hard-rock mining and smelting of tin and copper gave these Cousin Jacks, as they were known, wide repute as miners and smeltermen. They were welcomed with open arms in America's mining districts. In the '80s they moved into Butte by the hundreds from depleted American mining centers and directly from Cornwall.

Those of Irish descent were a close second to the Cornish in Butte of the '90s. Numbering 2,308,

Above: Hardly deserving the title in 1875, this was The City of Butte. By 1890 it claimed a population of nearly 24,000, and at the peak of its expansion in the Teens may have had 100,000 inhabitants.

Right: The first of the Copper Kings, William Andrews Clark, and Marcus Daly, far right. Montana Historical Society photos.

their influence was destined to grow to dominate the Mining City in terms of numbers, political power and cultural impress. At this time Germans (822) and Scandinavians (651) were the third and fourth largest groups.

Butte's ethnic mix expanded after the turn of the century with the addition of even more groups, with markedly greater numbers arriving from eastern and southern Europe. By 1920 residents included 1,273 Yugoslavians, 1,229 Finns, 964 Italians and other sizable contingents from more than a score of countries.

The immigrant character of Butte was amplified by the tendency for each national group to cluster, or as a local paper referred to it in 1910, to "flock together," in ethic neighborhoods. Rather than a single homogeneous city, Butte became an ethnic mosaic like larger industrial cities in the Midwestern and Eastern sections of the country.

American born were most numerous in neighborhoods west of Main Street. The more fashionable upper and middle class west side streets contrasted with the often more functional working class "foreign" tracts to the east. The sights, sounds and smells of these ethnic enclaves were just like those back in the old country. Despite persistent friction between them, Irish and Cornish concentrated to the north and northeast on the Hill, close to the mines. Places like Corktown and Dublin Gulch were once as Irish as their names, while both northern suburbs of Centerville and Walkerville had heavy concentrations of Cousin Jacks.

Lively and compact Finntown complete with its famous steam bath houses developed somewhat later. Chinatown, with everything from vegetable vendors and laundries to opium dens, occupied an area of several blocks on the south side of the central business district. The bright orange and brown tones of their buildings contrasted with the dreary green of the delapidated structures of the small, adjacent black ghetto.

Butte's entrepreneurial Lebanese were centered on East Galena within Little Lebanon. A much larger colony of Yugoslavians, including a big contingent of Serbs, clustered in several widely scattered neighborhoods where they celebrated their own holidays and recreated as much as they could of life back home. Bohunks, another name for these Slavic people, eventually dominated the McQueen and Boulevard additions. Suburban Meaderville east of town was originally populated by Welsh and Cornish, but later became known as "Little Italy" and as a mecca for gamblers.

The Cabbage Patch was a six-square-block slum area not unlike the more famous slums of London. Here down-and-outers from all nationalities tolerated each other. More than any other residential area, this was the melting pot of Butte.

Mining activity and population continued to build and peaked in the years during and just after World War I. Most of the stately masonry buildings of Uptown Butte were built during this period of rapid growth from the mid-'80s to the mid-Teens. The scale and architectural merit of these buildings are present-day reminders of the

grandeur and urban sophistication of a Butte that saw itself as *the* burgeoning western metropolis. No one knows for certain what the area's between-census population was in the late Teens peak, but local historians estimate there may have been almost 20,000 miners and as many as 100,000 residents. Despite this size and its status as one of the West's largest inland cities, Butte remained an interesting combination of frontier camp and modern, cosmopolitan city.

Contemporary writers graphically described the bustling industrialized Hill immediately north and east of the business district. This was the center of mining activity that continued round the clock. Its strictly functional landscape of mines, towering gallow frames, waste dumps, tangle of narrow gauge rails, rusty, smoke begrimed buildings and trestles and belching stacks were compared in appearance to a gigantic shipwreck.

Each shift change set loose an army of miners who flowed down the Hill ready to unwind. Many of the Butte mines had reputations as some of the nation's toughest with a combination of acid mine waters, die-hard shift bosses and the debilitating heat and humidity of ever-deeper shafts. By 1915 the High Ore was down to 3,400 feet, the Anaconda to 2,800, and many others to at least a half mile. "Ninety-by-ninety" conditions with temperatures of 90 degrees and humidity of 90 percent were not uncommon. After a shift underground the entertainment down the Hill was particularly inviting.

Butte in the Teens afforded the gamut of manly forms of rest and relaxation. Many miners were single and had little inclination to return to their spartan boarding houses until absolutely necessary. The action was in and along the streets and the action never stopped. Hundreds of saloons catered to thirsty miners, gambling joints were everywhere, and the red light district in the alleys behind Galena and Mercury streets regularly drew crowds that were rivaled only on parade days. According to the Butte classic, *Copper Camp*, its thousand girls ranked the district along with the Barbary Coast in San Francisco and Corduroy Road in New Orleans.

The labor unrest of the Teens intensified the rough and tough mining-camp side of Butte. It was a period of turmoil that included rival unions, company-union rifts, goon squads, strikes, bombings, murders, riots and the imposition of martial law and troops in the streets on more than one occasion. The war years coupled with Butte's polyglot nature tended to heighten the hysteria.

A town that produced one-fourth of the nation's and one-seventh of the world's copper, as well as substantial amounts of silver and zinc, obviously also had wealth. In 1915 the Anaconda was the world's largest silver producer and second ranking copper mine, and the Butte and Superior ranked as the greatest zinc producer. All totaled, the 150 active mines in the district annually produced approximately $1,000 for every Butte resident.

Major streets were paved with brick and granite and lined with concrete sidewalks by the mid-Teens. Handsome and substantial Uptown buildings were the norm. Structures like the towering eight-story Metals Bank Building, the ornate Curtis Music Hall, the unique Silver Bow Block with its Romanesque arches, distinctive eight-story Prudential Tower, and Moorish-looking Commercial Building are just a few remnants of this golden age of Butte. Closer inspection reveals the terra cotta, turrets, medallions, cornices and other architectural details of a prosperous and self-confident Butte telling the world it had arrived as a Western metropolis.

Up-to-dateness was important in Butte. Its merchants prided themselves on stocking wares worthy of a world-class city. The retail crown Uptown was Hennessy's, opened in 1898 and billed as "The Biggest, Best and Busiest Store in Montana." Retail space filled the basement and first three floors of this massive six-story building on the corner of Main and Granite streets. Even the town's most affluent could find what they wanted here, whether it be the latest silks from the looms of France, expensive evening gowns, or the finest in men's shoes.

In 1915 Butte's amusement houses included a first-class opera, two vaudeville theaters and eight "moving picture houses." Its public transportation system would be the envy of any modern-day Montana community. The electric street railway included 40 miles of track tying the city together and reaching into suburban areas. One of the most popular runs was the 20-minute ride to Columbia Gardens three miles east of town at the mouth of an attractive canyon. A large pavilion with a cafe, banquet room, refreshment booths, and a 62,000-square-foot dance floor dominated

Central Butte Hill and Dublin Gulch, about 1905. Montana Historical Society photo.

this 80-acre resort. Its grounds included greenhouses, trees, and a fantasyland of gardens, as well as picnic grounds, baseball diamonds and Garden Lake for swimming. Open air concerts by the highly acclaimed Anaconda Copper Mines Band were especially popular. Older Butte residents remember that on Thursdays children could ride to and from the park free. On a hot summer day 12,000 to 15,000 urban residents often escaped to this inviting resort complex.

The Anaconda Copper Mining Company (later Anaconda Minerals) came to dominate the Richest Hill on Earth. Butte became a company town and Anaconda set about building a Montana empire that reached well beyond the mine shafts at Butte. "The Company," as most Montanans knew it, eventually achieved an economic and political clout within Montana the likes of which the state had never seen.

Through their numerous Montana-owned dailies, including some of the state's largest circulation newspapers, the Anaconda Company propagandized their views and controlled what many state residents received by way of news. This "Company press" was so extreme that as late as 1952 one out-of-state journalist described Montana as "the last outpost in America of feudal journalism."

Even though Anaconda's Montana empire expanded beyond mining, Butte remained the crux of its operations. Over the decades inevitable change has come to the Butte mines. Increasing production from other domestic and overseas mines, the low grade of remaining ore, and expensive mile-deep shafts took their toll and forced changes. In 1955 the company began digging the Berkeley Pit east of Uptown. This area already had been honeycombed by shafts early in the century to mine the main high grade veins. Then again starting in the 1940s some areas also were mined with a new type of procedure using underground blasting.

Sept 10-1912

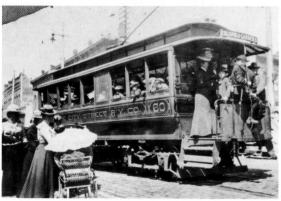

Top: Main Street of Butte in its heyday.
Bottom left: Early street car sometime before WWI.
Bottom right: The Columbia Gardens, about 1925.
Montana Historical Society photos.

As the pit grew it swallowed ethnic neighborhoods and nibbled at the edges of the historic Uptown area. The shift from underground to open-pit mining was completed in the mid-1970s. Shifting from labor-intensive underground mining to highly mechanized surface extraction in the world's largest truck-operated pit had detrimental implications for employment. In a three-month period more than 2,000 Anaconda employees were pink-slipped as the last underground mines were closed and production shifted exclusively to the growing Berkeley Pit.

Anaconda ceased to exist as an independent corporate entity in 1977 when it merged into the Atlantic Richfield Company (Arco). In the late '70s serious consideration was given to abandoning the entire Uptown to a devouring pit and building a new, futuristic central business district on the "Flats" below the Hill. But by then the pit's days were already numbered. In April 1982, citing low copper prices, Arco announced almost 300 Butte layoffs and the closure of its mammoth Berkeley Pit, then a 2,200-foot-deep crater more than a mile wide. Ore with less than one percent copper had become too expensive to mine. A reduced labor force shifted to the adjacent East Pit which had gobbled up the historic Columbia Gardens. There, 20 to 30 years of reserves, less overburden and associated molybdenum deposits looked more inviting.

Butte hadn't heard the last of its bad news. Within a year a world glut of copper and moly were major factors in the announcement that the company would suspend all mining and milling operations in Butte as of June 30, 1983, eliminating 700 jobs. Butte was stunned. Families that had been copper miners for four or five generations faced the prospect of a future without mining. Bold headlines in state papers carried details of the news to a surprised Montana public and wire services picked up on the story of one of the world's great mining centers facing the end of an era.

By the end of 1983 Arco's Butte employment may be down to 50. The shutdown is officially a suspension, but only the most optimistic expect Anaconda to return. Much higher copper prices, greater union flexibility, a quarter-billion-dollar modernization of the Butte ore concentrator, and evidence of a more sympathetic attitude from state government are four company prerequisites to reopening.

The Highland Mountains south of Butte. Rick Graetz photo.

The announcement of mining suspension in Butte was a shock, but not totally unexpected. Earlier signs that Arco was winding down its Montana operation included the September, 1980 announcement of the immediate closure of both its Anaconda smelter and Great Falls refinery, and the persistent decline in its Butte-area employment. These local cutbacks were a major factor in the ongoing loss of county population from more than 48,000 in 1950 to 38,000 in 1980. Arco's pullout is serious, but not a total disaster for the community. The 700 lost jobs represent approximately five percent of all employment in the Butte area. There will be a ripple effect felt through the regional economy with perhaps two to three other local jobs eventually lost for each position, but this isn't the coup de grace for Butte that many have suggested. It may even provide the necessary impetus to further diversify the local economy and attract less cyclical industries.

Butte isn't going to wait around to see if and when Arco decides to restart. Butte Chamber of Commerce and Butte Local Development Corporation are aggressively pursuing potential new employers. Boomer Chamber of Commerce literature from the Teens referred to Butte as "an excellent health resort" where "seldom is winter excessively cold" and a place where "persons from low altitude suffering from weakened lungs and other ailments frequently find the desired relief and renewed strength . . ." Today's chamber isn't trying to sell Butte as a subtropical health spa; they know the town's meteorological reputation has preceded them.

Instead they are emphasizing attributes like Butte's well-developed transportation system. A strategic location at the junction of I-15 and I-90, excellent scheduled air service from two national airlines, and the presence of two railroads (almost unheard of in Montana in the 1980s), are obvious pluses. Butte is home to the Montana College of Mineral Sciences and Technology, a 2,200-student school with a national reputation for excellence in its geology and engineering curriculum. Situated at almost 5,800 feet just below the Continental Divide, Butte enjoys one of the most striking natural settings of any Montana city. Outdoor enthusiasts can find almost unlimited recreational activities in the surrounding millions of acres of mountains and forests.

The quest for new employers centers on those providing fewer than 50 jobs. There is also interest in attracting new corporate headquarters. Butte already is home base for the Montana Power Company, now the city's largest employer. More than 1,000 MPC employees work in the company's eight Uptown buildings. The presence of the Montana Energy Research and Development Institute (MERDI) suggests a potential for high tech, and the National Center for Appropriate Technology has shown that national organizations can operate effectively out of the city.

Butte's special character and special people are certainly its most valuable qualities. These important characteristics too often are missed by outsiders who fail to look beneath a surface that most city residents would agree is a bit scruffy and dog-eared. Lately, out-of-state reporters who have jetted into Butte on a one-day whirlwind tour looking for an exhausted community and a dying-town story have been most myopic, although some state residents have been just as nearsighted.

More than a century of mining has left an indelible imprint on the cityscape that continues to contribute to the look and feel of Butte. Gallow frames, mine spoils, the gaping mineral-stained pit, and the tiny, closely packed homes of thousands of yesterday's miners are prominent elements in this admittedly somewhat obtrusive landscape. The sense of a big and brawny Butte is nowhere more apparent than Uptown where hulking 70-year-old buildings exude the community's masculinity. In his *Historic Uptown Butte*, an interesting architectural and historical analysis of the business core, Bozeman architect John DeHaas points out that Butte has a metropolitan character lacking in all other Montana cities. Butte definitely isn't a quaint restored mining area like so many tourist traps in the West. It's the real thing, where mining history isn't limited to a single street or little district; it permeates much of the community and its landscape. Walk the streets of Uptown and chances are you, too, will sense Butte's still broad shoulders and narrow waist.

Some residents have recognized the intrinsic value and significance of Butte's Uptown and

A

B

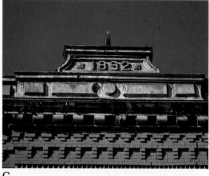

C

E

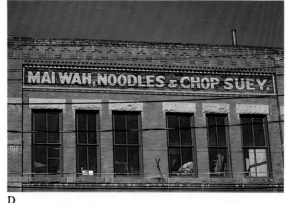

D

(A) The Hill. Tom Dietrich photo.
(B, C) Architectural detail harking back to the halcyon days. John Alwin photos.
(D) Evidence of the blend of nationalities that is Butte. John Alwin photo.

(E) Wide-open Butte spawned every entertainment known to the age. These are the "cribs," in the old red-light district. John Alwin photo.

efforts are ongoing to assure its commercial vitality. The area is a National Historic Landmark District, which makes possible substantial rehabilitation tax credits on historically important buildings. Thankfully, the rash of major arson fires in the Uptown finally seems to have ended. Janet Cornish heads the Uptown revitalization program for the city and is proud of what appears to be a "little Renaissance" in the central business district. The last three years have seen 80 businesses expand or move into the Uptown.

Butte's inhabitants have a reputation as rough and tumble as its landscape. Part of the image is that of a hard drinking, shot-and-a-beer town where bartenders don't get many requests for strawberry daiquiris. But statistics just don't seem to back up this almost sacred image. Per capita sales at state liquor stores aren't perfect indicators of consumption, but they do at least suggest general levels. Per person sales in Butte-Silver Bow aren't anywhere near those of Sheridan and Mineral counties and trail other rural counties including Glacier, Beaverhead, Sweetgrass and Toole. Perhaps this reputation is based on past laurels.

That's not to say that Butte bars don't pack them in. The community no longer has the estimated 500 saloons of its heyday, but there apparently is sufficient business to justify the 85 that remain. Saunter any Friday night to the Met, Five Mile, the Deluxe, Luigi's, Malley's, Marty's, Maloney's or the Helsinki Bar and Steam Bath and you'll see that drinking is still serious business in Butte. The tradition of those carrying a lunch bucket receiving a free shot of whiskey with their first beer may be gone, but some bars do continue the tradition of unlisted phone numbers to protect their patrons' uninterrupted privacy.

The M & M at 9 North Main is the grande dame of Butte bars, one of the last of its old-time saloons. It started serving drinks in the 1890s and today may have more regulars than any other drinking establishment in town. "We get them all" says owner Charlie Bugni, "everyone from M.D.s, lawyers, and stockbrokers to welfare people." Locals don't take out-of-town guests to the M & M to impress them with the community's sophistication. It's not one of those Naugahyde and chrome bars with wall-to-wall carpeting, subtle lighting and soft background music — it's a Butte institution. In addition to its well worn bar, there is a dinner counter along the opposite wall that provides inexpensive, filling, but by no means fancy, meals 24 hours a day. The back room is for round-the-clock gambling. Poker players humped over felt-covered tables from yesteryear, a floor littered with Keno cards and cigarette butts, and a wall-size Keno board give the place the look of a real joint.

There exists among Butte residents a brotherhood normally restricted to much smaller communities. Their pride in and loyalty to their city is so extreme as to seem alien to most Montanans. There aren't many Butte people who have much to say in a critical vein about their town.

Celebrations like St. Patrick's Day express the community's phenomenal pride, which is a partial explanation for why all hell breaks loose that day. All ethnic groups in town become Irish for a day. The community literally paints the streets green. Thousands of former residents and other visitors stream into town by bus and car, even from out of state, to partake of this extravaganza. As nearest neighbors, Anaconda residents are probably more aware of Butte's pride than any other non-residents. Inter-city high school sports competition is as intense as it gets anywhere in Montana. When the Anaconda High Copperheads come to town to take on the Butte High Bulldogs their spectator and team buses are given police escort!

Someone going to Butte looking for trouble will find it; others will experience one of the friendliest towns in the nation. Like so many other qualities of the community, this one is extreme. Tom Powers has lived in Butte since 1906 and saw thousands of residents during his 50 year career at the Metals Bank. According to him, "It's always been that way." A resident of 23 years, Mary Mollish echoes much the same sentiment. She has concluded that Butte residents have a "highly overdeveloped sense of hospitality and courtesy."

"Friendliness in Butte" would be a good topic for a sociological study. We can only guess at what makes its people so congenial. Perhaps it is a manifestation of the type of brotherliness seen within ethnic neighborhoods. It might also relate to having been through so many difficult times that people have pulled together and have genuine pioneer-like concern for others. Whatever the causes, Mary Mollish is sold on the community. "Butte is a super choice for a place to live. I've lived all over the world and Butte is best."

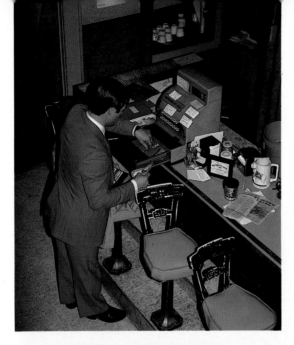

The brotherhood of Butte. At left customers make their own change in Gamer's restaurant. Below, St. Pat's day in the M&M. John Alwin photos.

THE MISSOULA-BITTERROOT

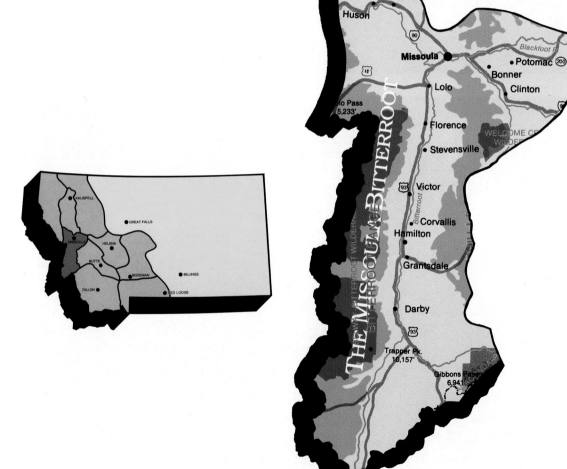

Even though geographically one of the smallest, the Missoula-Bitterroot's 100,000 residents make it the most populated of our nine western regions. The elongate area is anchored to Missoula on the north, with minor appendages of habitation to the east up the Blackfoot and east and west along the Clark Fork Valley. On the south the trough-like Bitterroot Valley is developing into a major population corridor that coalesces with the Missoula urban area on its north. A strong regional focus on Missoula, high levels of urbanization and population density, rapid rural population growth, a proliferation of subdivisions and a shared historical development form the basis for this region.

Owing partly to its Pacific Northwest location, this was the earliest center of continuous white settlement in Montana and became the westernmost portion of its historic core. At the request of the Salish, or Flathead, Indians who then resided in the Bitterroot, St. Mary's Mission was established outside today's Stevensville in 1841. Fur trappers and converted Indians working with the British fur companies had told the Flatheads about the Black Robes who could speak to the Great Spirit and who offered the "big prayer," the Indians' name for Mass. The arrival of Father Pierre-Jean DeSmet, S.J., that summer culminated the Flathead's decade-long effort which had included four pilgrimages to St. Louis to convince the Black Robes to locate among them.

St. Mary's Mission immediately became the nexus for embryonic Western Montana, an outpost in the wilderness. A settlement of Indians and a sprinkling of whites and half-breeds clustered around St. Mary's. The mission community claimed a number of Montana firsts. The oats, wheat and garden crops harvested in 1842 are considered the first in Montana. Likewise, the mission's use of irrigation and its cattle are assumed to have been the earliest, as were the flour mill and sawmill built in 1844.

St. Mary's was closed and sold to John Owen in 1850 for $250. He built the fort and trading post of Fort Owen on the site and greatly expanded its role as a center of commerce. Repeated Blackfeet Indian raids soon convinced him to relocate on nearby high ground behind a solid stockade of cottonwood logs, later replaced with a thick adobe wall.

An 1860 census of the Bitterroot, then in Washington Territory, shows several score non-Indians in the valley, with the largest concentration in the Fort Owen area. Occupations included traders, clerks, blacksmiths, harness makers, millers, carpenters, laborers and others consistent with the young frontier community. One man even gave his occupation as explorer. John Owen is listed as Indian Agent, and the former Hudson's Bay Company employee Richard Grant, then

Right: The Como Peaks from the Bitterroot Valley near Hamilton. Tom Dietrich photo.
Above: Long before the gold rush brought settlements to the southwest portion of Montana Territory, St. Mary's Mission had been established by Jesuits and claimed a number of firsts, such as Montana's first crops, first flour mill and first irrigation. John Alwin photos.

Top: Another of Montana's boom and bust stories was the Bitterroot apple orchard development around 1910. The real basis of the apple business was a land scheme. Shown here are some of the early results. Montana Historical Society photo.
Above left: The Bitterroot Valley is one of the state's most inviting for its mild climate, yet it is surrounded by some of the state's wildest country. This is above Trapper Peak. Mark Thompson photo.
Above right: Missoula's back yard is the Rattlesnake Mountains, recently designated as a wilderness area. Rick Graetz photo.

66, gave his profession as trader. Even though two years before the Homestead Act and more than a decade before the area formally was opened to agriculturalists, the census lists more than a dozen farmers.

Agriculture was destined to dominate the valley. By 1860 demand for foodstuffs in the rich Idaho diggings had suggested the potential of Bitterroot farming. Discovery of gold two years later in southwestern Montana accelerated development of the valley's already growing farming community. Like the Gallatin Valley to the east, the Bitterroot developed as an important supplier of food to Montana's mining camps and towns. Its fertile alluvial soils, broad flat nature and relatively long freeze-free season made it a leading producer of beef, vegetables and grain. The growing importance of agriculture was reflected in the July 23, 1862 entry in John Owen's diary: "Gold Gold Nothing is talked of but Gold. When will it End. The prospect of the farmer is flattering," he wrote. A year later Owen recorded, "Mr. Harris left this morning for the Stinking Water Mines [Virginia City, Montana, area] with two wagons loaded with vegetables and some ten or more head of Beef Cattle."

The influx of farmers into the Bitterroot accelerated during the remainder of the 1860s and for several decades in unison with Montana's growth and greater access to outside markets via improved transport. Fort Owen and St. Mary's Mission, re-established in 1866 by Father Anthony Ravalli, S.J., for whom the county is named, continued to draw many to nearby sections of the valley. The 1866 mission church and Father Ravalli's small log hospital/pharmacy still stand on the outskirts of Stevensville.

As the ranks of white farmers grew so too did their pressure on the federal government to remove the Flathead from the valley. In 1872 then Congressman and future president, James Garfield was sent to the valley to finalize the transfer of the Indians to the Jocko (Flathead) Reservation. Some were convinced to leave, but it was not until 1891 that the proud Flathead Chief Charlot finally succumbed to the inevitable and led the last of his people to the Jocko.

By the 1880s the Bitterroot's most famous resident was well on his way to establishing his immense country estate. The man was none other than Marcus Daly, one of Montana's Copper Kings. Daly had passed through the valley years earlier on a trip to British Columbia and was captivated by the panoramic beauty of emerald lowland tucked between the craggy raw mountains of the Bitterroot Range to the west and the softer, more heavily forested slopes of the Sapphire Range to the east.

Daly returned and built one of the finest stock farms in the world, modeled after Irish estates back in his

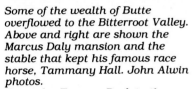

Some of the wealth of Butte overflowed to the Bitterroot Valley. Above and right are shown the Marcus Daly mansion and the stable that kept his famous race horse, Tammany Hall. John Alwin photos.
Far right: Trapper Peak in the Bitterroots. Rene Eustace photo.

homeland. According to Erma Owings, director of the Ravalli County Museum, Daly staked homesteaders to their claim and bought them out, allowing him to amass most of the 26,000-acre stock farm in one contiguous block just east of present-day Hamilton. World-class thoroughbreds, trotters and pacers trained at the estate's racetracks, which included a covered arena for winter workouts. Distinguished looking Tammany Hall, named for his most famous and favorite race horse, still stands as a local landmark.

Daly ruled his estate with its wooden fences and cottonwood lined highways (still visible today) from a hilltop Victorian mansion completed in 1890. Following his death in 1900 his widow had the structure completely remodeled and enlarged for an additional $40,000 into the imposing Georgian, or Southern Colonial, home that is now hidden from view behind locked gates and a jungle of vegetation. The mansion looks strangely out of place in Montana's Bitterroot, like something out of the set from "Gone With the Wind." Its three floors have 31 rooms and 13 bathrooms. The mansion remains in the family, but has fallen into disrepair. Some locals are concerned that if

action isn't taken quickly this most unique of Montana's historic mansions and a piece of the state's heritage will be lost permanently.

Agricultural euphoria and the number of newly arriving farmers peaked during the Bitterroot's colorful early 20th-century apple boom. Things really took off shortly after the 1905 start-up of construction of the Big Ditch, a 72-mile-long irrigation canal. Still a functional landmark, the ditch carries water from Lake Como at the head of a valley west of Darby, under the Bitterroot River and northward through the east bench areas as far as Florence.

Water from the giant scheme was to be used exclusively in orchards and the largely out-of-state land owners made sure there were plenty. Thousands of acres adjacent to the Big Ditch were sectioned into giant orchard complexes — "Paradise Heights," "Mountain Farm," "Sunny Side;" they sound like modern subdivisions. At least two were among the largest in the Pacific Northwest with more than 1,600 acres planted in trees.

The promoters' plans were simple — build the Big Ditch, lay out the apple orchards, subdivide them into

10-acre tracts (subdividing has a long history in the Bitterroot) and sell them to farmers lured into the area with an aggressive promotional program. Property that developers had purchased for $3.00 to $15.00 per acre would sell for up to $1,000 per acre. In typical boomer-literature fashion, the Bitterroot was billed as *the* fruit producing district in the Pacific Northwest, a place where 10 acres of fruit trees would annually provide a farmer with $5,000 and six months of vacation.

The ad campaign succeeded and even before the 1910 completion of the Big Ditch the east side was rapidly filling with apple boomers, most from the East and Midwest. As a result, county apple production skyrocketed from about 20,000 bushels per year at the turn of the century to more than 300,000 bushels in 1909. By then emphasis was on a large McIntosh variety that found a ready market, especially in New York City. During the height of the boom in the late Teens, 22,000 acres in the county were subdivided into orchards and annual production climbed to almost 400,000 bushels.

101

A

B

(A) St. Joseph Peak in the Bitterroots. Jim Romo photo.
(B) Agriculture remains an important component of the Bitterroot Valley economy. Tom Dietrich photo.
(C) Heart Lake and Pearl Lake on the Montana-Idaho divide. Jim Romo photo.
(D) Log yard of a log-home construction company near Stevensville. John Alwin photo.

C

D

Increasing competition from better suited areas closer to major markets, inability of the Bitterroot growers to develop new markets, and problems with soil fertility, frosts and inadequacy of water rights led to a decline in the valley's harvest. By the late 1940s production was down to a quarter of the all-time high. Most of the trees are gone now and the Bitterroot is no longer a commercial apple producing district, but hundreds of valley residents can trace their lineage back to the apple boomers of the early 20th century.

Orchardists and other farmers found that even though apples could be grown, the Bitterroot was better suited for commercial livestock and dairying. The number of cattle here is minor by state standards, but beef cattle and hay remain the cornerstone of Ravalli County agriculture in the 1980s. Proximity to Missoula and excellent irrigated pasture make the area a natural for dairying, and the county is in the top-three producers in Montana. The closeness of the large Missoula market probably also explains all the Bitterroot chickens, the largest flock among Montana counties. Combined cash receipts from animals and animal products account for more than 80 percent of all agricultural market receipts in Ravalli County.

In a process already seen in other Western Montana valleys, ranchers are being squeezed out by a new breed of subdivider. This time around instead of 10-acre orchard tracts, it is 10-acre ranchettes, which sometimes correspond to the very same 10-acre parcels surveyed in the Teens for the apple boomers.

Loyd Moran, who owns a 180-acre hay and grain operation nine miles northeast of Stevensville, had his place on the market in the summer of 1982. He moved to the valley in the 1950s and remembers that at that time it was largely an agricultural area, with most people living on small farms. "Things started to change in the early to middle '60s," he recalls and "by the late '60s and early '70s we got into a subdivision situation completely." Moran thinks that "basically, agriculture is done in the valley."

The state's Western Agricultural Research Center at Corvallis is emphasizing research with strawberries, raspberries and fruit trees, hoping to give area farmers new crops and possible alternatives to subdividing their ground. Statistics show the number of acres in county farms declining 16 percent between 1969 and 1978.

The ongoing land rush in the Bitterroot dwarfs the apple boom. During the decade of the 1970s county population increased from 14,400 to 22,500, a whopping 56 percent, ranking it first in Western Montana for growth rate. Only 500 of these 8,100 new residents lived in Hamilton and Stevensville, the valley's two largest communities. Almost all were rural residents and the majority settled in the northern half of the county, which has become a "bedroom community" of Missoula. These are the owners of cars with bumper stickers asking others to "Pray for me, I drive Highway 93."

Rural Ravalli County is experiencing a gentrification. Not uncommonly, new arrivals are economically upscale out-of-staters seeking immediate relief from Paradise Syndrome. Many are retirees. A love of horses and a desire for enough acreage to accommodate them is a prime concern. Consistent with Marcus Daly's equine passion, the Bitterroot may be the most horse-conscious place in Montana. Sections around Hamilton with their painted white fences and lush pastures look like they could be outside Lexington, Kentucky.

Six-hundred of the Bitterroot's new residents live in Pinesdale, 10 miles northeast of Hamilton. This 320-acre town, Montana's newest incorporated community, has no business district or residential sections. It is rural and residences are spread over the hillside site.

Pinesdale is populated exclusively by residents who consider themselves fundamentalist Mormons, although that Salt Lake City church has excom-

Left above: The newest crop in this field near Hamilton is a subdivision. The Bitterroot Valley has become Missoula's bedroom. John Alwin photo.
Left below: Main street of Hamilton. John Alwin photo.
Above: Well known to Missoula-area and valley hikers is Blodgett Canyon in the Bitterroots. George Wuerthner photo.

municated many of them for polygamy. Some still do practice polygamy, just as they adhere to other original principles of the Mormon religion as practiced in the 1880s. Polygamy was then considered one of the capstones of Mormon religious beliefs. Pinesdale residents feel that the mainline church has yielded to public pressures and drifted away from the original tenets. As one resident said, "truth doesn't change."

A few Pinesdale citizens are farmers, but most commute to jobs or their own businesses in Hamilton, Missoula or other nearby areas where they blend with non-members. The group runs its own private school and recently purchased a used fire truck. Since land sales are controlled by a Utah corporation, only those who share ideology are permitted to become new residents of this third largest of Bitterroot towns.

The Bitterroot also has attracted a sizable contingent of survivalists, people who want to be in the safest place possible in case of nuclear war or other disasters, including civil insurrection. Some have carefully plotted presumed Soviet targets in the United States and have mapped downwind areas of maximum nuclear fallout. These areas as well as major metropolitan areas, which are also assumed to be most susceptible to a breakdown of law and order, are shunned. Sparcity of population, suitability for farming, and adjacent unsettled forested areas, preferably mountainous terrain, where they might have to retreat even farther for a last stand, are viewed as essentials by the most extreme survivalists. Among the survivalist community the Bitterroot is known as one of these safe havens.

Urbane, "uptown," diverse. This is Missoula, Rattlesnake Mountains in the distance. Tom Dietrich photo.
Below left: Shopper in front of the old Missoula Mercantile, now The Bon, a modernized department store dating from the turn of the century. John Alwin photo.
Below right: Rock Creek in the fall. John Alwin photo.

Missoula

Plaid-shirted loggers, millworkers with lunch buckets, university intellectuals, businessmen in three-piece suits, hold-over hippies and more contemporary "granola people" — Missoula has them all. Butte may claim title to Montana's most mixed population of nationalities, but no community in the state comes close to Missoula's conglomeration of politics, philosophies and occupations. Missoula is a collage of free spirits, a pot that refuses to melt, and one of Montana's most interesting and stimulating cities.

For many around Montana, Missoula is synonymous with loggers, sawmills, plywood and pulp and paper mills. By all measures it is the center of the state's wood products industry. Forest products constitute the single largest component in the community's economic base making Missoula's economy one of the most cyclical of Montana's urban areas.

Five mills and plants in the area employ almost 2,300 people and account for most of the factory employment in the wood products industry. Champion International dominates the local scene with its three facilities, providing approximately 2,000 of these jobs. The efficiency of the modern forest products industry is evident in the company's Missoula operations.

Champion's plywood plant and sawmill at Bonner is the largest local facility with a payroll of 1,000. A substantial portion of the mill's timber is taken off the more than 650,000 acres of company owned or controlled land that lies in a discontinuous swath from just outside Helena to west of Kalispell. All peelable Douglas fir, larch and lower grade ponderosa pine logs are converted into plywood at this softwood plywood plant, the largest in North America. High-grade pine and unpeelable fir and larch logs are processed into lumber at the associated mill.

104

Champion also ships lumber-quality logs to its Missoula sawmill which provides another 200 jobs. Wood waste from the Bonner and Missoula facilities is converted into wood chips and sent to the company's 2,300-acre Hoerner Waldorf (Frenchtown) pulp and paper mill 12 miles west of Missoula. At the 700-employee mill, chips and sawdust from Champion and other mills, and additional chips from low-grade pulp logs produced at the site, are manufactured into linerboard, the two outer sides of cardboard. An almost continuous stream of 262 trucks per day haul in wood chips and lesser amounts of sawdust and logs. Chips that can't be used are burned as hog fuel to help run boilers, but most is processed through digesters, washers, evaporators, bleachers, pressers, and rollers to produce ten-ton rolls of paper, enough each year to fill 13,000 railroad boxcars.

White Pine Sash and Louisiana Pacific round out Missoula's major wood-products employers. The former employs 225, predominantly in the manufacture of window frames. Louisiana Pacific is Missoula's only particleboard mill. It depends entirely on shavings and chips from other mills within a 200-mile radius. What was once a waste product disposed of in tipi burners is used to manufacture a saleable commodity. Louisiana Pacific's market is primarily the furniture and cabinet industry.

In addition to the 2,300-plus millworkers, Missoula's forest products industry also employs hundreds of city-based loggers. Champion has its own logging crews employed in its timberlands division, but like others it also depends on private, contract help known in the trade as "gyppos." They are hired to do everything from felling trees in the woods to hauling logs to mills. Their logging rigs parked in residential areas with trailers stacked on the back of their trucks are a familiar sight in and around Missoula.

Federal workers for the U.S. Forest Service add even more to Missoula's forest-resource employment. Headquarters for the Forest Service's Northern Region is located in the city. Its staff of 600 oversees management of 13 national forests in Montana and three neighboring states just as an additional 170 Missoula-based employees at the Lolo National Forest headquarters supervise that sprawling two-million-acre forest.

Missoula is also synonymous with the University of Montana. It has been an element in

the community ever since Deer Lodge was permanently awarded the prized penitentiary and Missoula was "left" with the state university. Although established by the legislature in 1893, it was not until 1895 that the institution, with a teaching president, four faculty members and an 800-book library, opened its doors to the initial class of 50 students. A city grade school served as temporary quarters until the building of Science Hall and, in 1898, Main Hall. The latter, along with its former carriageway approach and now pedestrian walkway outlining "The Oval," remain the focus of this attractive 200-acre campus at the base of Mount Sentinel.

According to the legislation which established it, U of M's primary mission was liberal education. True to its charge, the College of Arts and Sciences is still the heart of the university. Its

Left top: Sudden growth to the south of Missoula has exceeded the capacity of the infamous Malfunction Junction at Highway 93 and South Avenue. John Alwin photo.
Left: Missoula's identification with forests and forestry is accented by the location there of Region One Headquarters of the U.S. Forest Service and its Smokejumper center. John Alwin photo.
Above: Champion International's pulp—or kraft paper—mill at Frenchtown employs 700. John Alwin photo.

programs include traditional subjects like Philosophy, History, Foreign Languages, Biology and Geography. But the U of M is a liberal arts university with a difference. Seven professional schools add a diversity not normally associated with a liberal arts institution. Students in the schools of Business Administration, Fine Arts, Education, Forestry, Journalism, Pharmacy and Law account for about half the enrollment.

The University of Montana is the second largest school in the state's six-unit university system. In 1982-83 its enrollment of 9,100 was an all-time high. Almost 30 percent of its students are from out-of-state, the highest among Montana colleges and attributable, in part, to the school's reputation for academic excellence which reaches beyond the borders of Montana. The Missoula school ranks right along with Stanford and the University of Washington, and above UCLA and

The University of Montana campus from Mt. Sentinel. Tom Dietrich photo.
The much photographed UM Main Hall. Tom Dietrich photo.

Berkeley as one of the top six west-of-the-Mississippi schools in terms of total number of Rhodes Scholars. Innovativeness is another hallmark of the university. The School of Law, for example, has become a model for rural legal education.

Campus teaching and research are augmented by two unique off-campus facilities. The School of Forestry's Lubrecht Experimental Forest 30 miles to the east in the Potomac Valley is the envy of other forestry schools. The 30,000-acre forest includes a new research building and a rustic complex where 45 to 50 forestry students spend the entire spring quarter each year. Lubrecht is entirely self-sustaining with income from timber sales and grazing leases.

The school's Biological Station at Yellow Bay on Flathead Lake is another valuable U of M facility. It was one of the earliest freshwater biological stations in the nation and today provides staff and students with an unrivaled research lab and field camp. In the late '70s and early '80s the facility served a central role in a comprehensive environmental assessment of the Flathead River drainage. It is assumed the station will continue to be at the forefront of Flathead Lake research and environmental monitoring.

Continuing education classes and the Montana Repertory Theater mean that thousands of

Montanans not attending classes at Missoula can benefit directly from U of M programs. Continuing education provided 164 classes in 36 Montana communities in the 1982-83 school year. Some 2,600 students enrolled in courses that year in towns as dispersed as Eureka, Plains, Anaconda and West Yellowstone, east to Havre, Glasgow and Colstrip. Thanks to the school's theater, the only repertory company between Minneapolis and Seattle, residents in 40 of the state's 56 counties were able to enjoy professional theater productions. The group is especially proud of its service to small towns — 80 percent of the communities on the tour had fewer than 3,000 residents. In these small centers performances became a real community event and averaged 450 people per performance. Thanks to the theater, Montanans who might not otherwise ever see a professional play are able to enjoy classics like "King Lear," "A Streetcar Named Desire," and "On Golden Pond."

Missoula is Rocky Mountain Montana's uncontested regional capital. Area population of 65,000 makes it larger than any other city in the state's westernmost third. Missoula has grown into a Billings- and Great Falls-scale city and now vies with those plains counterparts for dominance in easterly sections of Western Montana.

Retail trade has been a part of Missoula since its founding fathers, Christopher P. Higgins and Frances L. Worden, opened a store at Hell Gate, four miles west of today's downtown in 1860. Located on the Mullan Wagon Road connecting Fort Benton and Walla Walla, it served travelers and the white settlers who were just beginning to take up farming in the district.

Sending back the shoes that didn't fit or the wrong color bedspread from mail order catalogs has been an accepted part of life for most residents in Western Montana for generations. But population growth within Missoula and its trade area coupled with improvements in highway travel have convinced major retail chains to open full-fledged stores in Missoula. Western Montanans are willing to drive up to 150 miles or more one-way to shop in Missoula at least once or twice a year. The 1978 opening of Southgate Mall and its subsequent expansion program has added a new dimension to Missoula's business community and enhanced the city's role as a retail trade center. Even anti-mall types admit that if there must be malls, this 95-store complex is a satisfactory model with its abundance of greenery (some say more trees than Lolo National Forest), natural lighting, liberal use of wood and comfortable resting spots for shoppers. Unfortunately, Southgate Mall has adversely impacted other merchants in the city, especially those in the central business district.

Two-hundred physicians including open-heart and brain surgeons, the latest technologies and most up-to-date facilities make Missoula Western Montana's number-one medical center. According to Dominic Crolla, Director of Development and Public Relations at St. Patrick Hospital, Missoula has more physicians per person than any other city in the country. St. Pat's is the largest of the city's three hospitals. Its service, or catchment, area includes all of Western Montana and sections of north Idaho. Patients from smaller centers from Kalispell to Bozeman are routinely referred to St. Pat's, which is designated as a "tertiary" or highest level medical care center, for medical attention not available back home. Emergency transportation within a 160-mile radius is provided by helicopter ambulance service that delivers patients right to the hospital grounds.

Inconsistent with the Big-Sky, clean-environment image and with its role as a health center, Missoula has some of the most polluted air

in the state. An occasional commuter wearing a surgical mask, pollution alerts, school recesses cancelled because of unhealthy air, a local 24-hour pollution-alert hotline, and "air outlook" graphs in the daily papers sound like Los Angeles, but they are elements of life in Missoula. It is a serious problem. Past studies have shown a positive correlation between the monthly hospital admission rate for acute upper respiratory infection and the average monthly pollution level, and Missoula school children have been found to have lower lung function capacity when compared with their counterparts in Montana communities with cleaner air. The community is in violation of the Clean Air Act and already is under a federal moratorium on construction of major new pollution sources. The U.S. Environmental Protection Agency has threatened the loss or restriction of federal funding for such things as highways and sewer projects until compliance is attained. Air pollution is a serious enough problem to convince some people not to live in the city and to encourage others to leave.

Missoula's still-growing pollution problem can be explained by a combination of factors. Among these is a relatively large population squeezed into the narrow and restricted Missoula Valley, hemmed in on all sides by high mountains. In summer prevailing westerlies sometimes bring in odors from the west to remind residents of the wood products dominated economic base, but the community generally enjoys good air quality. Smoke, dust, auto emissions and other pollutants usually mix with cleaner air and are flushed from the valley by mountain breezes. Winter is an entirely different story.

With the arrival of cooler nights in fall Missoulians start turning to their wood-burning stoves. It is estimated that more than half of Missoula's homes, at least 13,000, burn wood for heat. By itself that might not be a problem if it weren't for the region's all-too-frequent inversions. With warmer air above capping the valley, wood smoke and other pollutants are trapped below. For residents of South Hill high on the mountain flank on the southeast side, the trapped blanket of pollution is viewed from above and sometimes looks almost thick enough to walk on. As air pollution increases and reaches a threshold particulate level it triggers a Stage I Alert by the Missoula City/County Health Department. An alert means people voluntarily are to refrain from using their wood-burning stoves unless it is their only source of heat. Residents are advised to limit driving to necessary trips and elderly, children and heart and lung patients are cautioned to reduce outdoor activity. Progressively higher particulate counts can lead to a Stage II Air-pollution Warning, Stage III Air-pollution Emergency, or even a Stage IV Air-pollution Crisis.

The growing problem prompted the county to adopt stricter air-quality laws in 1981. The health department has the authority to issue citations to homeowners who continue to burn wood once a Stage II warning has been issued. Missoula's air pollution generally does not exceed the Alert status, but such conditions can be protracted owing to meteorology and to homeowners who refuse to comply with voluntary requests to suspend burning. The longest pollution episode was a 19-day spell in 1977.

In 1983 the community was moving toward new, stiffer anti-pollution regulations. Much of the attention has been focused on wood-burning stoves and fireplaces, since they account for 50 to 60 percent of Missoula's air pollution. Some initial proposals were controversial. These included a permit system to assure that all new wood stoves would meet certain efficiency standards and required replacement of conventional, existing stoves within five years with new, "high tech" wood burners that emit substantially fewer particulates. In true Missoula style, a grass roots group called United Woodburners of Missoula formed immediately to protest, calling the proposals "un-American."

Wrangling over solutions to community issues extends beyond air pollution to traffic congestion, subdivisions, and most recently over a sign at the airport. Missoulians seem to thrive on controversy. According to Mayor Bill Cregg, controversy is as synonymous with his town as government is with Helena, grain is with Great Falls, and copper was to Butte. Says the mayor, "everyone is a quasi-expert on many subjects and is very outspoken . . . people are very involved in issues like peace, the environment, and minority rights." Cregg describes the city as "a tempest in a teapot."

Missoula has an interesting balance of working-class and professionals, a fine university, and access to outdoor recreation with one wilderness area just 1½ miles from a city bus stop. For most residents the community's argumentative nature is viewed as positive, air pollution solvable and the cyclic, wood products economy survivable.

THE FAR WEST

The Far West is Pacific Northwest Montana. Sights, sounds, and smells here are Northwest — mountains shrouded by lush and varied forests with towering coniferous trees, the whine of chain saws and the roar of logging trucks, the smell of sawdust and moss, and a pervasive wet, snowy and foggy clime.

The highest mountain peaks are mostly in the 7,000-foot range. Most summits reach elevations of 5,000 to 6,000 feet and are more rounded than in any other section of Montana. Nowhere else in the state are mountain slopes as nearly covered by trees. The Far West's forest estate blankets the region, extending across valleys and over most mountain crests. It is a prime element in the region's environmental character. The only sizable non-forested areas are higher reaches of the Cabinet and Bitterroot ranges above treeline and sections of cleared valley floors where only the efforts of man keep forests from re-invading. Both Lincoln and Mineral counties are more than 90 percent forested and neighboring counties aren't too far behind.

Forests of this region have no equal in Montana. The growth potential of commercial forest land is classified on the basis of cubic feet of wood growth per acre per year. Sites designated Class V, the lowest, produce only 20 to 49 cubic feet of wood per acre per year, while Class I yields more than 165 (an average single-family, wood-frame home contains about 900 cubic feet of wood). The 2.4 million acre Kootenai National Forest, which falls entirely within the Far West, ranks number-one among Montana's national forests in terms of growth potential. Thirty-six percent of the Kootenai is either Class I or II, whereas only six percent of the Lewis and Clark, five percent of the Gallatin, and zero percent of Custer National Forest are so designated. Sections of other national forests, including the Flathead, that extend into the region also rank near the top for productivity.

Not only are these forests prolific, they are also the most luxuriant and diverse in Montana. Moisture-loving trees like western red cedar, western hemlock, grand fir, western white pine and mountain hemlock add to the species mix. The Ross Creek Cedar Grove Scenic Area on the wet west flank of the Cabinets is an excellent spot to sense the productivity of these forests. Spared by the great fires that swept Western Montana early this century, this popular 100-acre grove still harbors forest monarchs more than 500 years old. Giant red cedars up to 12 feet in diameter and 175 feet tall, and towering hemlock and white pine produce a dense cover and a cool, humid and dark world. Farther north a few woodland caribou, an extremely rare species in the lower 48 states, may still subsist on their requisite diet of lichens that grow only on spruce and fir in mature forests.

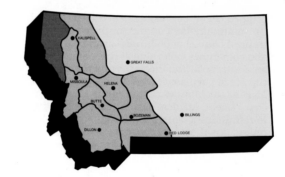

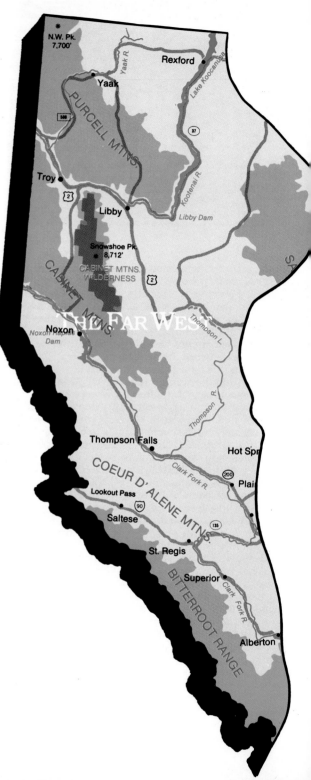

Right: Little Ibex Peak. Cabinet Mountains Wilderness area. Jeff Gnass photo. Top: Use of a CB radio is advised on the Yaak River road to learn of the approach of kamakazi log trucks. John Alwin photo. Bottom: Deer crossings, cattle crossings, yes, but how often do you see signs for bighorn sheep crossings. John Alwin photo.

A

B

C

(A) Vintage logging at an unknown date. Montana Historical Society photo.
(B,C) Logging isn't always big business. John Alwin photos.
(D) Although wood may be a renewable resource, it seems to take forever for the landscape to regain its beauty after logging operations. These are clearcuts east of Yaak. John Alwin photo.

The Far West's thriving forest lands account for approximately half of Montana's timber harvest. Lincoln County alone has generated almost 25 percent of state production in recent years. Lumber mills are everywhere and vary from unnamed, one-man enterprises to the huge St. Regis mill in Libby, the region's principal wood products center. Other sawmill towns include Thompson Falls, Superior, Eureka and Troy. Workers at these mills, loggers employed in the woods and truckers who haul within the region and to other mills in Kalispell, Columbia Falls, Missoula and Bonner dominate employment in the Far West.

If Montana is to continue to support a wood products industry, the Far West, not the commercially marginal forests of the Broad Valley Rockies or the Yellowstone Rockies, must be the main contributor. In 1983 environmentalists were concerned that at least the Kootenai National Forest was being expected to give too much. The proposed Kootenai National Forest Plan released that year projected timber harvest would increase from 215 million to 388 million board feet during the 50-year planning period, with greater access to timber provided by a doubling of road mileage. Vocal wilderness and wildlife groups focused on plans to build an additional 6,000 miles of roads which would bring the total system to 12,000 miles. One critic calculated that such a road building effort would leave the forest with a road every 350 yards

D

within the Kootenai's 1.6 million actively managed acres.

A roaded remoteness has been a Far West characteristic for decades, the legacy of a long history of logging. All recognize that access roads are a necessity of logging, but some feel the 1983 Kootenai plan went too far. The uproar had an impact on forest planners and new projected road miles are expected to be significantly less when the final forest plan is released in 1984.

Unlike our Yellowstone Rockies or Glacier-Bob regions, the Far West lacks extensive roadless areas hundreds of thousands of acres in size. Except for the Cabinet Mountains Wilderness and the proposed Scotchman Wilderness astride the Montana-Idaho border, few large sections are more than two or three miles from at least a primitive road.

The Yaak River Road is probably the region's most famous backcountry road. From the south it strikes north from Highway 200 just east of the Idaho border, past beautiful Yaak Falls, through tiny Yaak and then over to Lake Koocanusa. The narrow road winds through some of the most remote roaded country in the state. Extensive timber harvesting in the region means swift-moving logging trucks are common. Truck drivers announce their approach by calling out mile markers on CB channel 22, and motorists are advised to pull over and make room for these backcountry Mario Andrettis. Despite efforts by the Protect the Yaak Committee, the final 17 unpaved miles of the Yaak Road were being readied for hard surfacing in the summer of 1983.

Like its productive forests, the Far West's hydro-electric landscape is consistent with its Pacific Northwest nature. Abundant river flows, good stream gradient, and narrow valleys suitable for dam construction make this the prime area in Montana for major power dams. Along the Clark Fork the Montana

A

B

C

(A) The Yaak River south of Yaak. John Alwin photo.
(B) The Kootenai River. Rick Graetz photo.
(C) The Clark Fork River near Noxon. George Wuerthner photo.
(D) Settler's barn and cabin, Pleasant Valley, in the Kootenai National Forest. Jeff Gnass photo.

Power Company's run-of-river Thompson Falls Dam and Washington Water Power's Noxon Rapids Dam are major power producers. Although the dam is just across the border in Idaho, most of the reservoir behind Washington Water Power's Cabinet Gorge Dam is in Montana. As of the early 1980s the region's other major river, the Kootenai, was slowed only by the Corps of Engineers' Libby Dam. Completed in 1975, the multipurpose dam was permitted under the 1961 Columbia River Treaty, an agreement between Canada and the United States for the coordinated development and sharing of water-related benefits within the Columbia River Basin. The 91-mile-reservoir behind the dam, Lake Koocanusa ("Koo" for Kootenai, "can" for Canada, and "usa" for U.S.A.) reaches 42 miles into Canada. If power interests have their way, two new Kootenai River dams will soon join the Libby.

D

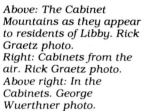

Above: The Cabinet
Mountains as they appear
to residents of Libby. Rick
Graetz photo.
Right: Cabinets from the
air. Rick Graetz photo.
Above right: In the
Cabinets. George
Wuerthner photo.

Plans for a Kootenai Falls dam and a Libby
reregulation dam are highly controversial. The
quarter-billion-dollar Kootenai Falls project has
received the greatest publicity. It has been proposed by
Northern Lights, Inc., an Idaho power cooperative, and
seven Montana cooperatives. It calls for construction of
a 925-foot-long, 30-foot-tall, concrete and steel dam
that would span the Kootenai River at the crest of
Kootenai Falls, 11 miles west of Libby. Even though a
run-of-river dam, it would back up the Kootenai for a
distance of 4.5 miles. Water within the reservoir would
flow into an intake structure and fall about 150 feet to
a tunnel that would carry it to an underground
powerhouse. Once through the generators a discharge
tunnel would return the water to the river about one
mile downstream from the dam. Maximum peak power
output would be 144 megawatts (approximately one-
third that of Libby Dam) and average output would be
58 megawatts.

The battle lines have been drawn in what has developed into a classic conflict between pro-and anti-development camps. Expressions by advocates and opponents to the project have been predictable. Proponents say their high unemployment region needs the 500 construction jobs the project would bring and that the power is needed if the region is ever going to see new industrial growth. Most would admit that the falls is scenic, but as one local lady says, "you can't eat it or pay your bills with it." One Libby resident feels that "every bit of water going over the falls could be producing electricity for the benefit of all. It is a shame it is going to waste." Another project backer in Troy believes that natural resources like Kootenai Falls "are God-given to be used as we need them."

Opponents point to the project's adverse environmental impacts that include altered aquatic and riparian habitats, impacts on fish, the Kootenai Falls bighorn sheep herd, and other wildlife. They cannot fathom destroying the Pacific Northwest's last falls on a major river for short-term economic benefits and only a few permanent jobs after completion. Those awed by the falls' beauty argue that a guaranteed minimum flow of 750 cubic feet per second over the falls, less than half the record low flow, would leave the falls aesthetically impotent. Northern Lights' proposal to use concrete structures textured and colored to mimic natural rock below the dam to direct flows and visually minimize dewatering of the falls adds insult to injury. Loss of archeological sites and the historic portage used by fur trader David Thompson and despoilation of an area sacred to the Kootenai Indians are additional issues raised by opposition.

Montana's Far West is a popular tourist area. Sightseeing, hiking, camping, horseback riding, fishing, hunting, boating, snowmobiling and skiing bring in thousands each year. Catering to these visitors is second economically to the wood products industry in most towns.

Lincoln County is now Western Montana's number-one mineral producer since the suspension of mining at Butte. Two large, world-class mines account for most production.

The older of the two is W. R. Grace Company's 200-employee vermiculite mine nine miles northwest of Libby. Vermiculite is a mineral with excellent insulative properties, and is also used in more than 100 other ways. Each year this operation vies with a South African counterpart for title of world's largest vermiculite mine. W. R. Grace markets its product internationally under the "Zonolite" label.

Seventeen miles south of Troy, on the west flank of the Cabinet Mountains, Asarco's new silver-copper mine employs 350 workers. Production began in 1981 and in 1982 it was the nation's largest silver producer

Montana's Amish

You get there by taking the bridge across Lake Koocanusa just south of Rexford. Heading north on the paved west-shore road, which doesn't show on many highway maps, watch for the sign directing you to the Kootenai General Store. In a few miles ease up on the accelerator — this is Amish country and their horse-drawn carriages regularly travel this stretch of road.

Montana's only Amish community began taking form in 1975 when three members purchased 2,700 acres just south of the Canadian border. Other Amish joined them, mostly from Midwestern states including Michigan, Ohio and Indiana, and today the settlement numbers more than 100 in about 20 families. A short supply of agricultural land limits ranching to three or four families; others find employment in an Amish owned buggy shop, harness shop, and sawmill-log home plants, while still others work in the nearby Tobacco Plains.

Amish are an Anabaptist group, like Montana's much more numerous Hutterites. "A lot of people figure we're just like the Hutterites," says 33-year-old Amish farmer Steve Kauffman, "but we're really quite different." A belief in adult baptism, pacifism, and a plainness of dress and household furnishings are shared characteristics, but some differences are conspicuous. Hutterites live communally in colonies several thousand acres in size and use all the latest technologies from

computerized milking systems to huge four-wheel drive tractors. Montana's Amish, on the other hand, live independently in single family homes on their own property. They shun modern innovations, depending on horse and buggy for personal transportation, live without electricity, radio or television, and rely on horses for farming.

Life in their Rexford community is slow-paced and closely knit, perhaps more the way it was in pioneering Montana. Women make most of the clothes worn by family members and put up much of the food they consume. Families tend to be large by non-Amish standards; a couple planning a "small" family might have four or five children. Babies are delivered at home by a midwife and without drugs, but with "lots of moral support," says expectant mother Linda Kauffman. Married men all wear beards and females over three years old wear a "covering," or bonnet.

Things spiritual and of the heart are paramount to the Amish. They have a strong sense of harmony and believe the elements of one's life should be in balance. "Things in excess aren't good," as one Amish put it. Their concern for avoiding idols explains their desire not to be the sole subject of a photograph.

Religious services are held in family homes instead of a church, which is the primary reason why Amish-built houses in the area are quite large with at least one generous room or pair of interconnecting rooms. Worship services are conducted on alternate Sundays with men and

Kootenai Country supports a relatively new settlement of Amish families. Believing in simplicity of dress and avoiding technology in their daily lives, they quietly farm and operate cottage industries such as the buggy and harness shop shown here. John Alwin photos.

women segregated on opposite sides of the room. On non-church Sundays members hold a singing and dinner for young people.

The Amish community maintains its own school, taught by an Amish teacher. After finishing the eighth grade or upon reaching age 16 children usually discontinue schooling. For many, the years between 16 and 20 are the most trying; this is the time when it is most likely that an individual will strike out on his own in the English, or non-Amish, world. At least half return.

Many, perhaps even a majority of, adults in this community have at some time in their lives held jobs in the outside, English world. Most are quite knowledgeable of the non-Amish ways. Although isolated from mainstream America by design, members may subscribe to newspapers, weekly news and other magazines and even occasionally take cross-country vacations by bus. They have chosen and adhere to their religion and its tenets, not out of ignorance, but out of personal preference.

Superior is almost in the shadow of the interstate highway, but its main street keeps a "hometown" feeling. John Alwin photo.

Thompson Falls is another community deep in the valleys of the Far West, so deep in fact that telephone service didn't reach from Thompson Falls to the Montana-Idaho border until the late '50s. John Alwin photo.

at 4.3 million ounces. The essentially flat Precambrian-age ore body is buried 1,000 feet below the summit of Mt. Vernon and measures 7,400 feet long, 1,800 feet wide and 60 feet thick. It is being mined by an underground method dubbed room-and-pillar which leaves sections of the ore body as supports every 45 feet. The method should allow mining of at least 80 percent of the ore over a projected 16-year life.

Asarco and U.S. Borax Corporation think the Cabinets may have additional commercial deposits of copper and silver. Both have been conducting very controversial mineral explorations and core drilling within the Cabinet Mountains Wilderness, permitted by law until December 31, 1983. The Forest Service has imposed strict controls on procedures, but environmentalists are concerned that the explorations and any subsequent mineral production, also possible under the Wilderness Act, may adversely impact the area's small and struggling grizzly population.

The Kootenai National Forest estimates that the entire Cabinet-Yaak ecosystem may contain only 15 to 20 of these bears, Montana's most threatened grizzlies. The relatively small size of their total available habitat, their semi-isolation from other grizzly populations, and the cumulative effects of mining, logging, and human habitation make their continued survival uncertain. Their small numbers alone may doom them. Some biologists think the population may already have slipped below the level necessary to maintain a healthy, reproducing gene pool. With numbers so precariously low, the loss of even one bear could be devastating to the entire population.

Agriculture is of minor importance in the Far West. Valleys are too narrow for extensive farming and forests too dense to provide much grazing. Lincoln and Mineral counties, both entirely within the region, have the least cropland of any county in the state. Combined they total 4,832 square miles, but have only about 20 square miles (approximately 14,000 acres) of cropland, most in the Tobacco Plains outside Eureka. All but 1,000 acres of the two-county total are planted in hay, a reflection of the overriding emphasis on livestock production.

A heavy regional dependence on the wood products industry, mining and tourism means the area's economy is subject to a pronounced boom-bust cycle. During periods of economic recession demand for wood and minerals is down. Difficult economic times also mean fewer tourists, especially since most travel considerable distances from out-of-state areas. The 1981-83 recession hit the region hard and counties in the Far West registered the highest unemployment in the state with figures for Lincoln County climbing to almost 40 percent in late 1982.

The Far West may be the closest thing to the woodsy, mountainous image most out-of-staters have of Rocky Mountain Montana. They sense that the Glacier National Park section of the Columbia Rockies is a one-of-a-kind area and relatively few visit the Bob Marshall Wilderness complex. The dryness and openness of the Broad Valley Rockies take most by surprise, but the heavily forested and closely-spaced mountains of the Far West, the winding roads switchbacking through huckleberry and lupine fields, and the occasional moose browsing in roadside streams fit preconceived notions. A sparsity of population and small towns limited to discontinuous stringers of habitation in narrow valleys also conform to the image.

Libby

The advertising slogan for Libby-brand fruits and vegetables used to be "if it's Libby, Libby, Libby, you will love it, love it, love it." That jingle aptly describes the reaction of most first-time visitors to the town of Libby, Montana.

Among Western Montana's towns, Libby may have infected a higher percentage of its visitors with Paradise Syndrome than any other community. The most flattering adjectives can't do justice to its setting — carved out of an engulfing coniferous forest landscape skirted by the Kootenai River with the dramatic western backdrop of the Cabinet Mountains' 7,000-foot peaks rising a mile high.

Libby has the look and feel of a Pacific Northwest municipality. This is Western Montana's only town-size community (population of more than 2,500) buried deep in the trees, not just near or next to the forest. It is reminiscent of comparable size communities in northern Idaho and western sections of Washington and Oregon. With these western counterparts Libby shares a Northwest-like climate, best described as modified Pacific maritime. Its winter climate is among the least severe in the state and must seem almost subtropical to residents of northeastern Montana. On the average, temperatures drop to zero or colder only 12 days per year and on just 38 days does it remain below freezing.

Consistent with its Northwest identity the wood products industry is Libby's major employer. The sprawling St. Regis mill on the south side of town is the largest with a payroll of approximately 700. Employment at the combination plywood plant-stud mill-sawmill peaked at almost 1,200 in the late '70s, but has dropped with plant modernization and increased mechanization. This aspect of the community's Northwest heritage is proudly proclaimed each July during Logger Days. The four-day celebration is now almost a quarter century old. Its competition in the manly arts of sawing, axe throwing, pole tossing and log rolling draw an international field of contestants.

Left: Libby enjoys the backdrop of the Cabinet Mountains. John Alwin photo.
Below left: St. Regis Company is the largest employer in Libby. John Alwin photo.
Above: Lake Koocanusa has added another dimension to the Libby area in the form of water recreation. This is the bridge across the lake near Rexford. John Alwin photo.

Efforts are underway to reduce the community's dependence on the extremely cyclical wood products industry. Two major mining operations have helped. W. R. Grace's vermiculite mine provides 200 high paying jobs and some Libbyites work at the Asarco copper-silver mine south of Troy, commuting the 65 miles round trip each day. As headquarters city for 2.4 million-acre Kootenai National Forest, Libby benefits with 230 local jobs.

Tourism is another mainstay of the local economy. Winter recreation is increasing, but visitor numbers are still strongly skewed to the summer months. It is hoped the proposed major Great Northern ski area 17 miles south of town will help boost winter recreational use.

The 1980 census tallied a population of 2,748 within the city limits, although the Chamber of Commerce counts 10,960 within a four-mile area.

Like many other Western Montana communities, Libby too, has experienced a recent influx of new residents from out of state. Rich Schneider, publisher of the local *Western News*, says his office is innundated by hopeful tourists looking for jobs. They fall in love with the area and want to live there. "Often people have just had some shocking experience back home and want to get out, leave the rat race and all the people," Schneider observes. "I really discourage them," he says, "jobs are really tough here."

According to locals, Californians are evidently most susceptible to Paradise Syndrome in the Libby area. Many of the large real estate transactions involve them. Debbi DeShazer, co-owner of Realty World-Fisher Realty, says that buying acreage with a private lake is especially popular. Such property in the 200- to 700-acre range sells for $500,000 to $1.5 million.

THE FLATHEAD

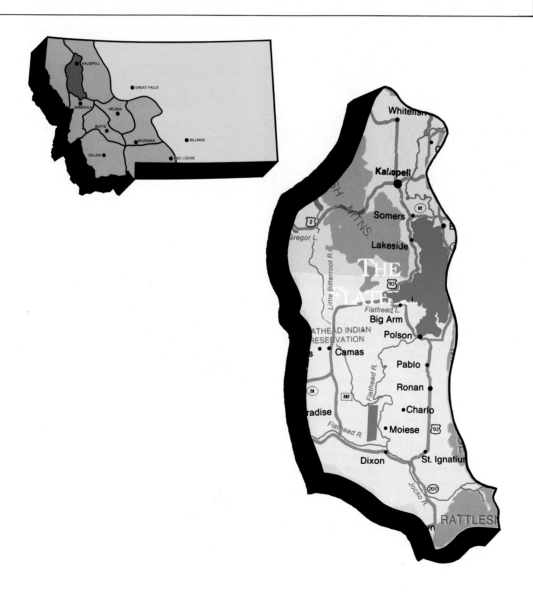

The Flathead is one of our smallest regions. Its boundaries are mostly topographic and trace the crest of a highland. Topography here is moderately diverse, but level to gently rolling terrain dominates and contrasts with the surrounding, heavily forested highlands. This is basically a land between the mountains. Noticeable exceptions include the comparatively low southern end of the Salish Mountains, the northern tip of the Swan Range and the Big Mountain portion of the Whitefish Range. All were included because of their strong tie to the central lowland.

Three major overlapping sub-regions take in most of the Flathead: 1) on the south a largely rural and agricultural Flathead Indian Reservation; 2) a central recreation-oriented Flathead Lake area; and 3) a more urbanized Upper Flathead Valley.

The Flathead Indian Reservation, Western Montana's only reservation, accounts for more than half our Flathead Region. Prior to the arrival of white settlers, this territory was home to the upper Pend d'Oreille tribe, although the friendly neighboring Kootenai, Kalispell and Salish (Flathead) also frequented the area. All except the Kootenai shared the Salish language, and enjoyed peaceful relations and a relatively prosperous life in and adjacent to this climatically moderate and wildlife-rich lowland.

Furs and religious zeal brought the area's first whites. White trappers previously had crisscrossed the area trapping beaver and other fur bearers and moved on without erecting permanent structures. Hudson's Bay Company trader, Angus McDonald, is credited with building the first trading post, Fort Connah, within the present reservation borders in 1846-47. This was the last Hudson's Bay Company post built in the United States and remained active until 1871, mainly under the charge of McDonald. Following its closure he spent most of the remainder of his life in the area farming and raising a family, the decendants of whom are numerous in the valley to this date. McDonald Peak in the Mission Mountains is named after this Montana pioneer.

Less than a decade after the establishment of Fort Connah, an even more important complex began taking form a few miles to the south, at a place the upper Pend d'Oreille Indians called "Snielemen." In the fall of 1854 the Jesuit Order's St. Ignatius Mission erected its first temporary buildings, one of which still stands. It quickly eclipsed Fort Connah as the nexus of local activity. Religious services began immediately, and before long, a water-powered flour mill and sawmill were in operation. Early experimentation with cropping proved successful, and soon productive vegetable gardens and large wheat and barley fields proved the area's farming potential. Eventually an

Above: A fresh snow highlights the Mission Mountains. Tom Dietrich photo.
Far left: The Flathead River. George Wuerthner photo.
Left: Young dancer ready for competition at the Elmo Pow Wow. John Alwin photo.

The Flathead is Western Montana's only Indian Reservation. (A) It was homesteaded by whites in 1910. This is Ravalli during the land boom. Montana Historical Society photo.
(B) Charlie McDonald, remembers the fences going up on his homeland.
(C) Agnes Vandenburg conducts a summer school in tribal customs. (D) Indian dancing at Elmo Pow Wow. John Alwin photos.

Indian school and hospital were added and a distinctly Indian community, the first within the reservation, developed. The large brick church that now dominates the community was built in 1891. Its renowned 54 frescoes were painted over a 14-month period by Brother Joseph Carignano, S.J., mission cook.

The Flathead Reservation came into being on July 16, 1855, with the signing of the Hell Gate Treaty. It designated the present reservation and left open the possibility of a detached and unspecified southern portion in the Bitterroot Valley as a reserve for three tribes — the Salish (Flathead), the upper Pend d'Oreille, and the Kootenai. The Pend d'Oreille and the Kootenai immediately settled in the northern reservation, while the last of the Flathead did not move onto the Flathead Reservation until 1891. The 1,243,000-acre reserve is now officially home to the "Confederated Salish and Kootenai Tribes."

Developments in the early 1900s explain much of the character of today's reservation. In May, 1909, the Flathead Reservation was thrown open for white settlement, but actual homesteading was not permitted

until 1910. During the previous several years each tribal member had been allotted 40, 80 or 160 acres. The approximately 1,000,000 acres that remained was the land open for settlement by non-Indians that year.

Eighty-six-year-old Charles McDonald of St. Ignatius, one of Angus McDonald's grandsons, recalls the surge of white homesteaders who fanned out across the reservation in 1910. He watched tents and tar-paper shacks sprout all around and the once open prairie being partitioned by a mesh of barbed wire fences. Suddenly cross-country horseback trips, especially after dark, became dangerous even on familiar paths. Charles remembers more than once coming up too quickly to an unexpected barbed wire fence that some new farmer had strung across the trail earlier in the day. These same farmers greatly expanded irrigation and planted trees where there had been only native grassland. Charles recalls that before the homesteaders the area "from Post Creek clear over to the Flathead River . . . was just one big prairie — not one tree except for one west of Charlo, a little old thorn bush."

The opening of the reservation to non-native homesteaders explains why today only 5,400 of its 22,000 residents are of Indian descent. Of that figure just 3,100 are enrolled members of the Confederated Salish and Kootenai tribes. In and around the small town of Elmo on the west shore of Flathead Lake most Indians are of Kootenai descent, while Flathead and Pend d'Oreille cluster around St. Ignatius and Arlee. The non-Indian population predominates in the major reservation towns of Polson, Ronan, Charlo and Hot Springs.

Non-Indians not only dominate the reservation in terms of population, they also own the majority of businesses, approximately half the area within the reservation boundary and most of the agricultural land. Reservation agriculture makes Lake County the state's biggest producer west of the Continental Divide in terms of cash receipts from crops and livestock. Emphasis is on cattle and feed crops, but potato production ranks second in the state and cherries have long been a specialty item in the Flathead Lake portion. If experimentation with vineyards on the west slope of the Mission Mountains east of Polson proves successful, grapes and wine could become new reservation products.

With the prevalence of non-Indians it takes an added effort by the tribes to perpetuate their cultural traditions and retain their Indian identity. That is why the work of 82-year-old Agnes Vandenburg is so important. Each summer, under the auspices of the reservation's cultural committee, she runs her own camp on the wooded east slope of Squaw Peak in the reservation's south end. Her summer campers call her "Ya-Ya," Salish for grandmother.

Cherry trees in bloom along Flathead Lake. Tom Dietrich photo.

Flathead Cherries

Mention Flathead in an agricultural context and most Montanans immediately think of Flathead cherries. This specialty crop has been a part of area agriculture for generations. A mid-summer excursion to buy cherries at stands along Highway 35 has become an eagerly anticipated part of the annual routine for hundreds of Montana families.

The presence of a Flathead cherry industry can be linked to Flathead Lake and the micro-climate this large water body produces. Water cools and warms more slowly than land. During winters Flathead Lake is chilled and occasionally freezes fairly extensively. With the arrival of balmier spring days, the lake heats up more slowly than land areas. This cold body tends to chill nearshore areas and retard the arrival of spring weather. Even if the lake doesn't freeze solid, the air remains cool enough to delay the budding of cherry blossoms, helping to minimize the danger of loss to late killing frosts. In the fall the warmed lake waters act as a heat sink, warming adjacent land areas and reducing the likelihood of early frosts that might kill trees.

Since prevailing winds in the area are out of the west, the "lake effect" is most pronounced along the east shore. Winds blowing across the water pick up moisture and make this the wetter side. This is where most cherry orchards are found, within a quarter-mile to one-mile-wide strip along the eastern shore. There are hundreds of orchards

Top: The industry depends on the labor of pickers, who call themselves "fruit bums." John Alwin photo.
Bottom: The orchards of Flathead, such as this one along the east shore, have tempted many a retiree into agribusiness. John Alwin photo.

in the Flathead Lake area, but most are small, and combined, total about 600 acres.

Many orchards are owned by hobby farmers for whom the cherry business is strictly supplemental to their main livelihoods. A large number live outside the region and even out of state, lured into the Flathead cherry business by the prospects of summers in the country, the area's outstanding scenic qualities, tax write-offs, and theoretically, additional income.

By early July an army of migrant workers begins swarming into the area to hand-pick the harvest. The majority are professional pickers, or "fruit bums," who move from region to region following the harvest of various fruits. Many pickers are

from Washington fruit-belt cities like Yakima and the Tri-Cities, others from as far away as California, Arizona, Texas and Mexico. "We get everything from some pretty tough characters to real nice people," says 40-year cherry veteran, Walt Staves at the east shore Big Sky Cherries packing plant. Since July is somewhat of a slack season in many western U.S. fruit areas, adequate labor usually is not a problem.

Workers normally pick from 600 to 1,400 pounds per day and in the 1982 harvest were paid an average of $2.00 for each 20-pound capacity box, called a lug. Locally, experienced Mexican workers have a reputation for speed and can net more than $100 a day.

Picked cherries are speedily trucked to four packing plants where they are washed and cooled, hand sorted and packed for shipment. The Kalispell plant is the largest. During its two and a half to three weeks of operation per year it employs 425 people in two shifts. Marketing of Flathead cherries is handled through a broker in Yakima, Washington. The Lambert sweet cherries are sold in New York, Florida, Texas and California, and Canada, Japan, Taiwan, Hong Kong and Sweden.

On a national scale Flathead cherry production is small-time generally accounting for only one to two percent of the harvest. But locally it's a major industry. Between 1973 and 1982 the annual crop averaged around 2,200 tons and had a value of just under $1.5 million.

Walt Staves at the Big Sky plant is pessimistic about the future of the cherry industry. He doesn't think there will be an east shore cherry industry in 20 years. High costs of land, orchard equipment and supplies and labor, he believes, will be the demise of the industry. Part-time orchardist Harry Medland has 10 acres of trees on the east shore. "I'm not optimistic about the future of cherries in this area," he admits. He points to persistent problems with hail damage and the all-too-frequent late rains which split open the fruit. Another handicap for Flathead cherries is their late season. "By the time we come onto the market people back East have been looking at cherries in the market for 45 days," Medland points out. Other locals identify subdivisions and summer home development as the greatest threats to the industry. The narrow, near-shore strip that is well suited to cherry growing is also the most highly regarded recreational land.

Above: Another attempt by the tribes to control their identity within the reservation is the new Salish Kutenai College in Pablo. John Alwin photo.

Above: West St. Mary's Peak. David Hall photo.
Middle, top and bottom: St. Ignatius Mission. Tom Dietrich, John Alwin.

"What I'm trying to do is get my tribe back where it should be," Agnes says, "people are trying to be too modern." At the camp visitors learn traditional Indian ways including tanning hides, making snowshoes and saddles, use of herbs, and local legends and tales. "I teach them everything that I know," says the Ya-Ya. During its May to August operation in 1982 more than 800 attended, mostly Indians.

The challenge of retaining traditional ways and at the same time moving the tribes forward into the last decades of the 20th century is apparent in the list of courses offered at the reservation's Salish Kootenai College in Pablo. The catalog for the 400-student school lists courses including Hide Tanning, Drum Making, Beading, and Dancing Outfit Construction, along with Word Processing, Advanced Programming, and Aerial Photo Interpretation.

Few reservations in the country can rival the spectacular and varied natural environment of the Flathead — the towering 9,000-foot peaks of the Missions, the verdant valleys and the crystal-clear waters of the southern half of Flathead Lake. Even with half its original lands deeded to non-Indians, the sprawling Flathead Reservation remains resource rich. The tribes control about 400,000 acres of forested land and 69,000 acres of surface water. Oil and gas have yet to be found in commercial quantities, but in early 1983 a California drilling company announced its intention to drill a 15,000-foot well south of Flathead Lake to test this section of Montana's Overthrust Belt. The reservation's own team of environmental planners and other contracted specialists should help assure wise resource development.

Flathead Lake is the focal point within our Flathead region. The 37-mile-long beauty, with more than 185 miles of shoreline and an area of 188 square miles, is the largest natural freshwater lake west of the Mississippi River. It is one of Western Montana's most prized natural recreational resources and is a national treasure.

An ancient Indian legend attributes the lake's great size and its Flathead River outlet to the work of a giant beaver that once inhabited an earlier, smaller lake long before the arrival of Indians. As the legend goes, the lake originally did not drain out of the south end, but rather emptied to the west, via Big Arm Bay. As the beaver grew to gargantuan proportions, so too, did his need for water. Eventually his higher dams caused water to run out the lake's lower south shore. He swam to that end and built a gigantic dam that spanned the valley from the mountains on the east to those on the west. Water filled behind the dam forming an even larger lake until one night a big chinook melted a deep snowpack resulting in a huge torrent of water breaking the dam at its weakest point. Water poured out the gap, forming the Flathead River.

If the word glacier is substituted for beaver, this Indian legend is a fair approximation of the evolution of Flathead Lake and River. The lake once did drain to the west via Big Arm and a large glacially deposited ridge (Polson Moraine) dammed the lake and was bisected by the Flathead River which still drains to the south.

Thanks to the work of the Flathead Lobe during the last Ice Age, or the more recent efforts of a giant beaver if you are a supporter of the Indian legend, the valley is blessed with one of the state's most popular water recreation and resort areas. Large size and outstanding scenery make Flathead especially cherished by boaters. Three marinas, one each at Lakeside, Polson and Woods Bay, sailing yacht clubs at Somers and Polson and more than a dozen public boat-launching ramps serve the lake's flotilla of watercraft.

Ralph Hoyt, owner of Lakeside Marina on the west shore, describes the lake as "the last frontier." He is originally from the East Coast and still is amazed at the relatively light use of Flathead compared to even the most marginal waters back home. Sparsity of regional population and great distances to major metropolitan centers help keep density down to the semi-private level to which most state residents are accustomed.

To the chagrin of locals, word is out that Flathead provides some of the finest lake trout fishing in the country. "People pull out 30-pound lake trout left and right" is the way one local puts it. Lake trout fishing is so consistently good that there are guides on the lake who will refund clients' money if they aren't successful. Trophy fishermen are still trying to better the state record, a 43-pounder caught by Dave Larson in the east shore area in 1979. Kokanee salmon and Dolly Vardon, or Bull Trout, also are popular with fishermen, although their numbers have been down lately.

Lakeside camping at the nine state parks and state recreation areas and the many private facilities is another summer favorite with both locals and tourists.

Wild Horse Island in the southwest part of the lake is the state's largest island and is now also one of Montana's newest state parks. Thanks to the help of the Nature Conservancy, a non-profit conservation organization, and the generosity of the Bourke MacDonald family of Butte which previously owned Wild Horse, most of the 2,150-acre island is part of the state park system. Approximately 50 half-acre and one-acre lots remain in private hands, and about a third of these have summer homes.

The island's name comes from the horses that were set free when the old Hiawatha resort complex, the ruins of which remain on the island's east shore, was closed early this century. Unchecked, their numbers grew to 100 by 1954, but were reduced by starvation during two harsh winters that followed. A later trapping program removed all but one horse and one mule. As of 1982 an old black Arabian stallion was the sole survivor.

The island is most noted for its sizable herd of Rocky Mountain bighorn sheep. Two yearlings, a male and a female, were introduced in 1939 and six more were added in 1947. By 1954 their numbers had grown to 90, and to 300 by 1973. A long history of overgrazing by horses and later by bighorn sheep and deer led to

The Flathead Valley spells recreation. Above, the scenic Polson Golf Course. Rick Graetz photo. Far left: A proud pike fisherman. Alice Blood photo. Left: Competitor barely keeping his head above water in the Mad River Kayak Race near Bigfork. Tim Church photo.

repeated winter die-offs from starvation. Removal of animals as part of an organized state management program should allow vegetation to recover. As of the early 1980s the bighorn sheep herd ranged between 55 and 58, deer numbered from 15 to 30, and wild horses, one.

Unlike most state parks this one is managed strictly as a day-use area, with no camping, fires or pets allowed. Picnickers are welcome but no tables are provided. Hiking on the forested half of the island is more difficult than on the rolling grassy hills that cover most of the island's south half. The trails are not maintained. A park ranger lives on the island from spring to fall to monitor sheep and answer questions.

Montanans are concerned that a proposed open-pit coal mine along the Flathead's North Fork in southeastern British Columbia may adversely impact Flathead Lake. The prospect of Canadian mining was a major impetus for initiating the five-year, $2½ million Flathead River Basin Environmental Impact Study completed in June of 1983. Findings reveal that water quality is exceptionally good, but ominous trends were

discovered that potentially could be accelerated by the Canadian mine.

The Cabin Creek Mine would be located on a major tributary of the North Fork of the Flathead River just north of the Montana border. Specifics have changed as the project has moved through the planning process, but would involve the removal of approximately 132 million tons of coal over a 20- to 30-year period from two pits that each eventually would grow to one mile across and 1,000 feet deep.

The Impact Study provided baseline information that will allow researchers to detect any serious future degradation of the Flathead watershed if the project gets the go-ahead from the British Columbia government. Researchers are especially concerned that a poorly managed mine would add silt to the North Fork and, eventually, Flathead Lake. Before the end of the federally funded study, Montana had established its own 15-member Flathead Basin Commission in April, 1983, as a watchdog group to monitor environmental conditions in the Flathead Basin.

One important finding of the study was that the lake is so clear because it has low levels of phosphorus. Preliminary analysis shows that 17 percent of the phosphorus entering the lake comes from domestic sewage, a non-natural source. Silt carried into the lake by erosion during spring runoff also contributes large amounts of phosphorus, but that source is limited to a brief seasonal surge. Large-scale surface disturbances at Cabin Creek could lead to a year-round inflow of silt-carried phosphorus.

Phosphorus fertilizes the lake, enhancing growth of algae. If unchecked, its buildup could lead to eutrophi-

Above left: For many years the only transportation around Flathead Lake was by steamer. This is about 1910. Montana Historical Society photo.
Above right: Flathead Lake — the largest, natural fresh-water lake west of the Mississippi. John Alwin photo.
Below: The Flathead Valley favors Christmas tree crops. John Alwin photo.

cation, a process that causes a lake to become unhealthy due to excessive nutrients that cause greater algae growth. Eventually algae clouds the water and robs the lake of oxygen, often leading to fish die-offs. Reports from long-time lake shore residents that algae now covers lake bottom rocks that were once clean and algae free corroborate the scientists' findings of rising phosphorus levels over recent years.

Sewage treatment plants at Kalispell, Whitefish, Columbia Falls and Bigfork are not now removing phosphorus. This would require upgraded plants capable of tertiary treatment, which removes nutrients

from waste water. Tertiary treatment is not legally required in Montana, but state and federal agencies are considering making an exception, requiring treatment for sewage water being discharged into the Flathead watershed.

The Upper Flathead developed later than the southern reservation section. No mission was established here and even though Hudson's Bay Company trader Joseph Howse built a post near today's Kalispell in 1810, it lasted but one trading season. The first communities to take root on the level plain north of the lake date from the 1880s.

By the late 1880s there may have been 2,000 settlers in the Upper Flathead. Their main transport link to the outside world was via steamboats on Flathead Lake and overland conveyance between the south shore town of Polson and the Northern Pacific main line still farther south. With a location at the head of steamship navigation on the Flathead River, Demersville prospered as a northern transport hub. The 1891-92 completion of the Great Northern Railroad across the valley meant the demise of this port community, but not until after rail construction sparked a local boom as the Great Northern brought in supplies by steamer and erected a warehouse.

With the railroad came full-fledged towns and a boost to commercial agriculture. Continued improvements in transport and the creation in 1910 of Glacier National Park added an important tourist component to the regional economy. Tourism has become vital to the Upper Valley's economy, and a varied agricultural sector that ranges from potatoes to Christmas trees remains important in this rapidly urbanizing area.

Hard on the Heels of Lewis and Clark
The Hudson's Bay Company Howse Expedition, 1810-11

As the first St. Louis-based American fur traders pushed up the Missouri into Eastern Montana and probed westward into the Three Forks area, British traders were firmly established to the north. Even before the arrival of Lewis and Clark in Montana, the Hudson's Bay Company and Northwest Company had well-developed trading systems that stretched westward to the eastern foothills of the Canadian Rockies. Hudson's Bay Company furs were floated downriver in wooden boats to York Factory on the west shore of Hudson Bay, and Northwest Company pelts were carried by canoe even farther to Montreal. It was these British traders who first tested the potential of Montana's fur-rich, west-slope country.

An interesting aside to this early British presence to the north is a yet unreported contemporaneous reference to the Lewis and Clark Expedition in the Edmonton House correspondence book. Writing to his commander in December, 1806, the post master of this Hudson's Bay Company fort at today's Edmonton, Alberta, conveyed Piegan-Blackfeet reports, writing,

"A party of Americans were seen last Summer where the Mississoury enters the Rocky Mountain and tis reported by the Muddy (or) Mississoury River Indians, that four of them [the Americans] set off with an intention to come here but that they killed one and the rest return'd."

The party seen near where the Missouri leaves the Rockies was probably the contingent led by Captain Lewis which had just crossed the mountains and descended the Sun River to the Great Falls. The smaller group of four that broke from the main body and headed northward would then have been Captain Lewis, Drouillard, and the two Fields brothers who had struck out for the Marias River. As students of the Lewis and Clark Expedition know, there was a clash with the Piegan along the Two Medicine River the morning of July 27, but the journals report that it was two Indians who lost their lives in the unfortunate skirmish. The Indian report of killing one of the Americans was evidently a face-saving fabrication.

In the early 1800s the Northwest Company's corporate organization and attenuated transport system depended on rapid expansion into new fur-rich areas. An 1807 quest for untapped territory led Nor'Wester David Thompson across the Rockies and into the southeastern corner of British Columbia where he built Kootenae House near Lake Windermere, the company's first post west of the Continental Divide. In the fall of 1808 he dispatched one of his trusted clerks, Finan McDonald, across to the Kootenai River and downstream to near the site of Libby, Montana, where another post was built. Impressed by the area's prospects, the following year Thompson established yet another Montana post, Saleesh House, on the Clark Fork River near today's Thompson Falls.

Since the company's Montana operation was based out of their post at Edmonton, the neighboring Hudson's Bay Company post commander was aware of his competitor's Pacific-slope endeavors. Post master James Bird contemplated that Hudson's Bay Company should follow suit, but was concerned with the difficulty of transport over the Rockies and the availability of provisions in an area so far removed from buffalo and the pemmican on which the fur traders had come to rely. Despite these problems the Hudson's Bay Company officials decided they had to counter and by 1810 were ready to move.

Officer Joseph Howse left Edmonton House in July 1810, with 16 others, bound for the west side of the mountains with instructions to establish a trading post. The Howse party included 10 other company employees, three Cree Indians, and three free traders. They took all the necessities for building a post, including three "falling" axes, hatchets, saws, planes, nails, hinges and padlocks. The entourage was well stocked with 51 kinds and varieties of trade goods. More than 480 pounds of tobacco was the most valuable item. Other important trade goods included nine 3-foot-long guns, 171 pounds of shot, 113 pounds of powder, and 46 gallons of English brandy with items of lesser value including buttons, bells, beads, shirts, combs and kettles.

Howse led his men up the north branch of the Saskatchewan and crossed the Continental Divide at what eventually became known as Howse Pass. Once over the main range he traveled up the Columbia River, portaged to the Kootenay, and descended that river to another portage where he crossed into the Flathead drainage. No one knows precisely where he built the wintering post of Howse's House, but in later years he corroborated its general location as shown on early nineteenth century Arrowsmith maps, which placed it just north of Flathead Lake in the vicinity of Kalispell.

The Hudson's Bay men spent a profitable winter trading among the Indians, probably mostly Pend d'Oreille, Kootenai and possibly Kalispell. They exhausted their entire stock of goods and even resorted to trading employees' personal blankets, knives and shirts! All totaled the take amounted to more than 1,100 beaver pelts and 1,600 muskrats. In December Howse and a few other men found time to travel with some Indians to the headwaters of the Missouri, presumably in the vicinity of Glacier National Park.

The Howse expedition returned to the Saskatchewan in 1811 with an impressive profit and glowing reports of beaver being "extremely numerous and spread over a great extent of Country." Despite favorable economic reasons to continue the lucrative Flathead trade, the Hudson's Bay Company did not return to the west side of the Rockies until 1821.

A major factor in abandoning this promising area was Piegan-Blackfeet threats. The Piegan had agreed to allow Howse to return safely, but vowed to stop all future efforts by white traders to supply their west-slope enemies with guns and ammunition. Not only did they threaten to plunder west-bound traders, they promised to kill them and make dried meat of their flesh.

The Nor'Westers' response in the fall of 1811 was to use the same route taken by Howse back over the mountains to Western Montana, but with the protection afforded by a large party of more than 30 men. The main body made it across that fall, but came upon their smaller advance party of six men who had been robbed, beaten and stripped naked (like Colter), but left alive by a band of Piegan. That year the Northwest Company established yet another post in Western Montana north of present-day Eureka.

The Indians' threat alone probably would have been enough to keep the more cautious Hudson's Bay Company on the east side, but another factor also weighed in their decision. After an earlier failure, the company was about to launch another thrust northward into the Athabaska Country, the fur trade El Dorado within the Mackenzie River Basin. This effort drained manpower from the upper Saskatchewan and ruled out any further west slope efforts. The Hudson's Bay Company did not operate beyond the mountains and in Western Montana until they acquired the Northwest Company's posts as a result of their 1821 coalition with the Nor'Westers.

Left: The Conrad Mansion, Kalispell. John Alwin photo.

Above left: Big Mountain Ski Area is the biggest in the northern portion of Western Montana. It has an international flavor resulting from the Canadian crowd it draws. Photos courtesy of Big Mountain Ski Area.

Kalispell, Whitefish and Columbia Falls

Charles E. Conrad is recognized as Kalispell's founding father. He and his brother arrived in Montana territory in 1868 via Missouri steamboat and settled in the bustling eastern Montana river town of Fort Benton. At the time this was entrepot to rapidly developing Western Montana and adjacent sections of Idaho and Canada. Before long the enterprising Conrad was a major force in the freight business on which the community subsisted. From its Fort Benton base, Conrad Brothers grew into one of Montana's largest freighting concerns. The company's steamboats soon linked Fort Benton to St. Louis and its horse, mule and oxen-drawn freight wagons tied the waterfront with communities throughout western and central Montana and eventually northward into Canada. Money generated by freighting and large cattle holdings made Charles Conrad one of the territory's wealthiest men.

By the 1880s it was obvious that the arrival of the railroad had ushered in a new transportation era, one in which the days of the river boat and oxen-drawn wagons were numbered. With the prospect of relocation in mind, Conrad traveled west in the spring of 1890 to check out Spokane. Enroute he and his wife stopped in the Flathead to visit relatives and fell in love with the place. They abandoned plans for Spokane deciding to make the Upper Flathead their new home.

If the arrival of the railroad at Fort Benton had led to lost opportunities there, its coming to the Flathead was to mean even greater wealth for Conrad. At the suggestion of James J. Hill, business acquaintance and railroad entrepeneur, Conrad began buying land in the projected path of Hill's Great Northern line. In 1891 the Kalispell townsite company was incorporated. The town's name chosen by Conrad referred to a "grassy place above the lake." By September of 1891 a Missoula newspaper reporter estimated there were more than 400 people in the embryonic community. Early that winter buildings from by-passed Demersville were loaded onto sleds and hauled the four miles into Kalispell. On January 1, 1892 the first train steamed into town, thereby assuring Kalispell's success and its future role as regional capital for Montana's far northwest.

Progress-minded Charles Conrad revivified and visiting Kalispell in the 1980s would be pleased with the development his city had made during his 80 years of absence. Most startling would be his discovery that the Conrad mansion still stands almost exactly as he left it. The Norman-style mansion was given to the city of Kalispell by his youngest daughter, Alicia, in 1975. It is operated as a historic site, visited by 20,000 people during its five-month viewing period each year. The home retains its architectural purity, never having been remodeled and always used as a residence. Much of the original furniture still graces its many rooms. Upstairs in the guest section is the Antique Room where guests including Charles M. Russell and Teddy Roosevelt slept.

The Conrad mansion is the number-one attraction in this tourist oriented community. Most tourist spots are outside the city, yet still close enough to assure Kalispell its share of the business generated by the million-plus visitors who pass through the area each year. Few places in Montana rival Kalispell in terms of proximity to unique and popular attractions. The western entrance to Glacier National Park is only a half-hour drive to the northeast, and on the south, Flathead Lake is even closer. Big Mountain, Montana's most popular downhill ski resort, is less than 20 miles to the northwest. The Flathead National Forest's more than two million acres encircles the entire Upper Flathead.

One distinctive component of tourism in Kalispell and all of Flathead County is the large percentage of Canadians. Here is a community where most merchants can tell you the daily exchange rate for Canadian dollars. Stebbins Dean, Executive Vice-President of the Kalispell area Chamber of Commerce, thinks Canadians account for up to 40 percent of all tourists by number and 60 percent of tourist dollars spent in the county.

An interest in making Canadians feel right at home explains why red, maple leaf flags are so numerous in Kalispell. Merchants even celebrate Canada Day, a national holiday across the border, decorating the town with more flags and courting Canadian shoppers. "The Saloon" on north Main, nicknamed "Moose's" for David "Moose" Miller who runs it, has become a popular watering hole for Canadians. According to one Kalispell police officer, "They love it — its swinging saloon doors, sawdust on the floor, peanuts and good pizza."

Kalispell is less dependent on the wood products industry than most Montana towns west of the Continental Divide. It does have its complement of sawmills and even a plywood plant, but this is not a one-industry lumber town. Its economy is diverse. A role as regional trade center for northwest Montana is reflected in the large number of people employed in the community's retail, trade, and financial businesses. Flathead Valley Community College with an enrollment of more than 2,000 is a major local employer, as is the U.S. Forest Service.

Local development corporations are working to further diversify area manufacturing. Factories turn out products ranging from lumber, house logs, treated power poles, roof trusses and evergreen wreaths, to wrought iron furniture, neon signs, metal and concrete products and even semi-conductor equipment. The chamber is looking for smaller employers, but wouldn't turn away a 500-employee plant. As with many Montana communities, one target is high-tech industry seeking a high-amenity area.

Left: Condominium and retirement-home development has followed the recreational trade in the Flathead. John Alwin photo.
Below: The Whitefish Kalispell-Big Fork axis seems to have as many artists per capita as loggers. This is potter Joanna Griffin at the Hockaday Art Center, Kalispell. John Alwin photo.

Ray Thompson returned to Kalispell in 1979 and established Semitool, Inc. His 50-person plant produces a rinser-drier used in the manufacture of computer chips. His customers include the big names in the semi-conductor field — IBM, Hewlett-Packard, Motorola, and Intel — and his product is marketed worldwide. In 1982 Semitool was working on developing a new product, an etcher for fabricating chips, that could result in an expansion of employment to 250 by 1984.

Thompson's move back to Kalispell was motivated by a strong desire to return home, but also by a need for a low-overhead operation and access to workers who are efficient, honest and dedicated, "the best," as he describes them.

He is bullish on Semitool's future, but isn't overly optimistic on the potential for high tech in general within Western Montana. "Right now our image isn't conducive to outside investing," he said and in some people's eyes, "Montana is equal to Siberia." He thinks there could be up to 2,000 high-tech jobs in Montana by the early 1990s, but doesn't see them replacing the region's traditional industries.

The Upper Flathead might not yet be Silicon Valley North, but Kalispell already is Montana's undisputed art center and some say "Art Capital of the Northwest." Thelma Powell credits her late husband and noted western artist, Ace Powell, with starting it all in Kalispell. He had spent all

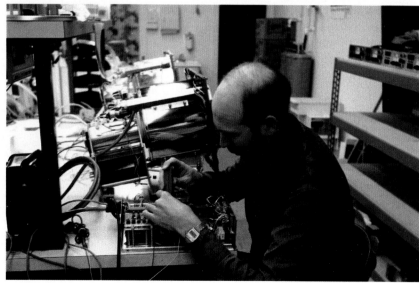

Above: Para-sailing on Whitefish Lake. Alice Blood photo.

Right: Like Missoula, Butte and Bozeman, Kalispell hopes to attract more amenity-seeking high-tech industry such as Semitool, Inc. already successfully operating there. John Alwin photo.

but three years of his life in the Flathead and according to Thelma, "Ace's dream in life was that this would someday be an art center." "He was a magnet," she says, and their home was like an open house 24 hours a day. Artists who stopped by were encouraged to locate in the area and those who did received free art advice from Ace on everything from technique to marketing.

Thelma estimates that there are more than 50 professional artists in the area who earn their living from painting, sculpting, carving, or working with clay and other media such as glass, leather and metal. There is an obvious emphasis on western art. The area's six bronze foundries constitute one of the largest concentrations anywhere in the country. In 1981 the foundries collectively poured five tons of bronze and did $1.5 million worth of business each month. The closely knit art community is geared to the annual fall Kalispell Art Show and Auction.

Census population figures for Kalispell are misleading. The 1980 tally shows only 10,648 residents. This figure is not indicative of the urban area's true size since it only includes those within the four-square-miles of the city's legal limits. Urbanization spills well beyond, and greater Kalispell's population is at least three times the city census figure. This is one of Montana's fastest growing city-centered regions. Suburban sprawl is a major concern to many residents, especially those from more urban sections of the country who were drawn to the area, in part, by its small-town and uncrowded qualities.

If Kalispell is a tourist town, Whitefish is even more so. A population of 3,700 makes it the second largest town in the Upper Flathead. Big Mountain, eight miles north of town, is Montana's most popular ski resort and one of only two destination downhill resorts in the state. The mountain's 27 trails and slopes have a combined length of more than 25 miles and a vertical drop of up to 2,100 feet.

Big Mountain Ski Resort is considering long-range expansion that would accommodate twice the mountain's average of 1,707 skiers per day recorded during the 1981-82 skiing season. The economic impact of such expansion on the community and the Upper Flathead is difficult to gauge, but a market study during the '81-'82 season showed skiers spent $23.9 million in the Flathead.

The Swan River flows through the heart of Bigfork. Tom Dietrich photo.

The presence of an Anaconda Aluminum smelter and several large saw mills gives Columbia Falls an industrial character not typical of most other communities in the Flathead Valley. John Alwin photo.

The Canadian presence is a large and growing element in Whitefish. A recent study at Big Mountain showed that at least half the skiers were Canadians, and almost half of those came from Alberta, especially Calgary. They evidently like what they see in Whitefish. Many are buying local businesses, houses, and condominiums. At some of the major condominium developments 50 to 100 percent of units belong to Canadians.

The chair-lift ride to the top of Big Mountain is a popular attraction, but most summer activity shifts to Whitefish Lake and the local 27-hole golf course.

Whitefish has its complement of smaller sawmills and log-home plants that are so ubiquitous in Montana's west slope area. Burlington Northern is another important, but shrinking local employer. As recently as 1980 Burlington Northern employed more than 500 at their Whitefish maintenance and repair facilities. Cutbacks and transfers had reduced that number to 300 by early 1983.

East across the north end of the Flathead Valley is Columbia Falls, the region's third-ranking community with 3,100 residents. In the past it advertised itself as "The Industrial Hub of the Flathead." That label is still valid, although it has been replaced by "Gateway to Glacier National Park and the fabulous North Fork of the Flathead."

The percentage of employment in manufacturing may be higher in Columbia Falls than any other Montana city. This is home to several wood products plants and Anaconda Aluminum's giant reduction works. Now owned by Arco, this complex has been the largest employer in the Flathead since the mid-1950s. Today the plant employs 1,100 people when in full operation and accounts for up to a third of Flathead County's entire tax base.

Original selection of the Columbia Falls site was linked to the availability of abundant and cheap hydro power. Power costs were a prime consideration since the reduction plant consumes huge amounts of electricity. At the time industrial consumers that located within a specified

distance of federal hydro dams, like Hungry Horse, were given a break in power costs. The plant still buys electricity from the federal Bonneville Power Administration at wholesale. This power runs the plant's five pot lines in which alumina, partly refined aluminum ore from Australia, is electrically reduced into aluminum. The final products are 16,000 pound ingots approximately 12 feet by 2½ feet by 1 foot deep. These are shipped by train to the company's Terre Haute, Indiana, plant where they are rolled into sheets for use in auto air conditioners and other consumer durable goods like washers and dryers.

Several large wood products plants add to a local manufacturing employment that approaches 3,000. Largest of these is Plum Creek, a Burlington Northern subsidiary. It employs approximately 1,100 at its giant Columbia Falls, complex with its integrated sawmill-fiberboard-plywood operation. Louisiana Pacific, F. H. Stoltze Land and Lumber Company and Superior Building Company added hundreds more to the local manufacturing component in 1983.

129

THE GLACIER-BOB

Straddling the Continental Divide from Highway 200 north to the Canadian line is the gigantic Glacier-Bob, a 160-by-60-mile wilderness world of superlatives. This largest of our Western Montana regions is almost uniformly characterized by rugged and remote mountainous terrain, spectacular scenery, extensive forests, abundant wildlife, and deep snows. Just two roads cross the region and only a few others penetrate its outer fringes. Almost all of the region remains unpopulated.

Most of Glacier-Bob falls within three regions. 1) Glacier National Park, 2) the Bob Marshall Wilderness complex, and 3) the Swan Valley. Glacier is one of the world's most highly regarded wilderness parks, renowned for its unequaled combination of precipitous peaks, glacier-carved valleys, alpine glaciers and lakes and a remarkable aggregation of wildlife suggestive of a resource abundance of another era.

The Bob Marshall Wilderness complex to the south is the nation's second largest and probably most famous. Combined, the Bob Marshall, Great Bear and Scapegoat wilderness areas form a contiguous wildland of more than 1.5 million acres. Visitors in quest of the wilderness experience are discovering this celebrated complex in record numbers.

The Swan Valley would be a candidate for its own regional designation if we had the luxury of dividing Western Montana into 15 or 20 regions. Within our framework of nine, its threshold wilderness nature and engulfing wildlands make it a logical extension of the Glacier-Bob. Highway 83 through the 90-mile-long valley is the only major north-south transportation corridor within the region. The approximately 1,000 year-round residents scattered along this route constitute the largest population grouping beyond the edge of 10,000-square-mile Glacier-Bob.

Because of its rugged landscape, harsh climate and isolation the area of Glacier National Park has been spared much of the human encroachment that has altered nearby areas. Even Indians back to pre-historic time did not view it as an attractive area for habitation or hunting. For most of thousands of years of human history this section of the Northern Rockies has been an area merely to be crossed, a natural barrier and buffer zone between neighboring tribes. It was not until the second half of the 19th century that serious exploration by white men began, and not until almost the turn of the century that the first residents settled within the confines of the present park border.

Writings of early explorers and visitors reveal that the Blackfeet Indians did frequent the eastern fringe of the region for hunting and religious purposes, but they were a plains people and their focus lay to the east on the buffalo-rich plains on which their subsistence depended. Even when tribes immediately west of the region looked to the east, they saw beyond the spectacular peaks to the more featureless grasslands. The Kutenai, Flathead and Kalispell tribes of the west slope were once plains dwellers, having been pushed westward like most tribes by a great continental chain reaction set off by the expansion of European settlement in the east. By the time of first white contact their adaptation to life in the forested valleys still wasn't complete, and they relied on regular expeditions back to the plains to hunt buffalo.

Hunting parties of these west-slope tribes regularly traveled over Marias and Cut Bank passes enroute to and from the plains. The importance of these forays outweighed the danger of almost certain attack from their bitter enemies, the powerful Blackfeet, who guarded the western approaches to their territory. The Piegan tribe of the Blackfeet confederacy used the same passes when dispatching war parties to raid west-slope tribes.

Canadian free traders supplied by and operating out of the Hudson's Bay Company and Northwest Company posts at present-day Edmonton, Alberta, may have been the first non-Indians to visit the area that became Glacier National Park. They are known to have frequented the Rockies and may have entered Glacier.

Specifics on the first visit of record come from the journal of Nor'Wester David Thompson. In 1810 Finian MacDonald and two other Northwest Company traders earned the distinction of being the first whites to enter the region when they accompanied an entourage of plains-bound Flathead Indians. MacDonald's party was attacked by the Blackfeet as were most others who dared venture into the area over the next several decades.

The U.S. government's railroad survey of 1853-54 marked the beginning of a half-century of organized exploration and mapping. Territorial Governor Isaac Stevens' charge was to ascertain the most practical and economical route for a possible railroad across the northern tier of the country, from the Mississippi River to the West Coast. The segment across the Continental Divide within Montana was the most worrisome along the projected route. The quest to find Marias Pass was unsuccessful and the defile's whereabouts continued to elude explorers for the next 30 years.

Hunters, prospectors, trappers, timber thieves and official government representatives visited the park area occasionally over the next two decades. Of special interest was the 1874 west-to-east traverse over Cut Bank Pass by two American lieutenants based at Fort Shaw, west of today's Great Falls. Lt. Van Orsdale was moved by the beauty he saw. Nine years later in a letter to the Fort Benton newspaper he suggested the area be set aside as a national park, the first published plea for park status.

Above: Lower Two Medicine Lake, Glacier Park. Tom Dietrich photo.
Right: Swan Lake, looking to the southeast. Rick Graetz photo.
Below: Entering the United States from Canada at Port of Chief Mountain. John Alwin photo.

The decades of the '80s and '90s proved to be monumental ones for the area destined to become Glacier. Two signficant developments stand out. First was the initial visit and subsequent involvement of George Bird Grinnell, noted naturalist and editor of the popular outdoor magazine, *Forest and Stream.* Grinnell made his first visit in 1885 and returned home to write a series of articles on hunting in the area. With his interest piqued, Grinnell returned in 1887 and then annually for years. He developed an affinity for the park area and a close personal relationship with the Blackfeet Indians.

When the U.S. government began negotiating with the Blackfeet in the 1890s for purchase of the westernmost section of the reservation, the portion of today's park east of the Continental Divide, Grinnell was a logical choice to serve as a negotiator. The tribe eventually agreed to surrender title in exchange for $150,000 worth of goods and services annually for a

131

(A) *Glacier Park Lodge at East Glacier. John Alwin photo.*
(B) *Many Glacier Hotel. Charles Kay photo.*
(C) *Sperry Chalet in the interior of the park. Tom Dietrich photo.*

A

B

C

10-year period. The existence of Glacier Park as we know it today would have been impossible without this eastern portion.

Following its purchase in the 1890s the Ceded Strip, like the west side, was incorporated in the gigantic Lewis and Clark Forest Reserve. Grinnell and others continued to lobby for more protection. The 1895 creation of Waterton Lakes National Park across the border in Canada added to the impetus for a similar designation for the adjoining American section. Grinnell's considerable wealth and influence were major factors in the push for national park status. Some consider him the father of the movement to establish Glacier. Park historians and conservationists point to his "Crown of the Continent" article in a 1901 issue of *Century Magazine* as a landmark publication in the movement.

The other major development of the two-decade period was the rediscovery of Marias Pass by railroad engineer John L. Stevens in December, 1889. Two years later James J. Hill's newly reorganized Great Northern Railway crested the Continental Divide at one of the easiest places in Montana. Even though the railroad only skirted the eventual park boundary, it became the dominant factor in Glacier's early development.

Luckily for park proponents the area's turn-of-the-century minerals boom was small and short-lived. Had a Cut Bank-scale oil field or mineralization like that under Butte been discovered, achieving park status might have been impossible. As it was, the 1901 Kintla oil rush in the northwest was a bust and the mineral development in the Swiftcurrent Valley proved only slightly more tenacious.

The first Glacier National Park bill was introduced in Congress in 1907, but it wasn't until the third try in 1909 that the legislation made it through both houses and eventually was signed by President Taft on May 11, 1910. Major William Logan headed west to assume his position as the park's first Inspector in Charge. The government's initial appropriation was $50,000 for the construction of roads and trails, hardly enough to transform Glacier into a "pleasure ground for the benefit and enjoyment of the people of the United States" as required by the enabling legislation. Developing the national park would be a long-term proposition, one that was helped along immensely in the early years by the Great Northern Railroad.

The 1892 completion of the Great Northern line over Marias Pass attracted far-sighted businessmen who sensed the area's outstanding tourist potential. None was more enterprising than George Snyder, who in the 1890s helped develop a road from Belton (West Glacier) to Lake McDonald and began steamboat service between the foot of the lake and his newly constructed hotel complex at the other end. By the '90s Great Northern passengers could ride a stagecoach from near Belton to the lake, catch a ferry ride to the Snyder Hotel and take horseback trips into the surrounding mountain country.

In his *Montana's Many-Splendored Glacierland*, Warren Hanna pointed out that railroad magnate Hill's son, Louis Warren Hill, "did more than any other to put Glacier Park on the map, to enhance its scenic and recreational appeal, and to make its name a byword with the traveling public . . ." Yet until Hanna's book appeared in 1976, Hill's noteworthy accomplishments went largely unacclaimed by park history buffs. Hanna lamented that there is no mountain, pass, lake, valley or road named to honor this park pioneer, an individual Hanna considers "godfather to Glacier."

Louis Hill directed the Great Northern's major and critical involvement in Glacier during its infancy. The company led the way in the Teens, building accommodations, trails, and even some highways, with an emphasis on the east side. Through the railroad's Glacier Park Hotel Company, Hill oversaw the construction of the park's flagship inn, the rustic Glacier Park in 1913, and the Swiss-style Many Glacier two years later.

The Great Northern subsidiary also built and operated a chain of smaller chalets scattered about the park and opened three camps where guests slept on cots in authentic Indian tipis with the addition of wooden floors. The importance of Glacier to the Great Northern was suggested by the adoption of the Rocky Mountain goat as a prominent element in their logo—evidently Louis' idea.

As park facilities expanded, so, too, did visitation. The 4,000 tourists of 1911 grew to more than 22,000 just nine years later. One of the biggest boons to tourism was the 1933 completion of breathtaking Going-to-the-Sun Road, Glacier's first and only transpark road.

Disagreement about the best highway route over the Continental Divide was settled in 1917-18 when government surveyors recommended Logan Pass. A total of 12 of 50 miles between West Glacier and St. Mary had to be carved out of solid rock. The most spectacular section is nine miles immediately west of Logan Pass. This ribbon of concrete snakes its way up the nearly vertical Garden Wall, rising 3,000 feet before cresting the 6,664-foot summit. A half-century later the highway still is considered an engineering feat and the view it offers is as awesome as ever.

Going-to-the-Sun ushered in a new period of tourism in the park. Prior to its completion, most visitors toured the park on horseback. A transpark highway opened the interior and gave visitors an opportunity to experience a cross section of Glacier from the comfort

Top: Glacier is the national park a railroad built, or at least promoted into national consciousness. This is what used to be Great Northern's Belton Station at West Glacier. John Alwin photo.
Bottom: Glacier also is a trails park. This is Granite Park Chalet. Rick Graetz photo.

of their cars. This appealed to tourists, whose numbers increased dramatically, rising from 53,000 in the year before the road's completion to 210,000 in 1936. Except for an understandable drop during World War II, attendance has climbed steadily. Annual visitation rose to a half-million in 1951, and exceeded a million visitors for the first time in 1969. Despite a continuing energy crunch and high gas prices, 1981 was the peak year with 1,786,000 visitors.

Fully 80 percent of visitors see Glacier during the three summer months. Open between mid-June and mid-October Going-to-the-Sun Road is the dominant visitor-use facility, and Logan Pass the principal focal point. This highway and its summit area are especially popular with those having only a day to spend in Glacier, yet wanting to enjoy a cross section of park features.

It is impossible to see all of Glacier in one day. Noted naturalist and conservationist John Muir suggested

one should "Give a month to this precious reserve. The time will not be taken from the sum of your life. Instead of shortening, it will indefinitely lengthen it and make you truly immortal." Ideally, the best way to experience the park's wonders would be to start at the southern entrance of Walton and hike the entire length north to the Canadian border. Those lacking the inclination, not to mention the physical stamina and time necessary for such an expedition, can customize their introduction to Glacier that would fall somewhere between a hurried traverse across the park and the ultimate, extended backcountry marathon.

Staying at one of the park's grand old lodges is a vacation in itself. The remarkable "forest lobby" of Glacier Park Lodge with its towering 60-foot-tall trunks, the Swiss decor of Many Glacier Hotel right down to busboys in lederhosen, and the rustic hunting lodge atmosphere at Lake McDonald are all uniquely Glacier. These historic hostelries, as well as three newer inns in the park and the gabled Prince of Wales Hotel next door in Waterton, are operated by Glacier Park, Inc., a Greyhound subsidiary.

Those wishing to commune with nature on a more intimate level can choose from several camping options. Camping is especially popular in Glacier where, in 1982, campers outnumbered guests in hotels and lodges by approximately 250,000 to 100,000.

The largest and most accessible campgrounds are the eight reached by paved road. They have the most improvements and are especially popular with recreational vehicle campers who now constitute a majority. Apgar is the giant, accommodating almost a third of all tent and RV overnighters. For those desiring more primitive conditions and solitude, several campgrounds accessible by gravel roads are available. All but one are in the remote North Fork country, Glacier's least visited roaded section.

Some purists are convinced it isn't possible to experience the majesty of Glacier on a truly personal and spiritual level without spending at least a night or two under the stars in the serenity of the backcountry. With only 76 miles of paved road and even less unpaved roadway within the park's 1,583 square miles, travel by auto is limited — by design. Ninety-two percent of Glacier is roadless and managed as wilderness. It is only accessible via an outstanding 700-mile system of trails. Surprisingly few people camp in Glacier's remote interior and even that small number has been declining. Between 1979 and 1982 visitor nights in the backcountry dropped steadily from 25,432 to 16,198, only a little more than half the 1977 peak.

A wide range of summer activities is available to all visitors. Park interpretation programs including guided walks and campfire sessions are well attended and are all free. Some prefer to take to the trails on their own for hikes that don't require overnight stays. Especially popular are short self-guided nature trails, particularly those that head along well traveled Going-to-the-Sun Road. The Trails of the Cedars starts near Avalanche Creek Campground and takes hikers through a luxuriant, moss mantled world on the park's wet side. Two other popular short hikes are along Hanging Gardens Trail which guides visitors through the fragile arctic-alpine meadows of the Logan Pass area and Going-to-the-Sun Point Trail which rewards users with a long remembered scenic vista.

Among a multitude of exhilarating one-day hikes are the five-mile treks to Grinnell Glacier or Iceberg Lake in the Many Glacier area, Snyder Lake, 4.2 miles from Lake McDonald Lodge, and the 5.5-mile hike from Two Medicine to 7,600-foot Dawson Pass. Granite Park and Sperry chalets are accessible only by trail and provide backcountry travelers with food and lodging. The easy 7½-mile Highline Trail from Logan Pass north to Granite Park Chalet is one of the park's most used wilderness walks. Radiating trails, especially from Granite Park, make both chalets excellent bases for backcountry exploration by those who prefer a few creature comforts.

Canoeing and boating are popular in the park. There are restrictions on motor boating and swimming isn't recommended in the predictably ice-cold waters. Commercial excursion boat cruises are available on six lakes and carry more than 25,000 people each season. Launches on Swiftcurrent Lake-Lake Josephine, Two Medicine and Waterton lakes take passengers deeper into the park interior to places that otherwise are accessible only by trail. Anglers can try their luck free of charge once they have the required park fishing permit. Rainbow and brook trout are found in a number of lakes and streams, as is the rarer and more prized westslope cutthroat trout. The crumbly nature of the park's sedimentary rocks limits technical mountain climbing, but non-technical mountaineering is especially rewarding in this magnificent mountain world.

Visitation drops dramatically after Labor Day. Most American visitors are transcontinental tourists and are already on their return home by that holiday. Albertans, however, flock to Glacier at this time to enjoy the fall color of an uncrowded park. This is the time of year that vehicles with Canadian plates seem to dominate park roads. By mid-September the Logan Pass visitor center is closed for the season as are the park's main lodges and inns.

A lack of crowds and a richness of natural colors amplified by the lower sun angle of autumn make the mid-September to mid-October season one of the most pleasant times to visit Glacier. Going-to-the-Sun Road is kept open for visitors until October 15, as are east-side roads like that into the Many Glacier area.

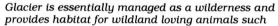
Glacier is essentially managed as a wilderness and provides habitat for wildland loving animals such *as moose, left, and bighorn sheep, right. Charles Kay photos.*

The gathering of eagles at McDonald Creek is the high point of the park's fall tourist season. Beginning in late September migrating bald eagles, mainly from Canada, join the few resident park pairs in a salmon feast that soon grows into the largest gathering of eagles in the 48 contiguous states. Peak numbers are reached in mid-November. To date, the record day count was 639 set in 1981, up from just 37 in 1939.

As many as 3,000 spectators, some from as far away as Europe, crowd the Apgar Bridge and Quarter Circle Bridge viewing areas during the height of this eagle extravaganza. The birds' quarry is Kokanee salmon, which swim to lower McDonald Creek from Flathead Lake to spawn in the gravelly creek bed and die at the end of their four-year life cycle. Ironically, this largest of American eagle concentrations outside Alaska is dependant on a non-native fish introduced into the Flathead system early this century.

Migratory eagles from as far north as the Arctic Circle have their fill of salmon before continuing on to winter areas in Montana and more distant states including Oregon, Utah, Nevada and California. In 1982 the peak eagle count had fallen to 306. Wildlife officials are concerned that reduced salmon numbers, in part owing to snagging of spawning salmon by fishermen downstream, may jeopardize this annual fall congregation.

Winter provides an opportunity to see and experience a different Glacier. Park roads are unplowed except the ten miles of Going-to-the-Sun between the park entrance at West Glacier and Lake McDonald Lodge.

While snowmobiles and other over-snow machines are prohibited, cross-country skiing and snowshoeing are encouraged and are growing in popularity. In 1982 rangers counted 6,607 skiers, up more than 163 percent over 1981. Winter recreationists find camping available at Apgar and St. Mary and other park areas by permit.

Preserving park environments while providing use and enjoyment for visitors presents Glacier's managers with continual challenges. At present the park is regarded fundamentally as a wilderness resource, unspoiled and largely controlled by natural processes. An annual invasion of more than 1½ million visitors, most in a period of a few months, must be carefully managed to minimize interference from human influence. Even with the best management plans visitation by such large numbers and disproportionate use of popular areas means some adverse impacts are inevitable.

Although wilderness camping is down, one-day hikes into the backcountry are on the increase, placing strains on more popular trails. Litter, trail erosion and trampling of fragile alpine vegetation is evidence of heavier use. People seem to gravitate toward water features. One consequence has been that some accessible portions of fragile lake shores and stream-beds have been adversely impacted. Large numbers of visitors also mean more auto emissions (576,401 cars in 1981) and campfire smoke with attendant air pollution. The increased number of tourists taxes sewage treatment facilities which can compromise water quality.

Unnatural and illegal feeding of animals can be expected to increase as visitor numbers climb. This has been a special problem with "roadside beggars" among bighorn sheep in the Many Glacier area. What seems an innocent and even well intentioned act may have serious consequences for these animals. The sheeps' health may suffer from the peanut butter and jelly sandwiches, crackers and candy bars offered them. It is possible that roadside feeding maintains an artificial summer population in the vicinity of the road at a time when the sheep normally would move to better quality range at higher elevations. Such a summer migration may be necessary for individual vigor and population quality. As sheep become more accustomed to human contact their likelihood of injury from vehicles increases as does their suscep-tibility to poaching.

No aspect of park management is more emotional than that dealing with grizzly bears. Six grizzly caused fatalities since 1967 and even more attacks and maulings have kept this a hot topic. Each human casualty sets off a flurry of heated dialogue on the park's bear policy and raises questions about the survival of grizzlies in the park. To keep abreast the Bear Management Plan is renewed annually.

Glacier National Park is home to approximately 200 grizzlies, evidently a stable and self regulating popu-lation. Contacts between people and the big bear were minimal until the late '50s after which increasing visitation and greater wilderness use by a backpacking public meant more incursions into the grizzly's domain. Potential for encounters are heightened by the fact that nearly all people arrive when bears are most active.

During the late '50s and '60s serious people/bear conflicts grew more common. Between 1956 and 1966 ten people were injured by grizzlies in seven different attacks. None of the attacks involved a raid by a bear on a campsite, campground or occupant of a sleeping bag. Most were defensive reactions of surprised sows guarding cubs. People/bear relations entered a new phase on the bizarre night of August 13, 1967. In two separate incidents grizzlies attacked without provoca-tion and mauled to death two young women while still in their sleeping bags. The gruesome tale of these attacks was told in Jack Olsen's popular *Night of the Grizzlies*, not recommended as bedtime reading for those tent camping in Glacier.

Another woman was killed in 1976 when a young grizzly ripped into her tent at Many Glacier camp-ground and dragged her away. Then in 1980 three people were mauled to death in two different incidents. A man and woman, park employees, camping in an unauthorized area only 200 yards from St. Mary Lodge, were killed in a 4:00 a.m. attack on July 24. That fall another grizzly killed and partially consumed a Dallas man on the shore of Elizabeth Lake in the northern part of the park.

The basic plan is to keep people and bears apart. A two-pronged program centers on educating and managing people while simultaneously dealing with problem bears. Informing visitors of the potential hazard of bears and making certain they know how to minimize that danger is accomplished in several ways. Educational efforts reach some people before they arrive in the park. The Assistant Superintendent regularly provides news releases for newspaper, radio and television presentations concerning bear safety in Glacier. People writing or calling the park requesting information be mailed to them prior to their visit will receive a bear alert handout.

Visitors entering Glacier are cautioned by the bear alert handout and prominent signs at all six entrance stations that the park is grizzly country. Signs are permanently posted at the entrance to each auto campground and at each trailhead. Evening camp-ground programs include specific comments on bear safety and every walk guided by park personnel begins with introductory comments on what to do if a bear is spotted. Each group obtaining backcountry permits receives oral warning of the hazards of camping and hiking in bear country. A pamphlet is provided along with a free plastic bag and directions to pack out all unused food and garbage.

Preventing bears from associating people with food is an important part of the education program. Aggressive bear behavior often can be linked to human food or garbage dumps. Clean camps in the back-country free of scraps and with food and garbage properly handled have a lower rate of bear incidents. In the frontcountry open dumps have been closed and bear-proof garbage cans are standard.

Glacier has a policy of computer logging sightings of bears throughout the park and in the adjoining Black-feet Indian Reservation. Sighting forms are distributed daily and scrutinized for potentially dangerous trends. Sufficient bear activity in an area can lead to temporary trail and campground closures before any attacks occur. Park personnel take additional practical pre-cautions at auto campgrounds with a history of bear problems. Frequency of grizzly bear activity in and near Many Glacier and Avalanche campgrounds has meant they are closed to all but hard-sided camper units. For the safety and convenience of backcountry hikers passing through the Many Glacier area the park provides a fenced bear-proof camping enclosure.

The park service has permanently closed Alder Trail to Granite Park Chalet. It passed through a small drainage near Logan Pass unofficially known as "Bear Valley" because of ever-present grizzlies. In 1983 Glacier was considering the possibility of a regular seasonal closure in the Apgar Mountain area where huckleberry-hunting grizzlies congregate in large numbers during a six-week period in August and September.

Bear management also entails relocation of problem bears and if necessary, their destruction. Bears that move into a visitor-use area but have not been overly familiar with people or caused an incident are transplanted within the park, but only once. Bears that have exhibited unnatural aggression, come to rely on non-natural foods or become overly familiar with humans are never transplanted within the park. A decision to destroy a bear is made only if specific conditions outlined in the current Bear Management Plan are met.

The National Park Service ranked Glacier as the country's most threatened national park in 1980. This unfortunate designation isn't based on unmanageable problems within its borders, but on actual and potential environmental intrusions from surrounding areas. It isn't likely anytime soon that Glacier will be left as an island of green surrounded by a wasteland. However, individual threats are insidious, and combined represent a very serious threat to one of the world's great wilderness parks.

Unluckily from a park perspective, it and adjacent sections are within the geologic Overthrust Belt, an area of active oil and gas exploration. Just across the border in Alberta the Belt has been a prolific producer and some think there is just as much potential in the circum-Glacier area. Thousands of acres have been leased on the national forest lands to the west and south. On the Blackfeet Indian Reservation several wells have been drilled just east of the park border and more are planned.

Another more chronic threat from the reservation side is the trespass grazing of Indian owned cattle. Livestock have been found up to 10 miles inside the park and as many as 700 head have been observed at one time from a helicopter. Domestic livestock places additional pressure on natural vegetation and thereby encourages less desirable exotic species. They also contribute to erosion and could transmit disease to wildlife. The Blackfeet Tribe maintains it has free access and use of the Ceded Strip by virtue of the 1896 treaty by which they sold that former section of their reservation. The Tribal Council has rejected a proposal to extend the fence that runs for only eight miles of the 64-mile common border for fear of jeopardizing treaty claims. Until treaty rights are resolved, a stepped-up range-rider program is all that keeps out a wholesale invasion of domestic livestock.

The North Fork of the Flathead River is remote country and most of its residents seem to want it to stay that way. A proposed paving project on the North Fork road has encountered heated opposition. George Wuerthner photo.

Upgrading and paving of the primitive road along the North Fork of the Flathead west of the park boundary threatens the wilderness character of the adjacent park area. The road is already paved for about 12 miles north of Columbia Falls, but Flathead County commissioners and some newer local residents want to see pavement extended. Environmentalists are concerned that a paved road eventually will reach the Canadian border and link with another extending westward through Waterton Park. This would complete the last segment in a circular highway that would pass through both Waterton and Glacier parks. Concern centers in the North Fork area where paved highway surely will mean increased logging, commercial developments and summer homes with their associated environmental consequences. Park personnel are concerned about high-speed access to the heart of Glacier's most wild and primitive area.

Another intrusion from the west has threatened Glacier National Park's Class I airshed. Federal law requires that areas with this highest quality clean-air designation maintain the standard as a national goal. Fluoride pollution from the Anaconda Aluminum plant at Columbia Falls is carried into the park's western edge by prevailing winds. A joint suit by the Forest Service and the park was filed against the company in 1978 for alleged fluoride damage on public lands. Anaconda has begun using a Japanese process to reduce fluoride emissions. Cutbacks to a fraction of full capacity at the Columbia Falls facility in the recessionary early 1980s has prevented a long-term test of this new equipment. Glacier's 14 fluoride monitoring stations will show park personnel just how effective the new emission-control equipment is as soon as the plant resumes full operation. Recently acid rainfall was detected in the park. Its specific area of origin is unknown but is assumed to be distant.

Perhaps the most difficult threats to deal with are those originating north of the border in Canada. One area of special concern is the Akamina-Kishinena Creek country of extreme southeastern British Columbia, a wedge-shaped area between the western border of Waterton and Glacier's northern edge. Conservationists think this section should be given park status. As is, they see it as a dagger pointed at the heart of Waterton-Glacier. Extensive roading and clearcut logging of mountain pine beetle-killed trees there have aesthetic and environmental implications for the adjacent national parks.

Another north-of-the-border concern is the Cabin Creek coal mine proposal. The open pit mine, less than 10 miles from Glacier's northwest corner, would be on a major tributary of the North Fork of the Flathead, which delineates part of Glacier's western boundary. There is fear of environmental damage in the Flathead drainage from acid wastes, siltation and other forms of pollution.

The prospect of open-pit mining in the Canadian section of the North Fork drainage provided part of the impetus for Congress to designate all three forks of the Flathead part of America's National Wild and Scenic River system in 1976. Testifying before the House of Representatives on September 27 of that year, Congressman Max Baucus stated "The U.S. Department of State has emphasized the importance of including the Flathead River as wild and scenic to strengthen their negotiating position in joint consultations with the Governments of Canada, British Columbia and Montana to determine means of preventing pollution." Hopefully designation of reaches of the North Fork as scenic and recreational rivers has helped convince Canadians of how highly these Flathead waters are regarded.

A conglomerate of environmental groups has rallied to fight these harmful intrusions. They view Glacier as one piece of a vast, as yet largely uninterrupted, wilderness complex that extends south out of the Canadian Rockies and reaches to Highway 200. Adverse impacts in one area have implications for other sections of this large international ecosystem.

Outside developments threaten park wildlife which depend on free uninhibited movement in and out of Glacier. This freedom of movement is essential to a stable and healthy wildlife population in the park. Recent sightings show that grey wolves utilize the park and adjoining areas at least part of the year, but there probably are not resident groups within the area. Reestablishment of breeding populations of this endangered species in the park and adjacent National Forest lands depends on southern migration of wolves from Canada where they are present in sizable numbers. This southward migration will not be possible if the continuity of wilderness is broken by development.

Glacier enjoys a well deserved reputation as one of the world's outstanding wilderness parks. It retains much of the extraordinary quality of primitive lands, flora and fauna for which it originally was created even though more than 38,000,000 people have visited it since its designation. Its worldwide significance was recognized formally in 1974 when it was made a unit in the international Biosphere Reserve system established by the United Nations Educational, Scientific, and Cultural Organization (UNESCO). Only a knowledgeable and involved public can assure that Glacier as we know it today will be enjoyed by future generations.

Almost half of the Glacier-Bob region south of the park is the 2,400-square-mile Bob Marshall Wilderness complex. The Bob Marshall (1,009,400 acres) is the. largest and most famous portion of this wilderness trio that also includes the Scapegoat (239,300 acres) to the south and the Great Bear (286,700 acres) on the northwest. All three share many features, including outstanding opportunities for solitude and an unrivaled wilderness experience.

This impressive country is unique among wildernesses. Among its distinctive features are several rare animal species including the westslope cutthroat trout, the nation's largest non-park grizzly population outside of Alaska, and at least periodic visits by the grey wolf. Other wildlife include elk, bighorn sheep, mountain goat, black bear, mule and whitetail deer, moose, mountain lion, wolverine and Canada lynx.

Unlike most other western wilderness areas relegated to the bare, rocky summits of mountain ranges, this complex has it all. Natural landscapes range from lush riparian meadows in generous glacially contoured 4,000-foot valleys, to scattered pine and bunchgrass parklands, heavily timbered slopes, and alpine tundra atop 9,000-foot peaks. Cliffs thrust up by almost inconceivable forces eons ago are left standing as sheer walls of limestone rising 1,500 feet and higher. Glaciers once covered the entire area and several active alpine glaciers still cling to a few high peaks in the Swan Range on the wetter west side. Sizable rivers grace these designated wildlands. The South Fork of the

A

B

D

C

E

Flathead originates in the Bob and weaves its way through the western section. To the north the Great Bear is centered on the Middle Fork that originates next door in the northern section of the Bob. The wilderness reach of both is designated as a "wild" river within the prestigious National Wild and Scenic River System.

The Bob Marshall was one of the nation's earliest wildlands to be set aside as an official wilderness area. Since its designation its name has been synonymous with the ultimate in western primitive lands. It has even been referred to as the "flagship of the wilderness fleet."

Given its gigantic size it is not surprising that the Bob's reputation has been primarily one of a horseman's wilderness. Summer use traditionally has been dominated by trail rides and fall use by a large invasion of big-game hunters. From throughout the country and even overseas, hunters flock to the famous Bob Marshall, a hunter's utopia, the virtues of which have been extolled in hunting periodicals. Elk is the primary quarry, nearly 100 percent of the hunts are stock supported and many are commercially guided.

Greater summer use and more hikers are two recreational trends in the Bob. Small groups of summer visitors in search of the challenge of long-distance hikes and total immersion in the wilderness have been using the Bob in increasing numbers. Like the horsemen they have discovered the grandeur of the Chinese Wall, irridescent Big Salmon Lake and the rugged Flathead Alps. Summer visitation may now exceed that of fall. While short, day hikes are commonplace in most Montana wilderness areas, the average stay within the Bob is almost six days, with a third of the users spending more than a week.

More than 1.5 million acres of wild land are contained in the contiguous Great Bear, Scapegoat and Bob Marshall wilderness areas.
(A) Great Northern Mountain, prized pinnacle of the Great Bear. Rick Graetz.
(B) Scapegoat Mountain near Augusta. John Krempel photo.
(C) Gateway Gorge atop the

Continental Divide in the Great Bear. Rick Graetz photo.
(D) The Middle Fork of Birch Creek, looking to the Rocky Mountain Front and the prairies of eastern Montana beyond. Rick Graetz.
(E) The Chinese Wall in the heart of the Bob Marshall Wilderness. Rick Graetz photo.

Top: Middle Fork of the Flathead River and Shafer Meadows airstrip, a hold-over from pre-wilderness days. Rick Graetz photo.
Bottom: The Bob Marshall is, more than any other wilderness in Montana, a horseman's wilderness. Near the head of Strawberry Creek. Rick Graetz photo.

Greater numbers of hikers in what traditionally has been a horseman's wilderness has caused some friction. Trail encounters of hikers and horse parties sometimes lead to a game of chicken to see who is going to yield. Hikers are aghast to see where stock have eroded trails into deep gullies, wide enough for four or five people to walk abreast. Dead or dying trees amid circles of horse-pawed ground are all too common evidence of improper horse use. Horsemen alone, however, are not responsible for the well-worn look in more frequented areas of the Bob. Litter, fire rings and other evidence of people also can be credited to hikers and an overall growth of visitor pressure. In 1982 the 178,200 visitor days tallied by the Forest Service represented a 14 percent increase over the previous year. As in most wilderness areas, the impact is amplified by highly uneven use patterns. Here the most used 25 percent of trail mileage carries about 95 percent of use. The trend suggests even heavier concentrations of use as visitors increasingly seek the more famous landmarks and better known hunting and fishing spots.

The Great Bear is the newest of the three wilderness areas of the Glacier-Bob. Efforts to protect this headwaters area of the Middle Fork of the Flathead River go back more than three decades. However, it wasn't until 1974 when threatened Forest Service roading and logging of the area appeared imminent that efforts shifted into high gear. Earlier discussions of the possibility of two large dams on the Middle Fork at sites identified by the U.S. Geological Survey, and an even more massive 405-foot-high Bureau of Reclamation dam, complete with a seven-mile-long tunnel to the west side of the Flathead Range, already had helped move wilderness proposals along. Congress formally set the Great Bear aside as wilderness in 1978.

The presence of the Forest Service's Schafer airstrip within the Great Bear adjacent to the Middle Fork introduces an added dimension. As many as 400 to 500 flights annually have touched down at the strip in recent years. Planes land for a number of reasons including day outings, freight hauling, charter flights, hunting, fishing, administration, and just the thrill of using a mountain strip. Many flights bring in river floaters for popular June-July raft trips down the Flathead's most challenging Middle Fork. Commercial outfitters account for half the downriver trips. Even with this additional approach, the Great Bear has a long way to go before its 57,300 visitor days of 1982 equal that of the Bob.

As of early 1983, wilderness advocates were lobbying for additions to the wilderness complex, a plan being touted as a "completion bill." Even with 1.5 million designated acres, more than 800,000 acres of de facto wilderness remain. The influential Montana Wilderness Association and others including the Bob Marshall Alliance are stressing the need to add an additional 400,000 fringe acres they believe should have been included in the original wilderness areas. Additions would include sections of the Rocky Mountain Front on the east, the Swan Range on the west, and acreage in the popular Monture Creek area along the southern edge of the Bob Marshall.

Extensive oil and gas leasing in the Front area especially worries environmentalists. An all-out effort by Montana's environmental community finally seems to have quelled the specter of oil and gas exploration within the designated wilderness areas, but adjacent land is still open to leasing. Wilderness designation hopefully would protect these additional areas from oil and gas impacts and complete the work started by conservationist Bob Marshall more than 50 years ago.

Accommodating wilderness-bound visitors is big business in the areas surrounding the Bob Marshall complex. Places like Augusta and Lincoln are considered gateway cities. They provide services to those

The Montana Wilderness Association

The Montana Wilderness Association is the oldest statewide wilderness preservation organization in the nation, formed in Bozeman in 1958 some six years *before* the passage of the Federal Wilderness Act. According to John Montagne, one of its founding members and past president, the MWA originally was established out of "concern for the lack of respect for the land." It started as a group with a general interest in quality outdoor recreation including non-wilderness-sounding subjects such as roadside picnic grounds. Over the years necessity has forced the group to emphasize wilderness preservation, although the members maintain an active interest in all of Montana's public lands.

This Helena-based, activist organization has been instrumental in the designation of millions of acres of wilderness in Western Montana. In 1983 it celebrated a proven track record that has spanned a quarter century of lobbying, commenting on various draft plans relating to the management of Montana's public lands, and supporting and encouraging more local and regional conservation groups. The organization has fought pitched battles and does not hesitate to resort to lawsuits when all else fails, although members realize that in the long-run the only thing that will save wilderness is a concerned public. Carrying the message of wilderness and wise management of our wildland resources to the public is a major thrust of the MWA. Public education efforts, including their popular summer Wilderness Walk Program, have introduced many to Montana's wildlands and help dispel the notion of wilderness users as strictly elitist eco-freaks.

The presence of more than three million acres of designated wilderness in Montana does not mean that the group has lobbied for its last bill or won its final battle. Unresolved wildland conflicts remain in Montana and in 1983 there are indications that they will become even more acute.

Bill Cunningham, Conservation Director of this 1,000-member organization, describes it as "a bona-fide, born-and-bred-in-Montana, grass-roots organization." Most members are Western Montanans, but a broadening, even national geographic base of support would be more consistent with the federally owned lands it works to protect. A modest annual dues entitles members to its bi-monthly newsletter and timely wilderness alerts on fast-breaking issues. The MWA's address is Box 635, Helena, Montana 59624.

entering and leaving the backcountry and are home to numerous guides and outfitters who earn at least a part of their living in the complex.

Not the largest, but one of the most unique gateways is Essex, where Sid and Millie Goodrich's Izaak Walton Inn has earned an excellent reputation among Montana's outdoor oriented public and is developing as one of the state's quality cross-country ski resorts. When they bought the abandoned railroad quarters they had assumed they would fix it up and sell it in a year or two — that was 10 years ago. "We just kept fixing it up and having a good time," Sid says. They have succeeded in creating a unique 24-room hostelry, a kind of hybrid New England inn and north-country lodge.

Glacier Park and the Great Bear Wilderness aren't the only attractions at Essex. The Burlington Northern maintains a helper operation here that provides two locomotives to assist heavy eastbound trains to crest Marias Pass. Helpers, trestles, snowsheds, tunnels and a mountainous setting have made the area a topic of articles in magazines catering to railroad hobbyists. During summers the basement lounge at the inn serves an interesting mix of wilderness vacationers, rail buffs, summer-home owners ranging from Hi-Line ranchers to school teachers from the Midwest, and passersby.

Swan Valley, which actually includes sections of the Swan and Clearwater river valleys, is the name given to the approximately 90-mile-long trough running from Clearwater Junction north to where Highway 93 breaks out of the mountains south of Bigfork. As in other areas fringing the Bob Marshall complex, this too, is a gateway to the wilderness. The trail into the Bob from Holland Lake is among the west side's most popular entry points. As well, most recreationists heading into the Mission Mountains Wilderness and the Mission Range west of the valley enter from the Swan side. Trails into Glacier, Turquoise and Cold lakes account for most visitor use.

The Swan also is a recreation area in its own right. With its forest-floored valley and heavy snow and fog, the place has a distinct Pacific Northwest quality. Its chain of glacially derived lakes including Lindbergh, Seeley and Salmon with their shoreline summer homes imparts an "On Golden Pond" feel to the area. Despite subdivision, the valley remains remote and sparsely populated. The off-season population probably isn't more than 1,000 and one-room school houses are not a thing of the past. Most of the valley is National Forest land or within the Swan River State Forest. This should help assure that the Swan's desirable qualities will be retained and that north-south highway travelers searching for an alternative to the Flathead's Highway 93 will be rewarded with one of the state's most scenic drives.

A

C

B

D

E

(A) Summit Lake in the Swan Valley, backed up by the Mission Mountains. Mark Thompson photo.
(B) The Tour of the Swan River Valley, known as TOSRV (toz-ruf) is a week-end romp from Missoula, up the Swan Valley. This shot was taken near Seeley Lake. Tim Church photo.
(C) Hunting guide in the Swan Range.
(D) The Swan Valley sometimes seems a world of its own, especially in winter. Salmon Prairie School in the northern part of the valley still has grades 1 through 8 in one classroom. John Alwin photo.
(E) Greg Morley of Morley canoes. Who would put such art in the water? John Alwin photo.

HELENA-CENTERED

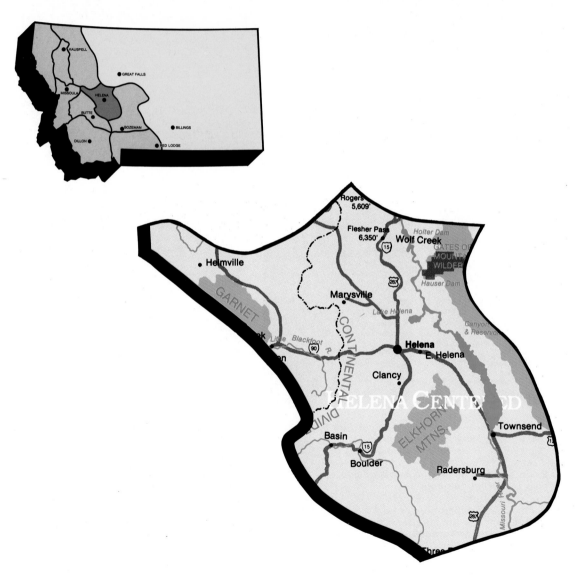

Sections of the Broad Valley Rockies that share a strong bond with Helena constitute this city-centered region. From the crest of the Big Belt Mountains on the east, west to Helmville and from the Wolf Creek area south to beyond Boulder, Helena dominates the region and is the hub of a radiating network of major highways. Its urban area includes more than 90 percent of the region's population.

Like the neighboring Mining Axis to the south, the Helena Centered region has a rich history of gold gulches and silver lodes, and today has some of Montana's best known ghost towns and near-ghost towns: Elkhorn, Wickes, Corbin, Diamond City, Rimini, Marysville and others are numerous enough to justify their own ghost town tour book. Things are again beginning to stir in some of these former mining centers as gold and silver prices of the early 1980s make remaining deposits look more alluring.

Owners of several mines in the Boulder area didn't wait for mining to return to their shafts. Some have opened their mines to those with arthritis, emphysema, bursitis, asthma and a wide range of other ailments. In the Merry Widow Mine sufferers bathe in natural spring waters. At the Free Enterprise, health seekers ride an elevator down to the 85-foot level, where they relax on cushioned seats in 400 feet of tunnelling while breathing radon gas. Believers refer to "negative ions in the blood," "stimulation of inner secretory glands" and "better utilization of oxygen" while explaining the alleged benefits of radon gas.

State Capitol Building. Tom Dietrich photo.

Below: Irrigation from the Missouri River system is critical to agriculture in the Helena Valley. This is near Helena looking toward Lake Helena. Rick Graetz photo.

Right: Ovando, on the southern fringe of the Bob Marshall Wilderness, could almost be considered part of the Bob Marshall-Swan Valley country. Tom Dietrich photo.

Far right: Harvesting dry-land wheat on the Toston Bench southeast of Helena. Rick Graetz photo.

The Montana Ghost Town Preservation Society

Though not one of Montana's largest organizations, the Montana Ghost Town Preservation Society is one about which more Montanans and others with an interest in the state's historical heritage should be aware. The non-profit group formed in Bozeman in 1969 with the primary objectives of helping to preserve Montana's remaining ghost towns and inform others about their condition.

More than 600 mining camps and towns existed at some time in Montana's past. Most were temporary encampments with shelter provided by tents, shacks, lean-tos and quickly built log cabins. Evidence of many of these ephemeral camps vanished almost as quickly as they had appeared. A few became full-fledged towns, and only a select group of these made the successful transition to modern 20th Century towns — Butte, Helena, Deer Lodge and Philipsburg to mention a few. Most mining-camps-turned-towns were less fortunate and they are now the subjects of ghost town books and the quarry of hordes of numerous tourists each summer.

The organization of the Montana Ghost Town Society took place at the time of a growing national interest in historical preservation. A heightened public reaction against sterile environments and things plastic turned the attention of victims of future shock back to things historical. The beginning of our national antique craze also dates from about this time. People grew uncomfortable with the rampant pace of change and began seeking out and prizing links with the past, digging for roots.

Ghost towns have a special appeal. Unlike many of the mansion homes of founding fathers and the masterpieces of famous architects, ghost towns are unpretentious. Whereas museum-quality historical sites seem to demand detachment and awe from visitors, ghost towns have quite the opposite effect. Visitors sense that what they are viewing and the streets down which they walk were produced by and for common folk. You won't

A

B

D

C

The ghost towns of Marysville, northwest of Helena (A,B), and Elkhorn (C), in the Elkhorn Mountains, are reminiscent of the area's roots in mining. (D) Other reminders of prospectors past can be seen in abandoned mine works and cabins throughout the area. This homestead is in Lump Gulch, near the abandoned Lump City, now a developing residential area serving Helena. (A) Rick Graetz. (B) John Reddy. (C) John Alwin. (D) Len Eckel.

find velvet ropes draped on chrome posts or clear plastic carpet protectors in ghost towns. Most of us feel at home here, and might even find ourselves kicking up some dust on the street in front of Skinner's Saloon at Bannack or dancing a private soft-shoe on the stage of the Fraternity Hall at Elkhorn.

Sensing the value of Montana's ghost towns and aware of the rapid rate at which they were disappearing, four concerned Bozemanites founded the preservation society — John DeHaas and Bert McCrowskey, both Montana State University architecture professors, geology professor Robert Chadwick, also at MSU, and attorney McKinley Anderson.

According to DeHaas, assault on ghost towns accelerated after World War II with the increasing popularity of jeeps which allowed people to get back to the remaining towns and cart off whatever they pleased. Later widespread adoption of motorbikes and snowmobiles only added to the problem. DeHaas is careful to point out that not all four-wheelers, bikers and snowmachine enthusiasts are ghost-town vandals. In fact, many have offered to serve as watch dogs to help prevent theft and destruction.

A still too-common attitude of "if I don't take it someone else will" is responsible for the demise of many ghost towns according to DeHaas. The problem became most acute beginning in the late '60s when weathered wood came into vogue for paneling in homes and businesses. Large trucks reportedly moved in from out of state and remains of entire towns were leveled overnight for their rustic wood.

Society summer projects have included stabilization and replacement of the roof on Superintendent Weir's house at Granite, stabilization of the hotel at Gallatin City, and extensive work at Garnet and Elkhorn. Each fall the society holds its annual meeting and banquet at a different Montana town. Field trips to historic sites are a part of every meeting. Between fall get-togethers a quarterly newsletter keeps members up to date on timely topics.

Membership in the society, which currently numbers around 125, is open to anyone with an interest in preserving Montana's past. Annual dues for an individual and immediate family are a nominal $6 per year. Other levels of membership up to a $250 lifetime membership are welcomed. The society's mailing address is Box 1861, Bozeman, Montana 59771.

A less controversial form of relaxation and health is water-based recreation on Canyon Ferry Lake, one of the region's dominant geographic features. This body of water 25-miles-long by 3-miles-wide was created by Canyon Ferry Dam. In 1957 the Bureau of Reclamation, which owns the reservoir and shoreline, signed an agreement with the state parks division that gives the Montana Department of Fish, Wildlife and Parks the authority to develop and administer recreational sites around the reservoir.

As part of the multiple use plan for Canyon Ferry, cabin sites were offered for lease at the north end of the reservoir in the late '50s. At the time the department had to beg people to sign up for lots at $25 to $35 per year. Today the 266 cabin sites are in great demand. Even though yearly rents are between $100 and $230 per year they are considered a bargain by leasees, some they are considered a bargain by leasees, some of whom have constructed homes in the six-figure range.

The 8,000-acre Canyon Ferry State Recreation Area surrounding the reservoir provides 26 recreational parks, eight of which include boat ramps. Residents from Helena, Butte, Bozeman, Great Falls and other cities within a 150-mile radius are regular visitors. Boating and fishing are especially popular on this, the second largest of Western Montana water bodies. Spring and fall trolling consistently reward fishermen with their limit of trout. Canyon Ferry's popularity among Montana's dry valley and semi-arid plains residents is reflected in its "visitor days" as measured by the Department of Fish, Wildlife and Parks. About half a million mostly in-state visitors enjoyed the waters of Canyon Ferry in 1982.

The 25-mile-long body of water impounded by Canyon Ferry dam draws recreational users from Helena, Great Falls, Bozeman and beyond. Rick Graetz photos.

143

Far left: Sunset over Helena, perched on the shoulders of Mt. Helena. Len Eckel photo.
Left: The Cathedral of St. Helena, certainly one of the most impressive in several states. Tim Church photo.
Below: Note the Moorish lines of Helena's Civic Center, built by the Shriners. John Alwin photo.

Helena

To Montanans their capital city is HEL-a-na, but to most out-of-staters, and almost all national newscasters, it's Hel-LEE-na. Like capital cities in other states and countries, it's not the most representative community within the political unit it administers. In addition to the obvious dominance of government employment and the local economic stability it helps foster, Helena also has a historical acuity and a tradition of urban sophistication not commonly seen in Montana cities. Helena is Western Montana, uptown style.

Montana's capital city started as a gold mining camp. The location of the July, 1864 discovery site is generally assumed to have been made in the downtown area in what is now an alley directly behind the recently restored Colwell Building on Last Chance Gulch. Helena's main street is so named because four Virginia City miners dubbed the little stream in the gulch as their "last chance" back in that summer of '64.

A fortuitous central location within a fabulously rich mining region and a strategic position on the Fort Benton-Virginia City Road helped assure Helena's survival long after the last of its diggings were exhausted. Almost immediately Helena became the financial hub and retail trade center, entertainment node and distribution point for residents in nearby mountain mining towns. Diamond City, Blackfoot City, Unionville, Park City and other towns as far away as Virginia City and Bozeman were within reach of Helena's long tentacles of trade and commerce. By 1870, at a time when neither Billings nor Great Falls existed, when Butte had but 241 residents and Bozeman 168, and after Virginia City's population had dwindled to 867, Helena was the undisputed number-one city in Montana with 3,300 residents.

Even then it showed a staying power unlike anything yet seen in the still young territory.

Transfer of the territorial capital from Virginia City to Helena in 1875 was testimony to its ascendance. The ongoing shift from placer mining to underground quartz operations in area mines during the 1870s and 1880s further intensified Helena's central role. Principal mining and refining centers such as Marysville, Wickes, Elkhorn and Rimini were tributary to Helena. Within four years of the 1883 arrival of the Northern Pacific, Helena was Montana's rail hub. Trunk lines carrying all east-west traffic passed through the city and branch lines radiated into surrounding mining districts.

Wealth and opulence peaked in a rapidly maturing Helena in the 1880s when the capital assumed title of "Queen City of the Rockies." Downtown, impressive brick and stone office buildings of the latest architectural styles crowded the winding contour of Last Chance Gulch. Mansard roofs, pediment windows, cornices, and even carved stone dolphin rain spouts graced handsome buildings where before more functional and less permanent log cabins and false-fronted frame buildings stood.

In the residential neighborhoods fringing the downtown, cattle barons, mining magnates, bankers, politicians and others among Montana's most wealthy and influential built their mansions. At the time Helena claimed more millionaires per thousand residents than any city in the country. Helena was clearly the most prestigious Montana address of the 1880s.

Ten miles west of town one of the most enterprising of the community's entrepreneurial

class, Charles Broadwater, completed his magnificent Broadwater Hotel and Natatorium in 1889. The scale and elegance of the resort complex was consistent with Helena in its golden era. Complementing the quarter-mile-long, 108-room hotel was the ornate natatorium. Built in a distinctive Moorish style complete with minarets

Left: One of the west's most luxuriant resorts, the Broadwater Hotel and Hot Springs, in post card from 1907.
Right: An idea of the size of the "natatorium" can be seen by the entrance alone.
Post cards courtesy of Len Eckel.

A powerful earthquake terrorized Helena on October 18, 1935, destroying a newly completed high school, damaging countless of Helena's lovely masonry buildings and killing four persons. Montana Historical Society photo.

and circular stained glass windows, this "aquatic theatre" as it was then known, housed the world's largest hot water pool, bigger than a football field. The flow from a natural hot spring was mixed with cooler waters and then cascaded into the pool over a 40-foot-tall ledge of granite boulders. Fountains and imported tropical plants added to the atmosphere of what the *Helena Daily Journal* described in 1891 as "the finest private bath house in the world — finer than those Caesar gave to Rome."

The pervasive air of optimism and the presumption of continued prosperity in Helena ended with the Silver Panic of 1893, which devastated silver producing centers tributary to the city. Helena's early census population peak was recorded in 1890 at 13,834. Historians estimate it may have climbed to 15,000 just prior to the collapse of silver prices. By 1900 the population had dropped to 10,770, while Butte, which some residents preferred to view as little more than a mining camp to its south, tripled in size during the decade of the '90s and stood at 30,470 at the turn of the century. To the north even the upstart town of Great Falls, only 15 years old in 1900, was almost 50 percent larger than the capital city. Helena was quite rudely awakened from its unrivaled dominance within Montana.

Even though a proliferation of strip developments, shopping malls and the inevitable golden arches have made Helena more like its sister cities of comparable size in Montana, enough remains from its rich past to provide the community with depth and continuity. Numerous

historic buildings and neighborhoods dating from its infancy remain to assure perpetuation of Helena's distinctiveness and sense of place. Montana's capital city remains an exciting city, in part, because of its collage of historical reminders.

One of the town's original cabins, built of hand-hewn logs and dating back to 1864, still stands at 210 South Park and is open to visitors. The Pioneer Cabin is furnished with authentic period furniture and is typical of the small miners' homes of the 1860s. Around the corner, Reeder's Alley remains as the last complete block of historic buildings still standing in Helena. Most of the unpretentious small stone and brick buildings probably date from the 1880s. Beginning in the 1960s this area was tastefully restored and provides one of the best examples of adaptive reuse in Montana. These former homes of miners and other laborers are now artists' studios, galleries and gift shops. The human scale of this preservation effort is especially appreciated by visitors in this era of freeways and highrises. Strolling down the narrow lane with its textured and intricate environment of lowrise buildings and tiny shops one can sense some of what Helena must have been like in the 1880s.

Downtown along Last Chance Gulch and intersecting streets some of the glorious old buildings still remain. Thanks to a sometimes controversial Urban Renewal and Community Development program, as well as private efforts by individuals, some of Helena's architecturally and historically significant buildings have been saved

223. Main Street, looking South, Helena, Mont.

Then and now: Looking south up Last Chance Gulch from the same spot. Today the southern two blocks of Main Street on the gulch have been transformed into a pedestrian mall. Post card, courtesy of Len Eckel. Photo by John Alwin.

and now serve useful purposes. The odd-shaped Diamond Block (1889) built to conform to the limits of a mining claim was among the first to be restored. Along Last Chance Gulch the one-of-a-kind Colwell Building (1888), the salamander-topped Atlas Block (1888) and solid Securities Building (1886) are among some of the restored edifices that date back to Helena in its bloom.

The old Fire Tower on Watchtower Hill just east of the Last Chance Gulch Pedestrian Mall, also dates from Helena's early days. In a town that almost lost its entire business district to fires three times during its first decade, this landmark became known as "Guardian of the Gulch." Today the tower is one of only a few left in the United States and has been adopted as the city symbol. In nearby residential areas fringing the downtown the 20- to 30-room mansions of the city's wealthy founding families are still numerous enough to dominate some streets, especially prestigious near west side drives like Madison, Stuart and Dearborn.

City resident Jean Baucus may have done more than any other person in Helena to introduce city residents and tourists alike to the rich heritage of Helena's cityscape. Her three inexpensive books

are a must for anyone interested in exploring Helena's many historic structures. *Gold in the Gulch* provides an excellent introduction to past and present Helena, with an emphasis on major buildings. Her two volumes of *Helena: Her Historic Homes* are useful guides to some of the capital city's Victorian masterpieces.

More than any other Montana community, Helena is a white collar town, dominated by well educated, young professionals. They prevail here just as mill workers do in Columbia Falls and miners used to in Butte.

State government is the largest employer with fully 3,600 of the state's total payroll of 10,500. The median age of these workers is in the mid-30s and educational levels are well above the statewide average. Surprisingly, the federal government is the city's second largest employer providing an additional 1,300 jobs. Like their state counterparts, workers with the Forest Service, Veterans Administration Hospital at Fort Harrison, Department of Agriculture and other federal agencies with offices in town tend to be professional, white collar workers. Other major employers add to the non-blue collar character of Helena. These include the 800 employees of

Mountain Bell, most working in the state headquarters, more than 450 at St. Peter's Hospital, and the 200 employed at Carroll College.

The Asarco lead smelter in next-door East Helena is the only major factory employer. It dates back to the height of the area's mining boom, having been built in 1888 to replace a smelter at nearby Wickes. It remains today as one of only a few lead smelters left in the country capable of processing complex ores of lead and silver. Originally the plant handled dominantly Montana ores, but today only 5 to 10 percent originate in the state. Most now come from South American mines. Ores are processed into 10-ton "pigs," or slabs, of 98 percent pure lead with trace amounts of gold and silver. From East Helena "pigs" go by rail to a refinery at Omaha, Nebraska, for final processing. The huge black slag pile paralleling Highway 12 is mute testimony to almost a century of the plant's operation.

With only minor dependence on the volatile wood products and minerals industries Helena enjoys one of Montana's most stable economies. During the height of the 1981-83 recession when unemployment in Mineral County neared 40 percent, the Helena-area figure stayed under nine percent. In addition to relative economic stability Helena also benefits from one of the highest average household incomes in the state, second only to Billings.

Census figures for Helena are misleading. They show a 1980 population of 23,938, up only five percent from the 1970 figure. The 1980 number does not include the thousands of people who have moved into adjacent suburban areas. Most populated of these is the Helena Valley, the unincorporated section north of town that includes everything from closely packed city lots to large suburban tracts 10 acres and larger. Helena commuters looking for a more forested and mountainous setting often opt for one of the many subdivisions to the south in the Prickly Pear Valley. Most of the development has taken place across the county line in the extreme northern end of Jefferson County. New residents of foothills subdivisions like Gruber Estates, Blue Sky Heights, and Forest Park Estates gave Jefferson County the second highest growth rate in Western Montana between 1970 and 1980. A proliferation of subdivisions in the Winston Flats area, formerly prime antelope range, has converted the extreme northwestern corner of Broadwater County into another Helena "bedroom community," and helped give that county one of the highest growth rates in Western Montana. If residents in these outlying sections of Helena's urban area are included, population probably approaches 50,000, a 30 percent increase over 1970.

Plans have been completed to develop Montana's largest planned community on a 4,100-acre site adjacent to Helena's southeast corner. The 1979 master plan for the entirely new community of Crossfire was completed by Wesplan Corporation of Missoula for its Helena developers, The Diehl Company. The innovative plan projects a population of more than 41,000 and includes sites for two high schools, elementary schools, neighborhood parks, a 27-hole golf course complex, equestrian center, and commercial/work space areas. A clustered style of development provides for maximum open space, leaving approximately 40 percent of the rolling grassland and ponderosa pine forest for recreational use or in its natural condition. Careful mapping of land-use capabilities including a consideration of slope, soil, vegetation and wildlife should help assure minimum impact and maximum harmony with the area's natural environment.

Top: In the Gates of the Mountains Wilderness. Rick Graetz photo.
Above left: I-15 north of Helena courses through some fascinating geologic formations in the Wolf Creek Canyon area. One can't help notice them for their proximity nearly overhead. John Alwin photo.

Above right: Frontier Town was created almost singlehandedly by the energy and showmanship of John Quigley to recapture the feeling of the old west. It sits just below the crest of MacDonald Pass, west of Helena. In the winter it serves local cross-country skiers. John Reddy photo.

At Marysville near Helena—Rick Graetz

*Wild Goose Island, St. Mary's Lake,
Glacier Country—John Reddy*

148

NEXT IN THE
MONTANA GEOGRAPHIC SERIES

A Study in Montana

YELLOWSTONE NATIONAL PARK

More than a picture book, this geographic will explore the important biological and physical treasures that make the Yellowstone area unique. The Yellowstone book is actually subtitled The Greater Yellowstone Ecosystem, and attempts to define the biological system surrounding and supporting the park. By Rick Reese, author of Montana Mountain Ranges and Director of The Yellowstone Institute.

THE MISSOURI RIVER

From Lewis and Clark to commercial float trips. From Fort Peck and its colorful construction to dissent over management of the dams on the river's upper reaches. From racing headwaters to the big muddy river of the east. This is the whole story of the Missouri River. Interviews with those who use it, live by it, take its waters for a living. Badlands, breaks, dams, history, outlaws, movies. All these things are the Missouri. By Bert Gildart, author of Montana Wildlife.

PRE PUBLICATION DISCOUNTS

If you would like to receive advanced notice of future geographics and qualify for our pre-publication discount, simply send your name and address to the address below and ask to have your name put on the Geographic Series mailing list. There is no obligation to buy. You can reserve a copy of any issue before publication and save up to 30 percent off the retail price.

OTHER TITLES IN PRODUCTION OR PLANNING

The Absaroka-Beartooth Mountains by Robert Anderson
The Yellowstone River by Bill Schneider
Montana's Historic Trails by Bill Lang
Montana Indians Yesterday and Today by Bill Bryan

To place your name on the
Geographic Series mailing list, write:

MONTANA GEOGRAPHIC SERIES

Box 5630
Helena, Montana 59604

MONTANA MAGAZINE
Tells The Whole Montana Story

The history, the wild back country, the people, the wildlife, the towns, the lifestyles, the travel — these things are Montana — unique among the states. Montana Magazine brings you the Montana story six times a year in a beautiful, long-lasting magazine.
Its hallmark is full-page color photography of Montana from the peaks to the prairies.

REGULARLY FEATURED DEPARTMENTS:

WEATHER
GEOLOGY
HUNTING
  AND FISHING
OUTDOOR
  RECREATION
HUMOR
PERSONALITY
GARDENING
DINING OUT

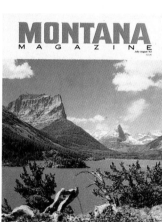

Montana Magazine
Because You Are
A Montanan

For subscription information write:
MONTANA MAGAZINE
Box 5630
Helena, MT 59604

About Our Back Cover Photo
This photographic mosaic was compiled from Earth Resources Satellite Photo passes made from a height of 570 miles. It was pieced together in black and white and interpreted in color by Big Sky Magic, Larry Dodge, Owner.
Commercial Color Adaptation © 1976 Big Sky Magic.

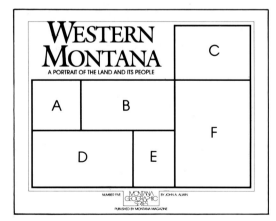

Front Cover Photos:

A. Log deck, Columbia Falls—John Alwin

B. Yellowstone River, Absaroka Range—William Koenig

C. The Como Peaks, Bitterroot Valley—Tom Dietrich

D. Polson, Mission Mountains, and Flathead Lake—John Alwin

E. Logger Bill Bennett East of Yaak—John Alwin photo

F. Granite Lake, "A" Peak, Cabinet Mountains Wilderness Area—Pat O'Hara